D1606492

WHY SIBLINGS MATTER

Many people grow up with at least one sibling. These siblings are often "fellow travellers" through adversity or significant life events; they can act as a source of support for some children and a source of conflict for others. For these reasons, siblings are a potentially powerful influence on development and this book is one of the first of its kind to provide an overview of cutting-edge psychological research on this important relationship.

Why Siblings Matter is a cornerstone text on siblinghood. Integrating findings from a ten-year longitudinal study alongside wider research, it provides a lifespan perspective examining the impact of sibling relationships on children's development and well-being. This text situates siblings in their historical, developmental and family context; considers the influence of siblings on children's development and adjustment; and provides an introduction to new research on siblings in diverse contexts. The authors discuss sibling relationships in varied populations such as siblings with disabilities, siblings in different cultures and siblings in non-traditional families, while also considering the practical implications of research.

Covering both classical studies and new results, this book offers take-home messages for promoting positive sibling interactions. It is invaluable reading for students and researchers in developmental psychology and family studies, and professionals in education, health and social work.

Dr Naomi White completed her PhD on the topic of siblings at the Centre for Family Research at the University of Cambridge, UK with funding from the Royal Society of New Zealand Rutherford Foundation and the Cambridge Commonwealth Trust. This work was part of a larger study led by Professor Claire Hughes that has tracked children's social and cognitive development from toddlerhood to the teenage years. She is currently completing clinical psychology training at the University of Otago, New Zealand.

Professor Claire Hughes is Deputy Director of the Centre for Family Research at the University of Cambridge, UK. She has now launched a new longitudinal study of the transition to parenthood and the role of early parent–infant interactions in mediating relations between prenatal well-being and the early development of executive control and self-regulation with collaboration from teams in the USA and in the Netherlands. Her studies are funded by the ESRC and the Wellcome Trust.

ESSAYS IN DEVELOPMENTAL PSYCHOLOGY

North American Editors:
Henry Wellman
University of Michigan at Ann Arbor

UK Editors:
Claire Hughes
University of Cambridge
Michelle Ellefson
University of Cambridge

Essays in Developmental Psychology is designed to meet the need for rapid publication of brief volumes in developmental psychology. The series defines developmental psychology in its broadest terms and covers such topics as social development, cognitive development, developmental neuropsychology and neuroscience, language development, learning difficulties, developmental psychopathology and applied issues. Each volume in the series will make a conceptual contribution to the topic by reviewing and synthesizing the existing research literature, by advancing theory in the area, or by some combination of these missions. The principal aim is that authors will provide an overview of their own highly successful research program in an area. It is also expected that volumes will, to some extent, include an assessment of current knowledge and identification of possible future trends in research. Each book will be a self-contained unit supplying the advanced reader with a well-structured review of the work described and evaluated.

PUBLISHED

White and Hughes: *Why Siblings Matter: The Role of Brother and Sister Relationships in Development and Well-Being*

Crone: *The Adolescent Brain*

Needham: *Learning about Objects in Infancy*

Hughes: *Social Understanding and Social Lives*

Sprenger-Charolles et al.: *Reading Acquisition and Developmental Dyslexia*

Barrett: *Children's Knowledge, Beliefs and Feelings about Nations and National Groups*

Hatano and Inagaki: *Young Children's Naïve Thinking about the Biological World*

Goldwin-Meadow: *The Resilience of Language*

Perez-Pereira & Conti-Ramsden: *Language Development and Social Interactions in Blind Children*

Bryne: *The Foundation of Literacy*

Meins: *Security of Attachment and Cognitive Development*

Siegal: *Knowing Children (2nd Ed.)*

Meadows: *Parenting Behavior and Children's Cognitive Development*

Langford: *The Development of Moral Reasoning*

Forrester: *The Development of Young Children's Social-Cognitive Skills*

Hobson: *Autism and the Development of Mind*

White: *The Understanding of Causation and the Production of Action*

Goswami: *Analogical Reasoning in Children*

Cox: *Children's Drawings of the Human Figure*

Harris: *Language Experience and Early Language Development*

Garton: *Social Interaction and the Development of Language and Cognition*

Bryant & Goswami: *Phonological Skills and Learning to Read*

Collins & Goodnow: *Development According to Parents*

For updated information about published and forthcoming titles in the *Essays in Developmental Psychology* series, please visit: **www.routledge.com/series/SE0532**

WHY SIBLINGS MATTER

The Role of Brother and Sister
Relationships in Development
and Well-Being

Naomi White and Claire Hughes

Routledge
Taylor & Francis Group

LONDON AND NEW YORK

First published 2018
by Routledge
2 Park Square, Milton Park, Abingdon, Oxon OX14 4RN

and by Routledge
711 Third Avenue, New York, NY 10017

Routledge is an imprint of the Taylor & Francis Group, an informa business

© 2018 Naomi White & Claire Hughes

British Library Cataloguing in Publication Data
A catalogue record for this book is available from the British Library

Library of Congress Cataloging in Publication Data
Names: White, Naomi, 1987- author. | Hughes, Claire, 1966- author.
Title: Why siblings matter: the role of brother and sister relationships in development and well-being / Naomi White and Claire Hughes.
Description: Abingdon, Oxon; New York, NY: Routledge is an imprint of the Taylor & Francis Group, an Informa Business, [2018] |
Series: Essays in developmental psychology | Includes bibliographical references.
Identifiers: LCCN 2017021859 (print) | LCCN 2017029583 (ebook) | ISBN 9781315630489 (ebook) | ISBN 9781138641440 (hbk: alk. paper) | ISBN 9781138641457 (pbk: alk. paper)
Subjects: LCSH: Brothers and sisters.
Classification: LCC BF723.S43 (ebook) | LCC BF723.S43 .W45 2018 (print) | DDC 155.44/3–dc23
LC record available at https://lccn.loc.gov/2017021859

ISBN: 978-1-138-64144-0 (hbk)
ISBN: 978-1-138-64145-7 (pbk)
ISBN: 978-1-315-63048-9 (ebk)

Typeset in Bembo
by Deanta Global Publishing Services, Chennai, India

CONTENTS

ACKNOWLEDGEMENTS

The Cambridge Toddlers Up study and so many of the findings in this book were made possible by funding from the Health Foundation and the Economic and Social Research Council. We'd like to acknowledge all those who have contributed over the past decade or more to this study. Special thanks go to Dr Rosie Ensor, Dr Alex Marks and Dr Rory Devine whose work underpins a number of the findings discussed in this book. Our thanks also go to everyone else with a PhD based on the Toddlers Up study: Dr Amanda Aldercotte, Dr Nik Darshane, Dr Martha Hart and Dr Gabriela Roman; as well as to Ms Sarah Foley (soon to become Dr Foley!), who played a pivotal role in the age 12 wave of the study. Without the support of participating families and schools, none of this would have been possible and so our very sincere thanks go to all those who've participated in the study over the years.

The Royal Society of New Zealand Rutherford Foundation and the Cambridge Commonwealth Trust funded Naomi's PhD and the cross-cultural study discussed in Chapter 8. We are very grateful to them and to the teachers and students in the UK and New Zealand who took part in this study. We'd also like to thank Dr Alison Pike, for her sage advice and encouragement along the way, and Professor Susan Golombok, Director of the Centre for Family Research, for her constant support.

Much of this book was written while the two of us were living at opposite poles of the earth and juggling many other commitments. So we'd both like to say a big thank you to the important people in our lives who've helped us to achieve this feat. For Naomi this is her parents – Phil and Helen – and friends (with special thanks to Eleanor Giraud, Valerie Tan and Elaine Reese whose support and encouragement at various stages of the project were invaluable). For Claire, this is her partner Andrew and their three children Alistair, Elora and Malaika, who are a constant reminder of the many ways in which sibling relationships bring both joy and support. Finally, it goes without saying that this book is dedicated to our own siblings, Nick, Liz, and David, and to brothers and sisters everywhere.

1

SIBLING RELATIONSHIPS

An introduction

Like a younger child in a large family, research on siblings has had to wait for its turn in the spotlight. Overshadowed for more than a century by research on parent–child relationships, research on sibling relationships is now flourishing within several disciplines, including family studies, sociology, psychology, human development, genetics, anthropology and psychiatry. The interdisciplinarity between these approaches adds vibrancy: sibling research now encompasses a broad range of topics of clear societal importance, as illustrated by a number of thought-provoking reviews (e.g., Conger, Stocker, & McGuire, 2009; Conger & Little, 2010; Dunn, 2011; Feinberg, Solmeyer, & McHale, 2012; Kramer, 2010; McGuire & Shanahan, 2010; McHale, Updegraff, & Whiteman, 2012; Volling, 2012; Whiteman, McHale, & Soli, 2011). In particular, while early research focused on the origins and consequences of individual differences in sibling relationship quality, recent work has brought a more contextualised approach that enables researchers to consider a wide range of new topics. These include: (1) the effects of parents' differential treatment of siblings on child and family well-being; (2) similarities and contrasts in sibling relationships across different cultures; (3) the interplay between nature and nurture on individual behaviours and social processes; and (4) interventions to reduce sibling conflict and to promote positive sibling relationships. Comprehensive coverage of all these topics is beyond the scope of this book. Instead, our goal is to provide a state-of-the-art review of research that highlights the breadth, rigour and complexity of contemporary studies in this field.

This introductory chapter aims to sketch out the history of research on siblings (in terms of both ideas and methods). This will, as indicated above, require a broad brush-stroke approach in order to bring together ideas from several different theoretical perspectives. As we ourselves are all too aware, time is increasingly a precious commodity. To assist the busy reader, this chapter, like the others in this book, is divided into headed sections. The first of these describes how although siblings have been included in at least three types of psychological studies over more than a century, the potential importance of sibling relationships for children's development and adjustment has remained largely overlooked. In the second section we summarise findings from recent large-scale, well-designed studies that, in general, challenge claims for the importance of birth order on child outcomes. The next four sections together illustrate the diverse ways in which researchers have portrayed siblings: as playmates, as attachment figures, as rivals and as role models. Following this, we move forward to more contemporary and contextualised approaches to studying siblings, describing the interplay between sibling relationships, other family relationships and the wider environment within which these relationships occur. The final section outlines key methodological challenges (and solutions) within research on siblings. We end this and all other chapters in this book with a bullet-point summary of ten key take-home messages.

Sibling relationships: Ubiquitous yet invisible?

Sibling relationships are a "fixture in the family lives of children and adolescents" (McHale et al., 2012, p. 913). Or, as vividly described by Shaw in an interview for Time magazine (Kluger, 2006, p. 2), "parents serve the same big-picture role as doctors on grand rounds. Siblings are like the nurses on the ward. They're there every day." Support for the ubiquity of siblings also comes from a national survey in the United States, which showed that youth aged 18 or under were more likely to be living with at least one sibling than with a father figure, with the percentages for each group being 82% and 78% respectively (King et al., 2010, as cited in McHale et al., 2012). Our fascination with siblings is reflected in their prominence in fiction. Literary portraits include siblings sharing adversity (e.g., *Hansel and Gretel* or Louisa M. Alcott's *Little Women*) and adventure (e.g., the Pevensie children in C. S. Lewis's *Chronicles of Narnia* or the Weasley brothers in J. K. Rowling's *Harry Potter* series). Stories about siblings also include darker images of persecution (e.g., *Cinderella*) or even fratricide (e.g., the Old Testament brothers, Cain and Abel).

Yet despite their ubiquity and importance, sibling relationships have long been eclipsed by the sheer volume of research on the influences of parents and peers on children's social development (e.g., Bowlby, 1958, 1969; Piaget, 1932). As trenchantly expressed by Irish (1964, p. 287), most of the academic literature on families "would lead one to conclude that parents rear their children one at a time – or in separate compartments". Using the online database, Scopus, to conduct a quick search of the literature up to 1999 we found that this neglect of sibling relationships was still very much in evidence by the end of the twentieth century: for the period up until 1999, the combined terms "sibling relationships" and "children" yielded just over a quarter as many hits as the term "mother-child relationships" (145 as compared with 563). In the twenty-first century, this gap has narrowed considerably: the same two searches for the period of 2000 to 2016 produced 450 and 763 hits respectively. Thus, when compared with all previous recorded years, the period of 2000–2016 produced more than a three-fold increase in papers about sibling relationships, but less than a one and a half-fold increase in papers about mother-child relationships.

While these numbers are likely to include medical studies, which involve siblings but do not examine the sibling relationship, and so should be viewed with caution, they do indicate that siblings have at last begun to attract psychologists' attention.

What is perhaps especially puzzling about the neglect of sibling relationships within psychological research in the twentieth century is that across this period at least three different strands of research actively involved siblings. The first of these strands concerns putative effects of *birth order*. Differences between siblings were first noted almost 150 years ago, when Galton's (1874) investigation of the characteristics of "men of science" highlighted the over-representation of firstborns among fellows of the Royal Society. Galton interpreted the inferred achievement gap between firstborn and laterborn sons as reflecting laws and mores around primogeniture. That is, the view that a father needed "an heir and a spare" led to inequities in the distribution of resources, with firstborn sons typically receiving the lion's share. Interest in birth order effects is still alive and well; an outline of current thinking in this field will be given later in this chapter. Note, however, that this research does not focus on the sibling relationship but rather on the impact of position in the family on children's experiences of family life and developmental outcomes.

The second line of research builds directly on Galton's early work and hinges on the value of *siblings as a research tool*, either to tease apart the effects of nature and nurture (by comparing identical and fraternal twins, or biological and adoptive siblings; e.g., Plomin & Daniels, 1987) or as a control for background factors that may underpin particular disorders in sibling case-control studies (e.g., Grimes & Schulz, 2005). Once again, however, each of these lines of research centres upon comparisons between siblings as individuals, such that the relationship between siblings is overlooked. One important finding to emerge from these studies is the striking variability between siblings who, as the saying has it, can be like "peas in a pod" or like "chalk and cheese". Variability is also a key feature of sibling relationship quality (see Chapter 3) and in part reflects the impact of structural contrasts, such as differences in age gap, gender composition or overall family size. These variables present a challenge for researchers seeking to draw overarching conclusions about the nature and significance of sibling relationships.

The third line of investigation also has a long history and does take seriously the impact of siblings on family relationships, but does so from a *psychodynamic* perspective in which theoretical interpretations typically supersede empirical data. Much of this work dates back to the early work of the psychoanalyst, Alfred Adler (1920/ 1923), who interpreted possible effects of birth order by highlighting children's experience of "dethronement" following the arrival of a new baby in the family. This term powerfully captures the feeling of displacement that can occur when children realise that they must share their parents' attention with the new arrival. Adler proposed that experiences of rivalry within the sibling relationship can lead to an *inferiority complex* (e.g., Mosak & Maniacci, 1999). Rivalry for parental attention was also prominent in Freud's (1900/1953, 1921/1955) writings about sibling relationships and, almost a century later, psychoanalysts have continued to draw heavily on the potentially traumatic experiences that are associated with becoming a sibling. These experiences, if sufficiently resolved, can be crucibles for children's development of character. For example, drawing on a longitudinal study of pre-school siblings two years apart in age, Neubauer (1982) suggested that the challenge of managing aggressive feelings associated with the birth of a sibling could be beneficial for ego development, while Kris and Ritvo (1983) argued that managing sibling rivalry and jealousy could help children deal with the frustration and conflict arising from the Oedipal conflict.

In contrast, Mitchell (2000, 2003) highlighted the inherent internal conflict in sibling relationships between love for someone who is like you, and the threat of replacement. At the same time, Mitchell also emphasised that in overcoming the fears of displacement associated with the birth of a new sibling and creating their own niche within the family, earlier-born children are able to develop both self-esteem and a sense of their unique identity, through differentiation from their sibling. While offering much food for thought, psychoanalytic conclusions are, by their very nature, impossible to test empirically, and so this psychodynamic work is beyond the scope of this book. Mitchell's work, however, deserves particular mention as, rather than viewing siblings in terms of their impact on the primary relationship between parent and child, she presents the relationship between siblings as worthy of attention in its own right. That said, in common with other psychoanalytic accounts (e.g., Freud, 1900/1953), Mitchell's work emphasises the *universality* of sibling experiences. In sharp contrast, the psychological studies reviewed in this book consistently emphasise the *diversity* of individual children's experiences with siblings.

Birth order and family size: Do they matter and why?

Earlier, we noted that research into birth order effects dates back to Galton's work almost 150 years ago. Today, interest in birth order as a predictor of achievement is alive and well within both sociological and psychological research. Reflecting the focus of research in this field, we restrict our review to the potential impact of birth order and family size on children's academic achievement (ending with a coda on the current status of findings regarding birth order and personality). Three main theories are used to explain effects of either birth order or family size on academic success (for a large sociological review, see Steelman, Powell, Werum, & Carter, 2002). The first account is the *resource dilution hypothesis* (Blake, 1981). According to this model, finite family resources mean that the addition of an extra child in the family reduces the resources available to each particular child. When testing this hypothesis, researchers typically assess three types of "household resources": cultural objects (books, music etc.); parental attention (teaching, support); and outside stimulation (e.g., trips to the library, park, museum). However, the first and third of these types are typically shared, such that all children in the family are likely to benefit, reducing the likelihood of birth order effects. Parental attention is potentially more specific, but often indexed by poor proxies (e.g., parental aspirations, maternal working hours). Unfortunately, as we shall see in Chapter 2, studies of children's transition to siblinghood have, to date, all involved samples recruited just prior to the birth of the second child. In other words, conclusions regarding the resource dilution hypothesis are difficult to draw, as direct comparisons of the quantity and quality of parents' interactions with firstborn and secondborn infants at the same age remain lacking.

The second account of effects of either birth order or family size on academic success is the *confluence hypothesis* (Zajonc, 2001; Zajonc & Markus, 1975). In this model, increases in family size lead to a combination of two mechanisms: a reduction in the level of intellectual stimulation for older siblings coupled with opportunities for learning through caregiving and teaching. As noted by Sandberg and Rafail (2014), these countervailing effects make this hypothesis rather difficult to test. According to the third account, the *admixture hypothesis*, genetic or environmental contrasts between families give rise to spurious negative associations between family size and achievement (e.g., Rodgers, Cleveland, Van Den Oord, & Rowe, 2000).

The focus of this chapter is on theory rather than empirical findings, but it is worth noting that these three accounts have been tested in several recent large-scale studies, with somewhat mixed results. Sandberg and Rafail (2014) examined detailed demographic data (for over 1,000 US children aged three to 18 in 2002) on children's time with parents, time spent using household resources and in outside activities, and time with siblings. Importantly, their analyses included the modelling of within-child changes (between 1997 and 2002) in cognitive scores with the addition of new siblings. Of the three accounts described above, their findings best fitted the admixture hypothesis. In a similar analysis of a simpler but much larger UK dataset (National Child Development Study, $n = 17,419$), Kanazawa (2012) reached exactly the same conclusion. That is, both studies suggested that unobserved differences between children's families that are associated with both family size and cognitive performance can explain why children from larger families, on average, are less academically successful than children from smaller families. Together, these findings highlight the methodological challenges of demonstrating clearly interpretable effects of family size (and hence of siblings) on children's academic achievement.

Turning now to the literature on birth order and personality, the most frequently cited work in this field is probably Frank Sulloway's (1996) book *Born to Rebel*, which portrayed firstborns as law-abiding and conformist and second or laterborn children as rebellious and creative. Rather than drawing on psychoanalytic theory, Sulloway's hypothesis is rooted in the evolutionary niche-finding model, in which children with different birth orders adopt contrasting behavioural strategies in order to secure maximal parental investment. This hypothesis has attracted considerable research attention and yet the results have, until recently, remained inconclusive. As discussed in a recent commentary on this topic (Damian & Roberts, 2015b), early studies in this field typically displayed several methodological weaknesses, including a widespread failure to control for two important confounds: (1) child age (children generally become less lawless and more conscientious with age and firstborns are, by definition, older than their siblings); and (2) sibship size (firstborns are more likely to be found in families with smaller numbers of siblings and so are also more likely to have educated and affluent parents). In their commentary, Damian and Roberts (2015b) argue that the findings from two large-scale studies have now settled the debate: birth order shows a tiny association with intelligence and a negligible relationship with personality. The first of these studies was their own: Damian and Roberts (2015a) used a representative US sample of 377,000 high school students that enabled them to control for potentially confounding effects of age, sex, sibship size, parental socioeconomic status and family structure and found that the average absolute association between birth order and personality traits was just .02. The second study was by Rohrer, Egloff and Schmukle (2015) and applied both between- and within-family designs to three large samples from the United Kingdom, the United States and Germany. The results from this international study revealed null effects of birth order on personality across the board, although self-reported intellect was slightly higher in firstborns.

Siblings as playmates and social tutors

Increasing the size of one's family is, as highlighted by the resource dilution model (discussed in the previous section), a costly business. Caring for an infant can also be extremely tiring. So why do so many parents with one child go on to have further children? One obvious answer is that most parents have memories of growing up with a sibling and so will know first-hand the delights of playing with a brother or sister. Observational research with preschool siblings highlights the uniqueness of sibling interactions in terms of both their quantity and their quality. Specifically, siblings spend significant amounts of time with each other (McHale & Crouter, 1996) and, by the age of 33 months engage in bouts of pretend play more frequently with their sibling than with a parent (Youngblade & Dunn, 1995). Few parents can say, in all honesty, that they love pretend games (be they fantasy rescues by firemen or simply pretend shopping trips or tea-parties) so much that they would gladly play the same game over and over again for days and weeks. In contrast, children really do love these games; as a result, having a sibling as a ready companion who truly shares the same view of what is fun (or funny – scatological jokes, anyone?) can mean instant access to entertainment.

Beyond the simple pleasure of a shared fantasy, joint pretend play provides a fertile arena for children to hone their communicative and collaborative skills (e.g., Howe, Petrakos, & Rinaldi, 1998). Perhaps it would be more accurate to say that these social and cognitive benefits arise precisely *because* children get such pleasure from shared pretend play. Specifically, the enjoyment derived from such play provides children with a powerful incentive to work their way through communication failures or even minor conflicts. In this regard, Dunn's early observational longitudinal studies (e.g., Dunn, Brown, & Beardsall, 1991; Dunn, Brown, Slomkowski, Tesla, & Youngblade, 1991; Dunn & Kendrick, 1982) had a seminal influence on theories about how children develop an understanding of their own and others' thoughts, feelings and intentions (also known as the acquisition of a "theory of mind"). In particular, accounts of individual differences in children's theory-of-mind skills have shifted in focus from nature to nurture (e.g., Hughes & Devine, 2017). Alongside Dunn's observational work, one particularly influential study in this respect was entitled *Theory of mind is contagious: You catch it from your sibs* (Perner, Ruffman, &

Leekam, 1994). The key finding in this study was that children with siblings typically passed a simple experimental paradigm (the object transfer false belief task) that has become the litmus test for theory of mind at an earlier age than children without siblings, with the benefit of each sibling being equivalent to approximately six months of age. This sibling advantage is all the more remarkable when one recalls that studies of birth order effects consistently show an advantage in academic achievement for firstborn children or children without siblings (see Steelman et al., 2002). Together with observational studies linking the quality of sibling interaction to children's success on false belief tasks (e.g., Brown, Donelan-McCall, & Dunn,1996; Dunn, Brown, Slomkowski, et al., 1991; Hughes, Fujisawa, Ensor, Lecce, & Marfleet, 2006), this finding has been the catalyst for numerous investigations of sibling influences on theory of mind. These are discussed in full in Chapter 6.

Siblings as attachment figures

Fertility rates have fallen significantly over the past century, leading to dramatic changes in family life (see Chapter 10 for further discussion). While children born in the twenty-first century Western world typically have only one or perhaps two siblings, those born in previous centuries would typically have had several siblings, some of whom might play a central role in caregiving (Davidoff, 2012). Indeed, when death in childbirth was relatively common, older siblings would often take on the role of surrogate parent. These experiences remain common in parts of the world in which both fertility rates and risks of maternal death are both high, and in traditional collectivist cultures more generally (see Chapter 9). A complete portrait of the sibling relationship therefore needs to go beyond the role of playmate to consider the extent to which siblings can also be key attachment figures.

John Bowlby's (1958, 1969) account of the parent-child relationship as an attachment relationship is probably the most influential theory within family research. By integrating ideas from psychoanalysis with observational methods developed by ethologists, Bowlby highlighted the evolutionary importance of parents as a "secure base" for children. A central tenet within attachment theory is that the caregiver-child relationship is a unique source of emotional security, enabling the child to explore the world safe in the knowledge that there is a warm and loving haven to which she or he can return. Within this perspective, however, sibling relationships have only a very secondary importance and so came to receive much less attention from psychologists.

That said, attachment theory has proved useful in understanding sibling relationships. For example, Bowlby (1969, 1973) argued that the attachment relationship provided a template for all other close relationships, positing that children drew on their experiences within the attachment relationship to form *internal working models* of relationships in general. In other words, children who enjoyed warm and supportive interactions with their caregiver were likely to view relationships as rewarding (and themselves as loveable), whereas children exposed to harsh or rejecting interactions with their caregiver were likely to anticipate rejection from others and so be less willing to invest effort or seek intimacy in their relationships with other family members. This led to the prediction that the quality of children's relationships with parents and siblings will be concordant, a prediction that has been supported in the literature (e.g., Brody, 1998; see Chapter 4 for a more detailed discussion of links between sibling and parent-child relationships).

Siblings as rivals and sparring partners

As noted earlier, in previous periods of history parents may have wanted a second child to have "an heir and a spare" (or, more simply, to have additional help at home or in a trade), but parents today are much more likely to want a second child in order to give their first child a playmate. Very few parents, we imagine, plan for a second child because they believe that their first child would benefit from having a rival. And yet, as made clear by the resource dilution model described above, this is exactly what siblings often appear to be. This view is quickly confirmed by typing the phrase "why do siblings" into Google: the most popular question generated is "why do siblings fight?"

Stories of sibling rivalry abound and date back to biblical times. Prominent examples from the Old Testament include the brothers Jacob and Esau (using an animal skin Jacob tricked his father into giving his blessing to him rather than to his more hirsute brother, Esau, and so effectively stole his brother's birthright), or Joseph, Jacob's son (whose coat of many colours drove his brothers into such a frenzy of envy that they considered fratricide). As noted earlier, theoretical accounts of sibling conflict hinged on psychodynamic interpretations of siblings as rivals for parental attention. However, these accounts are inherently untestable and so it is worth considering whether sibling conflict (which is undeniably real) is open to alternative (and more parsimonious) interpretations.

In particular, the sibling relationship is involuntary, enduring and characterised by a high degree of familiarity. Together, these features provide a simple explanation for why sibling interactions often have an emotionally intense "no-holds-barred" quality (Dunn, 1983; Howe, Ross, & Recchia, 2011). That is, while the fear of jeopardising a friendship will often restrain children's displays of frustration with a friend, children typically have far fewer inhibitions when they are upset or angry with a sibling. Indeed, the involuntary nature of sibling relationships means that, compared with children's relationships with either parents or peers, children's sibling relationships show an almost unique coupling of positive dimensions (e.g., warmth, closeness, mutuality, playfulness) and negative dimensions (e.g., hostility, aggression; Dunn, 1983; Howe et al., 2011). As Kramer and Bank (2005) put it:

> It is our brothers and sisters who see us as no-one else does, who are experts at how to both please and annoy us, and who bring out the best and the worst in us. Although not always providing a logical and consistent view of what transpires in families, the sibling world provides a critical window for understanding the ways in which children's experiences with their brothers and sisters may foreshadow variations in individual well-being and adjustment later in childhood, adolescence and well into adulthood.
>
> *(p. 43)*

In short, the unique nature of the relationship between siblings offers a simple explanation of why siblings are so important, without recourse to psychodynamic theories in which the sibling relationship only matters by virtue of its impact on the parent-child relationship.

Siblings as role models

As described above, sibling conflict is commonplace and often stressful for parents, but not necessarily a cause for real concern. More extreme forms of antisocial behaviour do, however, run in families and reflect both genetic and environmental influences (Moffitt, 2005). A key theoretical frame for research in this area is social learning theory, which was first developed by Bandura (1977). Whereas prior (behaviourist) accounts of learning emphasised the role of reward and punishment, a central tenet within social learning theory is that individuals can learn from a model without direct reinforcement, through processes of instruction or even simple modelling. In what has become a landmark study, Bandura (1977) showed that simply exposing children to live or filmed displays of adults hitting a large inflatable doll (Bobo) was sufficient to elicit similar behaviours from young children. A second tenet of social learning theory is that learning takes place in a social context, such that individuals are especially likely to copy significant others, such as family members. Sibling violence is the most common form of family violence (Tucker, Finkelhor, Shattuck, & Turner, 2013) and so is likely to contribute to the aggregation of antisocial behaviour within families.

Sibling influences on aggressive behaviour extend beyond direct modelling (i.e., "deviancy training"; Dishion, Spracklen, Andrews, & Patterson, 1996) to include coercive cycles of violence (Patterson, 1984) and interacting effects of both proactive and reactive aggression. Equally, role model effects have been identified in sibling studies of: (1) alcohol, tobacco and other drug use (Kothari, Sorenson, Bank, & Snyder, 2014); (2) gambling (Gupta & Derevensky, 1997); and (3) the onset of sexual activity and teenage parenthood (East, 1996; East & Jacobson, 2001; East & Khoo, 2005; Widmer, 1997).

Of course, siblings can also act as *positive* role models. In studies of typically developing children, evidence that siblings can serve as positive role models come from research on children's development of prosocial behaviour (e.g., White, Ensor, Marks, Jacobs, & Hughes, 2014) or boys' reading mastery (Telford, 1999), as well as from research into how adolescents achieve excellence in competitive sport (e.g., Fraser-Thomas, Côté, & Deakin, 2008). Overall, however, research into siblings as positive role models has probably been most active in studies of children with developmental disorders or disability. Chapter 8 provides a review of this field of research, highlighting the resilience of sibling relationships in the context of disability or chronic illness and outlining advances in intervention science that hinge on the positive effects of sibling modelling (e.g., Taylor, Levin, & Jasper, 1999). At the same time, the evidence reviewed in Chapter 8 also demonstrates the particular salience of resource dilution effects for families caring for a child with a disability.

The findings from this research field are likely to prove important not only in bringing about much-needed improvements in the effectiveness of societal care and support for families of children with disabilities but also as a means of deepening our understanding of contextual influences on sibling relationships.

Siblings as part of a family or community

Each new arrival in a family rapidly increases the number of different relationships. In two-parent families with one child there are three relationships; the arrival of a second child means that there are now six relationships; the birth of a third child brings the total number of relationships to ten, and so on. This complexity of family life is increasingly recognised in contemporary research on siblings, which typically draws on one of two theoretical models: (1) Bronfenbrenner's (1979) ecological model of development; and (2) family systems theory (e.g., Minuchin, 1988).

In Bronfenbrenner's (1979) ecological model, child characteristics are viewed as interacting with four different levels of the environment: micro-, exo-, meso- and macro-systems. Micro-systems refer to relationships with other people in a given setting, for example mother-child interactions at home. The next level up, meso-systems, refer to systems of micro-systems: the interrelations between the child's interpersonal interactions in different settings, such as their interactions with others at home, school and in the neighbourhood. More remote yet, the exo-system level refers to aspects of the physical environments (e.g., home, school) in which the child spends time. Finally, macro-systems refer to more abstract factors such as culture or class, which create a specific pattern of characteristics in micro-, meso- and exo-systems. For example, across cultural groups, individuals may show different styles of interpersonal relationships and may live in different physical environments. Although originally conceived to explain individuals' behaviour, Bronfenbrenner's (1979) ecological model has also been applied to examine social influences on sibling relationship quality (e.g., Brody, Stoneman, & Gauger, 1996; Jenkins, Rasbash, Leckie, Gass, & Dunn, 2012; Kretschmer & Pike, 2009). For example, Kretschmer and Pike (2009) showed that effects of household chaos (an exo-system factor) and socioeconomic status (a macro-system factor) on sibling relationship quality could be explained through their influence on maternal warmth and paternal harsh discipline (micro-system factors). In this book, Bronfenbrenner's (1979) ecological model emerges as useful in research on sources of variation in sibling relationships (see Chapter 3), on sibling relationships and adjustment in the context of disability or illness (see Chapter 8) and in cross-cultural comparisons of sibling relationships (see Chapter 9).

According to family systems perspectives, individual family members and dyadic relationships are interdependent parts of the larger family system. A particularly relevant example of this interdependence comes from research on the impact of differential parental treatment. Indeed, parents with more than one child will be well aware that their decisions (e.g., with respect to bedtimes, chores, treats and privileges) are likely to be carefully scrutinised. As discussed in Chapter 4, there is good empirical evidence that differential parental treatment, if perceived as unfair, is related to poor quality sibling relationships (Kowal & Kramer, 1997). Another important example of the interdependence within families comes from research on how behaviour in one relationship spills over into other relationships, leading to a clustering in the affective quality of individual relationships within a family. For example, using multi-level modelling, Jenkins et al. (2012) found a clustering in sibling relationship quality that was related to maternal warmth. Put more simply, in families where interactions between mothers and children are warm and affectionate sibling relationships are also likely to be positive. Conversely, marital conflict adversely affects both parent-child and sibling relationships (e.g., Brody, Stoneman, & Burke, 1987; Fauber, Forehand, Thomas, & Wierson, 1990; Gerard, Krishnakumar, & Buehler, 2006). As a result of this spillover, families develop specific patterns of interaction. Importantly, family systems theory recommends that sibling relationships be studied in relation to all other dyadic relationships within the family. Further support for the importance of adopting a whole-family approach comes from evidence that: (1) fathers play a key role in supporting positive sibling relationships (e.g., Volling & Belsky, 1992) and (2) including all the siblings in a family increases the explanatory power of models of sibling influences on adjustment (Marciniak, 2017).

Sibling research: Methodological advances

Alongside the variety of theoretical approaches described above, sibling research encompasses many different methodologies, reflecting, in part, the diverse foci of individual studies. Dunn's seminal studies with preschoolers typically adopted unstructured observations to give children a free rein; this work has been valuable in demonstrating how much effort and skill young children deploy in initiating and sustaining an activity they enjoy (e.g., Dunn & Kendrick, 1982). Other researchers have included more structured observational paradigms to investigate particular kinds of sibling interactions, such as exchanges that involve teaching (e.g., Howe & Recchia, 2009; Prime, Perlman, Tackett, & Jenkins, 2014). Methodological contrasts also reflect the longevity of the sibling relationship: observational methods are needed to investigate very early sibling interactions, but are much less likely to be necessary by middle childhood or adolescence. That said, several recent studies of adolescent siblings have used observations, typically involving a specific task (e.g., constructing a tower, discussing conflict, planning a fictional holiday), to index relationship quality, often in conjunction with parent- and self-report data (e.g., Iturralde, Margolin, & Spies Shapiro, 2013; Neiderhiser, Marceau, & Reiss, 2013).

Observations offer a number of advantages over other methodologies (e.g., self-report). They provide a more objective view of sibling relationships based on definitions of behaviour defined by the researcher (rather than by individual informants) and so are particularly useful for measuring specific behaviours or sequences of behaviour that informants may struggle, or be reluctant to report accurately (Furman, Jones, Buhrmester, & Adler, 1989; Gardner, 2000). In addition, observations can shed light on the "ABCs" of interactions (antecedents, behaviours, consequences) and so are useful in documenting reciprocal or transactional effects and behavioural contingencies, and in gathering insights about family dynamics. At the same time, observations can be influenced by day-to-day variability in behaviour, or by effects of the time of day (e.g., hunger, tiredness). That said, this sensitivity to small changes in behaviour and relationship quality can also be viewed as a strength (Aspland & Gardner, 2003): coupled with a reduced susceptibility to expectancy effects than parent- or teacher-report data (Aspland & Gardner, 2003; Patterson, 1982), this sensitivity to changes in relationship quality make observations particularly useful for assessing intervention effects.

Another common approach is the use of diary methods to record how much time children spend interacting with a sibling (e.g., McHale & Crouter, 1996; Updegraff, McHale, Whiteman, Thayer, & Delgado, 2005). Diary methods offer the advantage of ecological validity (e.g., Laurenceau & Bolger, 2005): direct observations are often conducted in artificial settings (e.g., a lab) and behaviour may be affected by the presence of the observer (e.g., reduced sibling conflict). Diaries can also be used to collect information over extended time frames and often include important contextual information. Note that diary-based methods include a variety of sampling techniques, ranging from fixed or pseudo-random interval sampling to event-based diaries that provide contextual information and meaning to pre-determined event categories (e.g., sibling squabbles). These methods do, however, place substantial demands on participants, and computerised systems such as "talk pedometers" that are beginning to be used in studies of parent-child interactions (e.g., Greenwood, Thiemann-Bourque, Walker, Buzhardt, & Gilkerson, 2010; Soderstrom & Wittebolle, 2013; Weil & Middleton, 2010) may prove useful in sibling studies to minimise the burden on families.

One advance in sibling research has been the increased use of methods that allow researchers to gather a "child's eye view" of sibling relationships, either through the use of questionnaires or semi-structured interviews (Deater-Deckard, Dunn, & Lussier, 2002; McGuire, Manke, Eftekhari, & Dunn 2000). This self-report method has the obvious advantage of economy, facilitating the collection of data from large samples of families, which is important both for reasons of statistical power (needed to provide an adequate test of study hypotheses) and to ensure the inclusion of a diverse array of families (needed to provide results that are generalisable to the overall population). Many questionnaires used in sibling research have already been well validated (Furman & Buhrmester, 1985a, 1985b; Stocker & McHale, 1992), but studies involving novel measures must ensure that these new instruments have been carefully constructed and have good psychometric properties (e.g., Rust & Golombok, 2009).

Beyond economy, questionnaire measures also provide information that observations cannot access, including information about relationship quality over a period of weeks and months and about subjective qualities of the relationship (e.g., Furman et al., 1989; Olson, 1977). In other words, self-report methodologies allow the researcher to understand the meaning of specific behaviours within a particular context or relationship. For example, a snatch or an aggressive gesture may have very different meanings for different sibling dyads. Indeed, children's *perceptions* of their sibling relationships may be more important for their well-being than the observed reality of the relationship.

Self-report questionnaires are most typically used with school-aged children and adolescents, but innovative methodologies have been developed to obtain a first-hand view of sibling relationships from children as young as four years old. For example, Sturgess, Dunn and Davies (2001) used a mapping procedure to measure five-year-olds' perceptions of closeness to their siblings, parents and friends. Likewise, several research groups have used puppet interviews, such as the Berkeley Puppet Interview (Ablow & Measelle, 1993) to obtain self-reports about sibling relationships from young children. In these studies children's reports showed good internal consistency, test-retest reliability and convergence with other family members' views of the relationship (Kretschmer & Pike, 2009; Pike, Coldwell, & Dunn, 2005; Ross, Woody, Smith, & Lollis, 2000).

Existing sibling research has made great progress in the development of both observational and survey methods, but several methodological weaknesses in the field remain. One clear gap is the lack of ethnic, social and cultural diversity in studies of siblings (see Chapter 9). Another important gap is the relative scarcity of studies that apply observational methods within a longitudinal design. Compared with other close relationships, sibling relationships are particularly dynamic, and the relative lack of observational longitudinal designs therefore limits our understanding of the mechanisms underpinning changes in sibling interactions. A third area that requires greater attention in future research is the embedded nature of sibling relationships. Several different analytical methods have been adopted for assessing dyadic measures of sibling relationships (for reviews on this topic see Hess, 2015; Whiteman & Loken, 2006), but ecological approaches also require consideration of the ways in which sibling interactions are nested within wider family, neighbourhood or cultural contexts, using multi-level modelling (Jenkins et al., 2012).

Finally, many of the chapters in this book draw on findings from a ten-year longitudinal study, the Cambridge Toddlers Up Study (see Hughes, 2011). As well as spanning a much longer developmental period than most studies (from toddlerhood through to pre-adolescence), the study stands apart from others in the field by virtue of the breadth and detail of the data collected, which include (1) detailed coding from video-observations of the children interacting with multiple social partners (mothers, siblings, friends, unfamiliar peers) and (2) interview- or questionnaire-based ratings from multiple informants (mothers, teachers and the children themselves). Moreover, each time-point in the Cambridge Toddlers Up study also included standard language ability assessments and batteries of experimental tasks, designed to capture variation in key cognitive skills such as executive functions (i.e., planning, working memory and inhibitory control) and social understanding (i.e., the ability to infer and predict others' thoughts and feelings). The richness of this longitudinal dataset provided a valuable arena in which the origins and consequences of variation in sibling relationship quality could be explored.

Take-home messages

1. As described by McHale et al. (2012, p. 913), sibling relationships are a "fixture in the family lives of children and adolescents" and yet have received far less attention than other family relationships.

2. Reports of birth order effects are greatly exaggerated and typically come from studies that did not include controls for factors that co-vary with position in the family (e.g., parental education, family size). More rigorously controlled studies show that birth order effects are typically very small in magnitude.

3. Siblings have also been used as research tools in both twin studies and clinical case-control studies as a way of controlling for general family factors.

4. Reflecting individual differences and age-related changes in the nature of sibling relationships, as well as historical shifts in ideas about siblings, several different models of sibling influence have been adopted. These include accounts of siblings as playmates, attachment figures, rivals and role-models.

5. Siblings are often children's preferred partners for pretend play and pretend interactions can provide enriched opportunities for discussing and thinking about mental states. Perhaps as a result, preschoolers with child-age siblings develop an understanding of mind more rapidly than other children (see Chapter 6).

6. Rather than demonstrating deep-seated rivalry and psychological insecurity, sibling conflict may simply reflect the involuntary and very familiar nature of the sibling relationship: whereas friendships are unlikely to survive sustained conflict, siblings remain siblings, providing licence for children to display negative feelings unchecked.

7. Research on siblings as role models has focused on adolescence and risk-taking behaviours, but siblings can also provide positive role models for prosocial behaviour (see Chapter 5) and academic achievement (see Chapter 6) and are increasingly included as models in interventions to support the development of children with disabilities (see Chapter 8).

8. Just as no man is an island, so no relationship should be examined in isolation from other relationships: sibling relationships both affect and are affected by other relationships within and outside the family (see Chapter 4).

9. Researchers investigating sibling relationships face multiple methodological challenges. While observational studies are generally considered a gold standard they are very time-consuming and do not assess subjective qualities of sibling relationships, such that for older children, survey-based studies may be preferred.

10. The Cambridge Toddlers Up study is unusual in applying observational methods within a 10-year longitudinal design. Many of the later chapters in this book will therefore draw on findings from this study.

References

Ablow, J. C., & Measelle, J. R. (1993). *The Berkeley Puppet Interview: Interviewing and coding system manuals*. University of Oregon, Department of Psychology. Eugene, OR.

Adler, A. (1900/1923). *The practice and theory of individual psychology* (P. Radin, Trans.). London: Routledge and Kegan Paul Ltd (Original work published 1923).

Aspland, H., & Gardner, F. (2003). Observational measures of parent-child interaction: An introductory review. *Child and Adolescent Mental Health*, 8, 136–143. doi:10.1111/1475-3588.00061.

Bandura, A. (1977). *Social learning theory*. Englewood Cliffs, NJ: Prentice Hall.

Blake, J. (1981). Family size and the quality of children. *Demography*, *18*, 421–442. doi:10.2307/2060941.

Bowlby, J. (1958). The nature of the child's tie to his mother. *International Journal of Psycho-Analysis*, *39*, 350–373. doi: 10.12691/ajap-4-2-1.

Bowlby, J. (1969). *Attachment and loss: Vol. 1. Attachment*. New York: Basic Books.

Bowlby, J. (1973). *Attachment and loss: Vol. 2. Separation*. New York: Basic Books.

Brody, G. H. (1998). Sibling relationship quality: Its causes and consequences. *Annual Review of Psychology*, *49*, 1–24. doi:10.1146/annurev.psych.49.1.1.

Brody, G. H., Stoneman, Z., & Burke, M. (1987). Family systems and individual child correlates of sibling behavior. *American Journal of Orthopsychiatry*, *57*, 561–569. doi:10.1111/j.1939-0025.1987.tb03571.x.

Brody, G. H., Stoneman, Z., & Gauger, K. (1996). Parent-child relationships, family problem-solving behavior, and sibling relationship quality: The moderating role of sibling temperaments. *Child Development*, *67*, 1289–1300. doi:10.1111/j.1467-8624.1996.tb01796.x.

Bronfenbrenner, U. (1979). *The ecology of human development: Experiments by nature and design*. Cambridge, MA: Harvard University Press.

Brown, J., Donelan-McCall, N., & Dunn, J. (1996). Why talk about mental states? The significance of children's conversations with friends, siblings, and mothers. *Child Development*, *67*, 836–849. doi: 10.1111/j.1467-8624.1996.tb01767.x.

Conger, K., Stocker, C., & McGuire, S. (2009). Sibling socialization: The effects of stressful life events and experiences. In L. Kramer, & K. Conger (Eds.), *Siblings as agents of socialization: New directions for child and adolescent development* (Vol. 126, pp. 45–60). San Francisco: Jossey-Bass.

Conger, K. J., & Little, W. M. (2010). Sibling relationships during the transition to adulthood. *Child Development Perspectives*, *4*, 87–94. doi:10.1111/j.1750-8606.2010.00123.x.

Damian, R. I., & Roberts, B. W. (2015a). The associations of birth order with personality and intelligence in a representative sample of U.S. high school students. *Journal of Research in Personality*, *58*, 96–105. doi:10.1016/j.jrp.2015.05.005.

Damian, R. I., & Roberts, B. W. (2015b). Settling the debate on birth order and personality. *Proceedings of the National Academy of Sciences of the United States of America*, *112*, 14119–14120. doi:10.1073/pnas.1519064112.

Davidoff, L. (2012). *Thicker than water: Siblings and their relations 1780–1920*. Oxford, UK: Oxford University Press.

Deater-Deckard, K., Dunn, J., & Lussier, G. (2002). Sibling relationships and social-emotional adjustment in different family contexts. *Social Development*, *11*, 571–590. doi:10.1111/1467-9507.00216.

Dishion, T. J., Spracklen, K. M., Andrews, D. W., & Patterson, G. R. (1996). Deviancy training in male adolescent friendships. *Behavior Therapy*, *27*, 373–390. doi:10.1016/S0005-7894(96)80023-2.

Dunn, J. (1983). Sibling relationships in early childhood. *Child Development*, *54*, 787–811. doi:10.2307/1129886.

Dunn, J. (2011). Sibling influences. In D. Skuse, H. Bruce, L. Dowdney, & D. Mrazek (Eds.), *Child psychology and psychiatry: Frameworks for practice* (2nd ed., pp. 8–12). Chichester, UK: Wiley-Blackwell.

Dunn, J., Brown, J., & Beardsall, L. (1991). Family talk about feeling states and children's later understanding of others' emotions. *Developmental Psychology*, *27*, 448–455. doi: 10.1037/0012-1649.27.3.448.

Dunn, J., Brown, J., Slomkowski, C., Tesla, C., & Youngblade, L. (1991). Young children's understanding of other people's feelings and beliefs: Individual differences and their antecedents. *Child Development, 62,* 1352–1366. doi: 10.1111/j.1467-8624.1991. tb01610.x.

Dunn, J., & Kendrick, C. (1982). *Siblings: Love, envy, and understanding.* London: Grant McIntyre Ltd.

East, P. (1996). Do adolescent pregnancy and childbearing affect younger siblings? *Family Planning Perspectives, 28,* 148–153. doi:10.1363/2814896.

East, P., & Jacobson, L. J. (2001). The younger siblings of teenage mothers: A follow-up of their pregnancy risk. *Developmental Psychology, 37.* doi:10.1037/0012-1649.37.2.254.

East, P. L., & Khoo, S. T. (2005). Longitudinal pathways linking family factors and sibling relationship qualities to adolescent substance use and sexual risk behaviors. *Journal of Family Psychology, 19,* 571–580. doi:10.1037/0893-3200.19.4.571.

Fauber, R., Forehand, R., Thomas, A. M., & Wierson, M. (1990). A mediational model of the impact of marital conflict on adolescent adjustment in intact and divorced families: The role of disrupted parenting. *Child Development, 61,* 1112–1123. doi:10.1111/j.1467-8624.1990. tb02845.x.

Fraser-Thomas, J., Côté, J., & Deakin, J. (2008). Understanding dropout and prolonged engagement in adolescent competitive sport. *Psychology of Sport and Exercise, 9,* 645–662. doi:10.1016/j.psychsport.2007.08.003.

Freud, S. (1953). The interpretation of dreams (J. Strachey, Trans.) *The standard edition of the complete psychological works of Sigmund Freud* (Vol. 4–5). London: Hogarth Press (Original work published 1921).

Freud, S. (1955). Group psychology and the analysis of the ego (J. Strachey, Trans.) *The standard edition of the complete psychological works of Signmund Freud* (Vol. 18). London: Hogarth Press (Original work published 1921).

Furman, W., & Buhrmester, D. (1985a). Children's perceptions of the personal relationships in their social networks. *Developmental Psychology, 21,* 1016–1024. doi: 10.1037/0012-1649.21.6.1016.

Furman, W., & Buhrmester, D. (1985b). Children's perceptions of the qualities of sibling relationships. *Child Development, 56,* 448–461. doi: 10.2307/1129733.

Furman, W., Jones, L., Buhrmester, D., & Adler, T. (1989). Children's, parents' and observers' perspectives on sibling relationships. In P. Zukow (Ed.), *Sibling interaction across cultures: Theoretical and methodological issues* (pp. 165–183). New York: Springer-Verlag.

Galton, F. (1874). *English men of science: Their nature and nurture.* London: MacMillan and Co.

Gardner, F. (2000). Methodological issues in the direct observation of parent-child interaction: Do observational findings reflect the natural behaviour of participants? *Clinical Child and Family Psychology Review, 3,* 185–198. doi:10.1023/A:1009503409699.

Gerard, J. M., Krishnakumar, A., & Buehler, C. (2006). Marital conflict, parent-child relations, and youth maladjustment: A longitudinal investigation of spillover effects. *Journal of Family Issues, 27,* 951–975. doi:10.1177/0192513X05286020.

Greenwood, C. R., Thiemann-Bourque, K., Walker, D., Buzhardt, J., & Gilkerson, J. (2010). Assessing children's home language environments using automatic speech recognition technology. *Communication Disorders Quarterly, 32,* 83–92. doi: 10.1177/ 1525740110367826.

Grimes, D. A., & Schulz, K. F. (2005). Compared to what? Finding controls for case-control studies. *Lancet, 365,* 1429–1433. doi:10.1016/S0140-6736(05)66379-9.

Gupta, R., & Derevensky, J. (1997). Familial and social influences on juvenile gambling behavior. *Journal of Gambling Studies, 13,* 179–192. doi:10.1023/A:1024915231379.

Hess, M. (2015). Methods in family and sibling research. In A. Sisler and A. Ittel (Eds.), *Siblings in adolescence: Emerging individuals, lasting bonds* (pp. 127–156). London: Psychology Press.

Howe, N., Petrakos, H., & Rinaldi, C. (1998). "All the sheeps are dead. He murdered them": Sibling pretense, negotiation, internal state language, and relationship quality. *Child Development, 69*, 182–191. doi:10.1111/j.1467-8624.1998.tb06142.x.

Howe, N., & Recchia, H. (2009). Individual differences in sibling teaching in early and middle childhood. *Early Education and Development, 20*, 174-197. doi: 10.1080/10409280802206627.

Howe, N., Ross, H. S., & Recchia, H. (2011). Sibling relations in early and middle childhood. In P. K. Smith and C. H. Hart (Eds.), *The Wiley-Blackwell handbook of childhood social development* (2nd ed., pp. 356–372). New York: Wiley.

Hughes, C. (2011). *Social understanding and social lives: From toddlerhood through to the transition to school.* London: Psychology Press.

Hughes, C., & Devine, R. T. (2017). Family influences on theory of mind: A review. In V. Slaughter and M. de Rosnay (Eds.), *Theory of mind development in context* (pp. 41–56). Abingdon, Oxon: Routledge.

Hughes, C., Fujisawa, K., Ensor, R., Lecce, S., & Marfleet, R. (2006). Cooperation and conversations about the mind: A study of individual differences in two-year-olds and their siblings. *British Journal of Developmental Psychology, 24*, 53–72. doi:10.1348/026151005X82893.

Irish, D. P. (1964). Sibling interaction: A neglected aspect in family life research. *Social Forces, 42*, 279–288. doi:10.1093/sf/42.3.279.

Iturralde, E., Margolin, G., & Spies Shapiro, L. A. (2013). Positive and negative interactions observed between siblings: Moderating effects for children exposed to parents' conflict. *Journal of Research on Adolescence, 23*, 716–729. doi: 10.1111/jora.12020.

Jenkins, J., Rasbash, J., Leckie, G., Gass, K., & Dunn, J. (2012). The role of maternal factors in sibling relationship quality: A multilevel study of multiple dyads per family. *Journal of Child Psychology and Psychiatry, 53*, 622–629. doi:10.1111/j.1469-7610.2011.02484.x.

Kanazawa, S. (2012). Intelligence, birth order, and family size. *Personality and Social Psychology Bulletin, 38*, 1157–1164. doi:10.1177/0146167212445911.

Kluger, J. (2006, July 10). The new science of siblings. *Time*. Retrieved from http://content.time.com/time/magazine/article/0,9171,1209949,00.html.

Kothari, B. H., Sorenson, P., Bank, L., & Snyder, J. (2014). Alcohol and substance use in adolescence and young adulthood: The role of siblings. *Journal of Family Social Work, 17*, 324–343. doi:10.1080/10522158.2014.924457.

Kowal, A., & Kramer, L. (1997). Children's understanding of parental differential treatment. *Child Development, 68*, 113–126. doi: 10.2307/1131929.

Kramer, L. (2010). The essential ingredients of successful sibling relationships: An emerging framework for advancing theory and practice. *Child Development Perspectives, 4*, 80–86. doi:10.1111/j.1750-8606.2010.00122.x.

Kramer, L., & Bank, L. (2005). Sibling relationship contributions to individual and family well-being: Introduction to the special issue. *Journal of Family Psychology, 19*, 483–485. doi:10.1037/0893-3200.19.4.483.

Kretschmer, T., & Pike, A. (2009). Young children's sibling relationship quality: Distal and proximal correlates. *Journal of Child Psychology and Psychiatry, 50*, 581–589. doi:10.1111/j.1469-7610.2008.02016.x.

Kris, M., & Ritvo, S. (1983). Parents and siblings: Their mutual influences. *Psychoanalytic Study of the Child, 38*, 311–324.

Laurenceau, J. P., & Bolger, N. (2005). Using diary methods to study marital and family processes. *Journal of Family Psychology, 19*, 86–97. doi:10.1037/0893-3200.19.1.86.

McGuire, S., Manke, B., Eftekhari, A., & Dunn, J. (2000). Children's perceptions of sibling conflict during middle childhood: Issues and sibling (dis)similarity. *Social Development, 9,* 173–190. doi: 10.1111/1467-9507.00118.

McGuire, S., & Shanahan, L. (2010). Sibling experiences in diverse family contexts. *Child Development Perspectives, 4,* 72–79. doi:10.1111/j.1750-8606.2010.00121.x.

McHale, S. M., & Crouter, A. C. (1996). The family contexts of children's sibling relationships. In G. H. Brody (Ed.), *Sibling relationships: Their causes and consequences* (pp. 173–195). Norwood, NJ: Ablex.

McHale, S. M., Updegraff, K. A., & Whiteman, S. D. (2012). Sibling relationships and influences in childhood and adolescence. *Journal of Marriage and Family, 74,* 913–930. doi:10.1111/j.1741-3737.2012.01011.x.

Marciniak, K. (2017). Variance distribution in sibling relationships: Advantages of multilevel modeling using full sibling groups. *Family Process, 56,* 189–202. doi:10.1111/famp.12157.

Minuchin, P. (1988). Relationships within the family: A systems perspective on development. In R. Hinde and J. Stevenson-Hinde (Eds.), *Relationships within families: Mutual influences* (pp. 7–26). Oxford, UK: Clarendon.

Mitchell, J. (2000). *Mad men and Medusas: Reclaiming hysteria and the effects of sibling relations on the human condition.* London: Penguin Press.

Mitchell, J. (2003). *Siblings – Sex and violence.* Cambridge: Polity Press.

Moffitt, T. (2005). The new look of behavioral genetics in developmental psychopathology: Gene-environment interplay in antisocial behaviors. *Psychological Bulletin, 131,* 533–554. doi:10.1037/0033-2909.131.4.533.

Mosak, H., & Maniacci, M. (1999). *A primer of adlerian psychology: The analytic-behavioral-cognitive psychology of Alfred Adler.* New York: Taylor and Francis.

Neiderhiser, J. M., Marceau, K., & Reiss, D. (2013). Four factors for the initiation of substance use by young adulthood: A 10-year follow-up twin and sibling study of marital conflict, monitoring, siblings, and peers. *Development and Psychopathology, 25,* 133–149. doi:10.1017/S0954579412000958.

Neubauer, P. B. (1982). Rivalry, envy, and jealousy. *Psychoanalytic Study of the Child, 37,* 121–142.

Olson, P. H. (1977). Insiders' and outsiders' views of relationships: Research studies. In G. Levinger and H. Raush (Eds.), *Close relationships: Perspectives on the meaning of intimacy.* (pp. 115–135). Amherst, MA: University of Massachusetts Press.

Patterson, G. (1982). *A social learning approach: Vol 3. Coercive family process.* Eugene, OR: Castalia.

Patterson, G. (1984). Siblings: Fellow travelers in coercive family process. In R. Blanchard and D. Blanchard (Eds.), *Advances in the study of aggression* (Vol. 1, pp. 173–215). Orlando, FL: Academic Press.

Perner, J., Ruffman, T., & Leekam, S. (1994). Theory of mind is contagious: You catch it from your sibs. *Child Development, 65,* 1228–1238. doi:10.1111/j.1467-8624.1994.tb00814.x.

Piaget, J. (1932). *The moral judgement of the child.* New York: Academic Press.

Pike, A., Coldwell, J., & Dunn, J. (2005). Sibling relationships in early/middle childhood: Links with individual adjustment. *Journal of Family Psychology, 19,* 523–532. doi:10.1037/0893-3200.19.4.523.

Plomin, R., & Daniels, D. (1987). Why are children in the same family so different from one another? *Behavioural and Brain Sciences, 10,* 1–60. doi:10.1017/S0140525X00055941.

Prime, H., Perlman, M., Tackett, J. L., & Jenkins, J. M. (2014). Cognitive sensitivity in sibling interactions: Development of the construct and comparison of two coding methodologies. *Early Education and Development, 25,* 240–258. doi: 10.1080/10409289.2013.821313.

Rodgers, J. L., Cleveland, H. H., Van Den Oord, E., & Rowe, D. C. (2000). Resolving the debate over birth order, family size, and intelligence. *American Psychologist, 55,* 599–612. doi:10.1037/0003-066X.55.6.599.

Rohrer, J. M., Egloff, B., & Schmukle, S. C. (2015). Examining the effects of birth order on personality. *Proceedings of the National Academy of Sciences of the United States of America, 112,* 14224–14229. doi:10.1073/pnas.1506451112.

Ross, H., Woody, E., Smith, M., & Lollis, S. (2000). Young children's appraisals of their sibling relationships. *Merrill-Palmer Quarterly, 46,* 441–464.

Rust, J., & Golombok, S. (2009). *Modern psychometrics: The science of psychological assessment* (3rd ed.). New York: Routledge.

Sandberg, J., & Rafail, P. (2014). Family size, cognitive outcomes, and familial interaction in stable, two-parent families: United States, 1997–2002. *Demography, 51,* 1895–1931. doi:10.1007/s13524-014-0331-8.

Soderstrom, M., & Wittebolle, K. (2013). When do caregivers talk? The influences of activity and time of day on caregiver speech and child vocalizations in two childcare environments. *PLoS ONE, 8,* p. e80646. doi:10.1371/journal.pone.0080646.

Steelman, L. C., Powell, B., Werum, R., & Carter, S. (2002). Reconsidering the effects of sibling configuration: Recent advances and challenges. *Annual Review of Sociology, 28,* 243–269. doi:10.1146/annurev.soc.28.111301.093304.

Stocker, C., & McHale, S. (1992). The nature and family correlates of preadolescents' perceptions of their sibling relationships. *Journal of Personal and Social Relationships, 9,* 179–195. doi: 10.1177/0265407592092002.

Sturgess, W., Dunn, J., & Davies, L. (2001). Young children's perceptions of their relationships with family members: Links with family setting, friendships, and adjustment. *International Journal of Behavioral Development, 25,* 521–529. doi: 10.1080/01650250042000500.

Sulloway, F. (1996). *Born to rebel: Birth order, family dynamics, and revolutionary genius.* New York: Pantheon.

Taylor, B. A., Levin, L., & Jasper, S. (1999). Increasing play-related statements in children with autism toward their siblings: Effects of video modeling. *Journal of Developmental and Physical Disabilities, 11,* 253–264. doi:10.1023/A:1021800716392.

Telford, L. (1999). A study of boys' reading. *Early Child Development and Care, 149,* 87–124. doi: 10.1080/0300443991490107.

Tucker, C. J., Finkelhor, D., Shattuck, A. M., & Turner, H. (2013). Prevalence and correlates of sibling victimization types. *Child Abuse and Neglect, 37,* 213–223. doi:10.1016/j.chiabu.2013.01.006.

Updegraff, K., McHale, S., Whiteman, S., Thayer, S., & Delgado, M. (2005). Adolescent sibling relationships in Mexican American families: Exploring the role of familism. *Journal of Family Psychology, 19,* 512–522. doi:10.1037/0893-3200.19.4.512.

Volling, B. L. (2012). Family transitions following the birth of a sibling: An empirical review of changes in the firstborn's adjustment. *Psychological Bulletin, 138,* 497–528. doi: 10.1037/a0026921.

Volling, B. L., & Belsky, J. (1992). The contribution of mother-child and father-child relationships to the quality of sibling interaction: A longitudinal study. *Child Development, 63,* 1209–1222. doi:10.1111/j.1467-8624.1992.tb01690.x.

Weil, L. W., & Middleton, L. (2010). Use of the LENA tool to evaluate the effectiveness of a parent intervention program. *SIG 1 Perspectives on Language Learning and Education, 17,* 108–111. doi:10.1044/lle17.3.108.

White, N., Ensor, R., Marks, A., Jacobs, L., & Hughes, C. (2014). "It's mine!" Does sharing with siblings at age 3 predict sharing with siblings, friends, and unfamiliar peers at age 6? *Early Education and Development, 25,* 185–201. doi:10.1080/10409289.2013.825189.

Whiteman, S. D., & Loken, E. (2006). Comparing analytic techniques to classify dyadic relationships: An example using siblings. *Journal of Marriage and Family, 68*, 1370–1382. doi:10.1111/j.1741-3737.2006.00333.x.

Whiteman, S. D., McHale, S. M., & Soli, A. (2011). Theoretical perspectives on sibling relationships. *Journal of Family Theory and Review, 3*, 124–139. doi:10.1111/j.1756-2589.2011.00087.x.

Widmer, E. D. (1997). Influence of older siblings on initiation of sexual intercourse. *Journal of Marriage and the Family, 59*, 928–938. doi:10.2307/353793.

Youngblade, L., & Dunn, J. (1995). Social pretend with mother and sibling: Individual differences and social understanding. In A. Pellegrini (Ed.), *The future of play theory: Essays in honor of Brian Sutton-Smith* (pp. 221–240). New York: SUNY Press.

Zajonc, R. B. (2001). The family dynamics of intellectual development. *American Psychologist, 56*, 490–496. doi:10.1037/0003-066X.56.6-7.490.

Zajonc, R. B., & Markus, G. B. (1975). Birth order and intellectual development. *Psychological Review, 82*, 74–88. doi:10.1007/978-1-4615-8765-1_12.

2

BECOMING A SIBLING

A time of crisis?

How young children respond to the transition to siblinghood is a topic that has interested a small but distinguished group of researchers for almost three quarters of a century. In an early review of this field, Legg, Sherick and Wadland (1974) noted that, for the preschool child, everyday life is full of surprise and novelty: some new experiences bring delight, but other new situations, such as the arrival of a new baby, have the potential to cause confusion, fear and stress. To emphasise this point, Legg and colleagues cited Freud's (1900/1953, p. 252) view that children harbour death wishes towards their new sibling, such that "hostile feelings towards brothers and sisters must be far more frequent in childhood than the unseeing eye of the adult observer can perceive." Although this claim is, of course, intrinsically untestable, in this chapter we shall examine Winnicott's (1964, p. 133) more moderate proposal that "it is so usual as to be called normal when a child is upset at the birth of a new one."

First, however, a few historical shifts in the context of children's experiences in becoming a sibling deserve note. In particular, compared with previous generations, expectant parents today face much less uncertainty: medical advances have dramatically reduced infant mortality rates and ultrasound screening provides expectant parents with direct reassurance of their new baby's healthy development in the womb. Coupled with a raised awareness of the psychological upheaval that a new baby may bring, these technological advances mean that parents today are likely to be more confident and more motivated to prepare their firstborn children for this important transition. Moreover, in contrast with the situation described by Legg et al. (1974), today's parents (in the Western world, at least) can readily find a wide range of developmentally appropriate picture books that provide an engaging but accurate picture of life with a new baby. As a result, the task of preparing young children for the arrival of a sibling is much less challenging than it might once have been. The period of separation associated with staying in hospital to give birth is now also very much shorter. For example, 42% of mothers giving birth in a hospital in 1975 stayed for seven or more days (and 68% stayed for four or more days): corresponding figures for 2005–2006 were just 3% and 13% (Richardson & Mmata, 2007). Moreover, in the 1950s and 1970s, children were not always allowed to visit their mothers in hospital (and if they were, the visit might involve interacting through a pane of glass). In contrast, hospitals today have frequent visiting hours and are typically designed to be reassuring for families.

Thus, for a host of reasons, the experience of becoming a sibling in the 1960s (when Winnicott was writing about this life-changing period) was much more likely to be traumatic than it is today. Convergent evidence for the prevalence of distress following the birth of a new sibling comes from other early studies that did not adopt a psychoanalytical perspective. For example, in a longitudinal study of temperament in 110 typically developing children followed from the first month of life, Thomas, Birch, Chess and Robbins (1961) noted that ten of the 18 children who experienced this transition to siblinghood during the course of the study displayed either developmental regressions (in socialisation, feeding, sleeping or toileting) or aggressive behaviour towards the new baby. Importantly, these children were not only typically younger than those who showed no sign of trauma during this transition but had also displayed a less adaptable temperament from the first few months of life. Likewise, in a later pilot study of 21 preschoolers who had recently experienced the birth of a younger sibling, Legg et al. (1974) reported that developmental regressions were common, as were signs of jealousy and resentment when the new baby was being breastfed. Two further interesting findings from this study were that: (1) parents rarely prepared children below the age of two years for the arrival of a new sibling; and (2) distress was conspicuously diminished when fathers took an active role in caring for the older child. In discussing the first of these findings, Legg et al. (1974) offered a number of practical suggestions for minimising the stresses associated with other changes to family life associated with the baby's arrival, such as changing sleeping arrangements or moving home. In relation to the second of these findings, Legg et al. (1974) made a plea for more studies into the developmental consequences of fathers' involvement in childcare during this transitional period. Strikingly, our search through the literature indicates that researchers did not respond to this challenge for another 40 years; the findings from this long-awaited research by Volling and her colleagues (Kolak & Volling, 2013; Song & Volling, 2015; Volling et al., 2014) are discussed later in the chapter.

Although, as discussed above, external factors adding to the trauma of the transition to siblinghood are now much less common, it is worth noting that this transition is typically experienced during toddlerhood or the early preschool years, a period of profound change in children's lives (e.g., starting nursery) and in their ability to make sense of and regulate their behaviour and emotions, developmental milestones that may contribute to the much-famed "terrible twos" (Meltzoff, Gopnik, & Repacholi, 1999). Moreover, the lack of sleep and stresses associated with caring for a new-born infant often take their toll on parental sensitivity (Teti, O'Connell, & Reiner, 1996). Within this context, it is unsurprising that the appearance of a new baby can evoke ambivalent emotional responses from young children.

However, in keeping with the theme of striking individual differences in the quality of children's sibling relationships, which will be a recurring motif within this book, responses to the transition to siblinghood vary dramatically across children. For some (and perhaps most), this transitional period is predominantly positive, with the new baby providing an enchanting source of entertainment, and parents and other family members remaining reassuringly consistent and available. The following excerpt from an interview with a mother of two girls B, aged nine and M, aged seven and a one-year-old boy (J) illustrate some of these positives:

> When we first told them that they were going to have a baby brother, one of M's first responses was "Oh great! I'm not the youngest anymore!" […] and she ran around the room just really pleased. (And when J arrived) it was like they were, it was so maternal, they were […] lying on the bed with him for hours and just kind of holding him and looking at him and just very slow and attentive like you are as a new mother almost. […] They're so proud of him, so, again, that's why they feel a bit like parents, you know, he, he's only just standing up on his own, I mean literally in the last week […] and they have the excitement that I do, and they kind of, they rushed in and told their teacher "J's standing!", you know, they're really proud.

For other children, however, Freud's account of the reaction of Little Hans, "the stork can take him away again" (1900/1953, p. 251) may seem, in comparison, remarkably polite and restrained. Young children's initial reactions to a new sibling appear telling: in an early study Kendrick and Dunn (1982) found that children's reactions three weeks after the birth of a younger sibling predicted their reactions to mother-infant interactions just over a year later. Of particular concern, young children who appeared withdrawn following the arrival of a new baby were more likely to develop poor sibling relationships over time (Dunn & Kendrick, 1982).

One goal of this chapter is to outline the factors that predict these individual differences in young children's experiences and reactions to becoming a sibling. First, however, we will briefly outline a few of the theoretical models used to understand family transitions (for a more detailed account, see Volling, 2012). One of the very first models of families experiencing stressful transitions was developed to explain how families coped with fathers being drafted into the army during the Second World War (Hill, 1949). This early model portrayed family adaptation to a stressful transition as hinging on the balance between an individual's resources (in terms of finances, education, health and social support) and the demands of the family and community: stressful transitions impose a drain upon these resources, such that "going into the red" effectively precipitates a family crisis.

Life-stage researchers offer a rather different view of transitions in which changes to an individual's biological, cognitive, affective or behavioural functions occupy centre-stage. Perhaps more relevant for the transition to siblinghood however, is Bronfenbrenner's (1979) ecological model, which highlights changes in both an individual's role and in the immediate social context, with the interplay between these two domains contributing to individual differences in outcomes. From this perspective, life stressors serve as turning points that, while challenging, can lead to positive as well as negative changes. Indeed, life stressors may simply accentuate prior tendencies. That is, as noted by Rutter (1996, the experience of a transitional event "may be positive, negative or neutral, depending on whether the experience alters the person's life in a way that matters and in a direction that runs counter to the previous life trajectory or pattern of psychological functioning." (p. 612)

Overall, the findings from the 23 longitudinal studies included in Volling's (2012) empirical review indicate that the transition to siblinghood is, in fact, rarely experienced as a family crisis and is a turning point for some but not all children. Both child and parental characteristics contribute to this variability. For example, early work showed that the transition to siblinghood is more challenging when the firstborn is still very young; more recent studies have documented the effects of temperamental characteristics, such as emotional reactivity, and cognitive milestones such as children's understanding of others' thoughts and feelings (see Volling, 2012). With regard to parental characteristics, both mental health (e.g., post-partum depression) and self-efficacy appear to matter.

Interestingly, what is meant by "self-efficacy" is likely to be very different for new parents and for parents expecting a second child. While the former group are likely to worry about their general competence as parents, the latter group are more likely to express doubts about their ability to be fair and impartial in loving and raising two children (Walz & Rich, 1983). Of course, this birth order effect may depend on the profile of the parent. For example, the responses to informal interviews we have conducted with colleagues expecting a baby (i.e., individuals with specialist qualifications or experience related to children) suggest that, across birth order, concerns focused on the impact of the arrival of a new baby on existing relationships within the family. To illustrate this point, two short extracts from these interviews are given below. The first comes from a mother expecting her first child; the second comes from the mother of B, M and J (from the earlier excerpt) interviewed before the birth of her third child (J) as she compares her concerns before the birth of her second child (M) with those regarding J's arrival.

> I'm not the greatest sleeper in the world so I'm aware that that sleeplessness will cause me to maybe become more tense and that might rub off in terms of my relationship with my husband and we might become snappy with each other, but he's very good at not holding onto grudges and things like this, so I hope we won't butt heads too much. (Mother expecting first child)

Mother: I think I was much more apprehensive about how it'd impact on her [B] [...] because she was so little and, you know, she had that closeness to me [...]

Interviewer: And so were those fears unfounded?

Mother: They, they probably were but I found the divided attention quite difficult to do at the beginning. It was quite overwhelming having such small children, you know, they both need your time whereas I'm not worried about that this time […] I think there might be a bit of a pull, you know baby on the one hand, I think while he's a baby it will be quite easy actually because they just sit around and don't do too much but when they're a bit older and they have different needs I think that might stretch me a little bit. (Mother expecting third child)

Perhaps for everybody, however, what changes as families grow in size is the importance parents attach to achieving perfection. As the adage goes, with a first child we can be the kind of parents we dream of being, but with a second child we are often the kind of parent we hoped we would never become. Supporting this view, numerous longitudinal studies (and in particular the seminal work of Dunn & Kendrick, 1982) have shown that the birth of a second child is often accompanied by a drop in maternal positive affection, attention and responsiveness, coupled with an increase in negative control and conflict. The news is not all bad, however, as findings from at least two early studies indicate that the birth of a younger sibling is also typically accompanied by an increase in the frequency and richness of mothers' talk to their firstborns (Dunn & Kendrick, 1982; Field & Reite, 1984).

More recently, in the first large-scale study to include father-infant-sibling interactions as well as mother-infant-sibling interactions (in a well-educated sample of 224 families with one-month-old infants living in Michigan, United States), Volling et al. (2014) applied person-centred analyses to analyse firstborns' behaviour in a situation designed to provoke jealousy. Triadic mother-infant-child and father-infant-child free-play sessions in this study were filmed back-to-back on the same day and both mothers and fathers were instructed to be overtly affectionate towards the infant in order to ensure that the interaction attracted the attention of the firstborn. The authors found that the majority (60% for interactions with mothers, 55% for interactions with fathers) of young children showed a positive profile of regulated exploratory play. For interactions with both parents, just under a third of the sample showed an "approach-avoidant" profile, less than 3% showed high levels of disruptive behaviour, and approximately 6% showed "anxious-clingy" profiles.

Interestingly, despite the contiguity and consistency across sessions, children often showed very different profiles with each parent. In particular, children who were anxious-clingy with one parent were very unlikely to be anxious–clingy with the other parent). Overall, however, the proportion of children in each group was quite similar for sessions with mothers and fathers – the one difference was the emergence of a fifth group of "attention-seeking" children in response to fathers' interactions with the infants. In seeking to explain why attention-seeking behaviours were specific to the father sessions, Volling et al. (2014) note that fathers have been found to be more likely than mothers to respond punitively to children's negative emotions (Nelson, O'Brien, Blankson, Calkins, & Keane, 2009) and so may be less tolerant of clinging behaviours or displays of distress. As a result, children may learn to achieve emotional reassurance at a distance from fathers.

In other work with the same sample, Volling and colleagues (Kolak & Volling, 2013; Song & Volling, 2015) have uncovered interesting interactions between the quality of co-parenting and children's temperament as predictors of firstborns' adjustment shortly after their sibling's birth. Kolak and Volling (2013) showed that firstborns' negative reactivity (an aggregate of both parents' prenatal ratings) predicted their internalising behaviours one month after their sibling's birth, but only when parents showed high levels of undermining co-parenting in a family free play session. Similarly, negatively reactive children also showed high levels of externalising behaviour over the transition when parents showed high levels of undermining, and low levels of supportive co-parenting behaviour.

Song and Volling (2015) reported a similar interaction between the quality of co-parenting and children's temperament as predictors of cooperative behaviour during an observation in which the mother changed the one-month-old infant's nappy (diaper). Specifically, over and above the effects of child age, gender and maternal education, prenatal ratings of low child soothability predicted observational ratings of low cooperation during the nappy-change session, but only for families with high undermining and low cooperative co-parenting. Importantly, parallel aggregate prenatal ratings of child anger did not predict children's cooperation, highlighting the importance of soothability and regulation of distress (rather than frustration) as a foundation for cooperative behaviour. In discussing the interaction between soothability and cooperative co-parenting as predictors of child cooperation, Song and Volling (2015) note that low cooperative co-parenting not only indicates a lack of positive role-models for children's cooperative behaviours but may also index either an antagonistic family climate (that might exacerbate the stresses associated with becoming a sibling) or low paternal involvement (such that the drop in maternal responsiveness to the firstborn following the birth of the infant is not compensated by positive attention from fathers). These proposals all fit within a second theme that will run through the chapters of this book, namely that family interactions represent a complex interplay of interacting systems, such that sibling relationships cannot be studied in isolation but instead need to be examined within the rich matrix of family life (see Chapter 4).

With this lesson in mind, it is worth noting that the stresses associated with the arrival of a new baby in the family are likely to be less marked for laterborn children, who are much less likely than firstborn children to have experienced an extended period of undivided parental attention. One obvious limitation of research in this field is that existing studies have focused exclusively on the impact of the arrival of a sibling on a firstborn child. Given this narrow focus on how firstborn children react to becoming siblings, it is worth noting that epidemiological studies offer opportunities for investigating the impact of a sibling's arrival within larger families.

A good example of this work can be found in Lawson and Mace's (2009) analysis of data from the Avon Longitudinal Study of Parents and Children (ALSPAC), in which both maternal and paternal behaviours were tracked over the first decade of life. This analysis focused on parental investment, measured as the frequency of engagement in key care activities over the first decade of life. As predicted, maternal investment was biased to daughters and paternal investment was biased to sons, and an increase in family size was associated with a drop in parental investment per offspring for both parents. Worryingly, the presence of a non-biological father figure was associated with lower investment from both parents. Another important finding to emerge from these analyses of data from 13,176 British children was that the decline in parental investment in families with more children was particularly marked for laterborn children. That is, while the arrival of a new baby may present laterborn children with less psychological upheaval than that experienced by firstborn children, across the first decade of life laterborn children typically receive significantly less parental attention. On a more positive note, as we hope the later chapters in this book will illustrate, this drop in parental attention may be balanced by positive influences (e.g., caregiving, tuition) from older siblings.

This point brings us neatly to the next topic within this chapter, namely the ways in which the arrival of a younger sibling provides opportunities for children to acquire a more advanced understanding of others. While it is intuitively obvious that younger children frequently learn new skills and acquire a more mature understanding of the world through interacting with their older sibling, there are also ways in which the presence of a younger sibling can facilitate children's socio-cognitive development. Indeed, the conversational analyses within Dunn and Kendrick's (1982) seminal study highlighted the frequency with which mother-child talk focused on what was acceptable and unacceptable behaviour. Understandably, the mothers were very protective towards the new baby and young children's natural curiosity sometimes led to rather rough investigations of their new sibling. As a result, the transition to siblinghood was associated with a clear increase in the frequency of verbal and non-verbal conflict between mothers and their firstborn children. While mothers often attributed this rise in conflict to their own fatigue and depleted reserves of patience, observational coding indicated that the conflict often followed episodes of children's demanding or deliberately naughty behaviour that, strikingly, were three times as common when mothers were involved in caring for the new baby than when they were not. At the same time, as noted earlier, this study also showed that the transition to siblinghood was characterised by a marked increase in the frequency of mother-child conversations about others' needs, emotions and desires. An example of such talk, given in a review by Dunn and Hughes (2014), is included below:

Mother to Baby (who has been crying for a long time): I don't know what we're going to do, do you?
Child: Smack [spank] him.
Mother: He's too little to smack.
Child: Smack him.
Mother: Can't smack him, 'cause he doesn't know any better.

(p. 24)

In this excerpt, the mother not only provides guidance regarding acceptable and unacceptable behaviour (i.e., that smacking a baby is not an option), but also highlights the baby's lack of intentionality and so draws the child's attention to differences in the child's and the baby's understanding of the world. As noted by Dunn and Hughes (2014), this kind of mother-child talk displays at least two features that are likely to facilitate young children's understanding of moral issues. The first of these is the explicit, clear and reasoned nature of the messages mothers give to children about the kind of behaviour they want from the child. The second is the emotional tenor of these conversations: they are not neutral exchanges but reflections on emotionally charged situations that the child is likely to remember for some time. As one might expect, there were marked individual differences in both the absolute level and magnitude of change in mental state talk following the birth of a new baby (Dunn & Hughes, 2014; Dunn & Kendrick, 1982). In families in which the mothers commented frequently on what the baby's cries might mean and made several suggestions about what might cheer up the baby the firstborn child often became an enthusiastic partner in caregiving activities.

The benefits of such talk about thoughts and feelings are not just immediate, but also more long-term. For example, children from families who frequently engage in mental state talk have been shown to develop in their social and moral understanding more rapidly than their peers, even when other predictors such as age, gender and maternal education are taken into account (for a recent narrative review and meta-analysis, see Devine & Hughes, 2016; Hughes & Devine, 2017; see also Chapter 6). While there is good evidence for a robust association between the frequency of mothers' conversational reference to thoughts and feelings and children's later performance on tests of social understanding, the processes and mechanisms underpinning this association have yet to be established (e.g., Hughes, White, & Ensor, 2014). As noted by Dunn and Kendrick (1982), mothers who frequently engaged in this kind of talk were also more likely than other mothers to give justifications for their disciplinary responses to the firstborn's misbehaviour, to use language for complex cognitive purposes and to join the child in games of shared pretend play.

This cluster of findings is important as it indicates a general style of interacting that is well-tuned to children's thoughts and motivations and that in turn is likely to facilitate children's entry into the "community of minds" (Nelson, 2005). If, as the evidence suggests, the birth of a younger child is typically associated with a sharp increase in opportunities for discussing thoughts and feelings, then the transition to siblinghood brings with it cognitive benefits as well as emotional challenges. Moreover, variation in children's socio-cognitive skills helps explain variability in how children respond to emotional challenges. For example, a recent longitudinal study that tracked firstborn children from before the arrival of a new baby and across the first year of siblinghood showed that children's prenatal levels of aggression were related to their later antagonism to the baby both directly (reflecting stable individual differences in levels of aggressive behaviour) and indirectly, with children who showed poorer theory of mind (i.e., poorer understanding of others' thoughts and feelings) displaying greater antagonism (Song, Volling, Lane, & Wellman, 2016).

Parallel analyses of data from the same longitudinal study of the first year of siblinghood (Oh, Volling, & Gonzalez, 2015) showed that only 8% of the firstborn children were antagonistic towards their baby sibling at the four-month visit: while these children also showed high levels of positive engagement, this early antagonism remained high across the first year and was accompanied by a steep increase in avoidance behaviours and so acted as an early marker for later problems. A larger group of children (40%) showed an increase from low to high levels of antagonism across the first year, but the majority of firstborn children showed high levels of positive engagement coupled with low levels of both antagonism and avoidance. For most families, then, worries about how young children will respond to a new sibling appear needless. Moreover, early levels of sibling antagonism were associated with low parental self-efficacy and more punitive disciplinary styles. Together, these findings suggest that interventions that build parents' confidence and equip parents with positive strategies for managing conflict in the first year of the sibling relationship should help foster positive sibling relationships that, as discussed in the later chapters of this book, contribute to children's social and cognitive development.

Take-home messages

1. The cultural context surrounding both the transition to siblinghood and parent-child interactions has changed dramatically over the past half century. As a result, early reports of children's distress and trauma following the birth of a sibling may reflect difficulties evoked by prolonged separation or lack of preparation rather than an intrinsic part of becoming a sibling.
2. In a recent study in which mothers and fathers were invited to make overt displays of affection to the newborn infant, the majority of firstborns showed positive adjustment and regulated exploratory play.
3. The family dynamic changes with the addition of a new child. Empirical evidence suggests that there is (at least temporarily) a drop in parental positivity and sensitivity following the birth of a second child.
4. Parents should not blame themselves for an increase in conflict with their firstborn following the birth of a second child. Firstborns are more likely to transgress when parents are caring for the new baby, suggesting that conflict is often initiated by the firstborn testing boundaries (or reacting to the novel situation of no longer being the centre of attention).
5. Life stressors serve as turning points that, while challenging, can lead to positive as well as negative changes. Indeed, life stressors may simply accentuate prior tendencies.
6. A smooth transition to siblinghood is not simply a question of finding the perfect age gap (although younger children may find the transition more challenging). Individual differences in firstborns' soothability (rated by both mothers and fathers before the birth of the second child) predicted individual differences in cooperative responses during a nappy-change paradigm.

7. Highlighting the importance of family context, this effect of temperament was particularly clear in the context of negative (or low positive) co-parenting.
8. Fathers matter and may be particularly crucial once there are two young children to care for. Evidence about the quality of co-parenting demonstrates that family influences can operate even when the father is not directly present.
9. How firstborns react to their parent playing with the new baby may be quite different when they are with their mothers versus their fathers. For example, displays of anxiety or clinginess were typically only evident with one parent, while displays of "attention-seeking" behaviour were restricted to children's interactions with fathers.
10. Preparation is key: parents can use picture books and help their child to think about the new baby as a social being with needs, desires and interests. Longitudinal findings highlight the importance of this understanding in enabling children to avoid antagonistic interactions with their siblings.

References

Bronfenbrenner, U. (1979). *The ecology of human development: Experiments by nature and design.* Cambridge, MA: Harvard University Press.

Devine, R. T., & Hughes, C. (2016). Family correlates of false belief understanding in early childhood: A meta-analysis. *Child Development.* Advance online publication. doi:10.1111/cdev.12682.

Dunn, J., & Hughes, C. (2014). Family talk about moral issues: The toddler and preschool years. In C. Wainryb and H. E. Recchia (Eds.), *Talking about right and wrong: Parent-child conversations as contexts for moral development* (pp. 21–43). New York: Cambridge University Press.

Dunn, J., & Kendrick, C. (1982). *Siblings: Love, envy, and understanding.* London: Grant McIntyre Ltd.

Field, T., & Reite, M. (1984). Children's responses to separation from mother during the birth of another child. *Child Development, 55,* 1308–1316. doi: 10.2307/1130000.

Freud, S. (1953). The interpretation of dreams (J. Strachey, Trans.) *The standard edition of the complete psychological works of Sigmund Freud* (Vol. 4–5). London: Hogarth Press (Original work published 1900).

Hill, R. (1949). *Families under stress: Adjustment to the crises of war separation and reunion.* New York: Harper.

Hughes, C., & Devine, R. T. (2017). Family infuences on theory of mind: A review. In V. Slaughter and M. de Rosnay (Eds.), *Theory of mind development in context* (pp. 41–56). Abingdon, Oxon: Routledge.

Hughes, C., White, N., & Ensor, R. (2014). How does talk about thoughts, desires, and feelings foster children's socio-cognitive development? Mediator, moderators and implications for intervention. In K. Lagattuta (Ed.), *Children and emotion. New insights into developmental affective science* (pp. 95–105). Basel: Karger.

Kendrick, C., & Dunn, J. (1982). Protest or pleasure? The response of first-born children to interactions between their mothers and infant siblings. *Journal of Child Psychology and Psychiatry, 23,* 117–129. doi:10.1111/j.1469-7610.1982.tb00057.x.

Kolak, A. M., & Volling, B. L. (2013). Coparenting moderates the association between firstborn children's temperament and problem behavior across the transition to siblinghood. *Journal of Family Psychology, 27,* 355–364. doi: 10.1037/a0032864.

Lawson, D. W., & Mace, R. (2009). Trade-offs in modern parenting: a longitudinal study of sibling competition for parental care. *Evolution and Human Behavior, 30,* 170–183. doi:10.1016/j.evolhumbehav.2008.12.001.

Legg, C., Sherick, I., & Wadland, W. (1974). Reaction of pre-school children to the birth of a sibling. *Child Psychiatry and Human Development, 5,* 3–39. doi:10.1007/BF01441311.

Meltzoff, A., Gopnik, A., & Repacholi, B. (1999). Toddlers' understanding of intentions, desires and emotions: Explorations of the dark ages. In P. Zelazo, J. Astington & D. Olson (Eds.), *Developing theories of intention: Social understanding and self-control* (pp. 17–41). Mahwah, NJ: Lawrence Erlbaum Associates.

Nelson, J., O'Brien, M., Blankson, A., Calkins, S., & Keane, S. (2009). Family stress and parental responses to children's negative emotions: Tests of the spillover, crossover, and compensatory hypotheses. *Journal of Family Psychology, 23,* 671–679. doi: 10.1037/a0015977.

Nelson, K. (2005). Language pathways into the community of minds. In J. Astington & J. Baird (Eds.), *Why language matters for theory of mind.* Oxford, UK: Oxford University Press.

Oh, W., Volling, B. L., & Gonzalez, R. (2015). Trajectories of children's social interactions with their infant sibling in the first year: A multidimensional approach. *Journal of Family Psychology, 29,* 119–129. doi: 10.1037/fam0000051.

Richardson, A., & Mmata, C. (2007). *NHS maternity statistics, England: 2005–2006.* London, UK: National Statistics. Retrieved from http://www.hscic.gov.uk/catalogue/PUB01682.

Rutter, M. (1996). Transitions and turning points in developmental psychopathology: As applied to the age span between childhood and mid-adulthood. *International Journal of Behavioral Development, 19,* 603–626. doi:10.1177/016502549601900309.

Song, J. H., & Volling, B. L. (2015). Coparenting and children's temperament predict firstborns' cooperation in the care of an infant sibling. *Journal of Family Psychology, 29,* 130–135. doi: 10.1037/fam0000052.

Song, J. H., Volling, B. L., Lane, J. D., & Wellman, H. M. (2016). Aggression, sibling antagonism, and theory of mind during the first year of siblinghood: A developmental cascade model. *Child Development, 87,* 1250–1263. doi:10.1111/cdev.12530.

Teti, D. M., O'Connell, M. A., & Reiner, C. D. (1996). Parenting sensitivity, parental depression and child health: The mediational role of parental self-efficacy. *Infant and Child Development, 5,* 237–250. doi: 10.1002/(SICI)1099-0917(199612)5:4<237::AID-EDP136>3.0.CO;2-5.

Thomas, A., Birch, H. G., Chess, S., & Robbins, L. C. (1961). Individuality in responses of children to similar environmental situations. *The American Journal of Psychiatry, 117,* 798–803. doi:10.1176/ajp.117.9.798.

Volling, B. L. (2012). Family transitions following the birth of a sibling: An empirical review of changes in the firstborn's adjustment. *Psychological Bulletin, 138,* 497–528. doi: 10.1037/a0026921.

Volling, B. L., Yu, T., Gonzalez, R., Kennedy, D. E., Rosenberg, L., & Oh, W. (2014). Children's responses to mother-infant and father-infant interaction with a baby sibling: Jealousy or joy? *Journal of Family Psychology, 28,* 634–644. doi: 10.1037/a0037811.

Walz, B. L., & Rich, O. J. (1983). Maternal tasks of taking-on a second child in the postpartum period. *Maternal-Child Nursing Journal, 12,* 185–216.

Winnicott, D. W. (1964). *The child, the family, and the outside world.* Harmandsworth, Middlesex, England: Penguin Books.

3

DEVELOPMENTAL CHANGES AND INDIVIDUAL DIFFERENCES IN SIBLING RELATIONSHIPS

Sibling relationships come in all shapes and sizes. A brief examination of families in literature demonstrates the diversity of sibling relationships. In some cases, literary siblings highlight the bitter conflicts and rivalries that can exist between brothers and sisters, as in, for example, the stories of Cain and Abel or Katherina and Bianca Minola in Shakespeare's *The Taming of the Shrew*. Other stories, such as those of the March sisters in Louise May Alcott's *Little Women* emphasise the role of sibling support in overcoming adversity. The quality of individual sibling relationships also differs within families. In Jane Austen's classic, *Pride and Prejudice,* the close supportive relationship enjoyed by the two older sisters, Elizabeth and Jane, is in stark contrast to the bickering between the two youngest Bennett sisters, Kitty and Lydia. What explains this variation in sibling relationship quality? In the case of the Bennett sisters we might explain the more positive relationship enjoyed by Jane and Elizabeth by their increased age and maturity relative to Kitty and Lydia. Alternatively, we might consider the different temperaments or personalities of the individual sisters in each relationship.

In this chapter, we consider some of the factors that contribute to the dramatic individual differences in the quality of children's sibling relationships. First, we consider sibling relationships from a developmental perspective, examining how the quality of children's relationships with their brothers and sisters changes from the preschool years to adolescence and beyond. A key theme of this section is *heterotypic continuity*: that is, while the specific types of sibling behaviour and the function of sibling relationships may change over time, individual differences in the *quality* of the relationship remain reasonably stable. The second section of this chapter draws on an ecological framework (Bronfenbrenner, 1979). As described in more detail in Chapter 1, from this perspective the child's (or the sibling dyad's) behaviour is viewed as a product of interactions with various levels of their environment. Broader environmental influences from other family relationships and cultural values are considered in Chapters 4 and 9, respectively. By contrast, in the current chapter, we explore effects of gender, age gap and child temperament to investigate how sibling relationship quality may vary with characteristics of the sibling dyad and the children within it.

A developmental perspective on sibling relationships

Early childhood. The foundations of sibling relationships are laid very early on in life. As described in Chapter 2, Dunn and Kendrick's (1982) study showed that children's reactions to their newborn siblings predict the quality of their later relationships. Specifically, firstborn children who demonstrated interest and affection towards the new baby showed more friendly behaviour towards their sibling 14 months later, while children who showed withdrawal after the birth of their sibling exhibited more unfriendly behaviour 14 months later. Interestingly, the younger child's behaviour followed a similar pattern – that is, younger children showed more friendly behaviour at 14 months if their older sibling had shown interest and affection towards them after their birth – pointing to strong partner effects in sibling interactions. Alongside this stability of individual differences, the early years are also characterised by an overall increase in sibling interaction as the younger child develops the physical and social skills to be an interesting playmate to their older sibling. In a diary study examining family activities before, immediately following and a year after the second child's birth, mothers reported an age-related increase in the time children spent interacting together (Lawson & Ingleby, 1974). Similarly, Lamb (1978b) showed that preschool children were more willing to interact with their infant sibling in a laboratory setting when they were 18 months' old compared with six months previously, and there was substantial stability in individual differences in sibling relationship quality over this six-month period.

Sibling relationships are characterised by ambivalence, and this holds particularly true in early childhood when siblings may change from playmates to sparring partners seemingly in the blink of an eye. Effects of birth order are also particularly evident at this age. Older siblings typically take the lead in interactions, and tend to initiate most prosocial interactions and most instances of conflict or teasing (Dunn & Munn, 1986b; Howe, Ross, & Recchia, 2011; Pepler, Abramovitch, & Corter, 1981). At this age, sibling conflict may often result in physical aggression, and here birth order effects remain: older siblings are more likely to use physical force, whereas younger children, perhaps noting their physical disadvantage in this area, are less likely to respond with aggression (Dunn & Munn, 1986a; Perlman & Ross, 2005). Rivalry may also be commonplace: for example, as noted in chapter 2, older children may become clingy or demanding when their mother's attention is directed towards the younger child (Dunn & Kendrick, 1982). Sibling relationships in early childhood also feature many positive interactions. The relative similarity in children's ages and hence in their interests (at least relative to parents) means that siblings are ideally placed to be playmates, and often engage in extended and complex pretend play narratives (e.g., Hughes, 2011). Moreover, the contrast in abilities between the two children provides opportunities for sibling teaching, and observational studies show that, as discussed in more detail in Chapter 6, older siblings are effective teachers, while younger siblings are active learners (e.g., Howe, Brody, & Recchia, 2006).

Although rapid improvements in the younger child's cognitive and social capabilities dramatically increase their capacity to engage in sibling interactions over the preschool period (Lawson & Ingleby, 1974), longitudinal studies suggest that individual differences in the quality of sibling relationships show some stability over the preschool period. Specifically, Stillwell and Dunn (1985) showed that observational measures of sibling relationship quality when the younger child was 14 months' old were linked to mothers' reports of their children's behaviour towards each other when the younger child was four years old. Moreover, there was stability across the whole four-year period: mothers' reports of the older child's positive interest in their new sibling shortly after birth were associated with the older child's own positive comments about their sibling four years later (Stillwell & Dunn, 1985). In contrast, other researchers have found little stability in siblings' observed prosocial and agonistic behaviours over a similar developmental period when younger children were aged two to five years old (Abramovitch, Corter, Pepler, & Stanhope, 1986), perhaps reflecting lower stability of the frequency of specific observed behaviours.

Middle childhood. Further work by Dunn suggests that individual differences in sibling relationship quality remain stable from preschool to early adolescence. In a seven-year study beginning when siblings were aged three and five years old, Dunn, Slomkowski and Beardsall (1994) showed that mothers' reports of the older child's positive and negative behaviour towards their younger sibling at age five and age 12 were moderately correlated over time. Similarly, mothers' reports of younger siblings' positive and negative behaviour both showed consistency from three to six years and from six to 10 years (although they were not correlated across the whole seven-year period). At this point it is worth noting that while a moderate correlation (typically defined as a correlation of .3 to .5) indicates a degree of convergence between two variables, the corresponding proportion of shared variance (calculated by squaring the correlation coefficient, such that a correlation of .3 indicates .9% shared variance) is still smaller than the proportion of unshared variance. Thus, while these studies show some stability in individual variation in sibling relationship quality, there was also considerable change in ratings that likely reflect both changes in the sibling relationship and random error associated with measurement.

The moderate stability found by Dunn and colleagues was replicated in an observational study following families from when their secondborn children were one month old, until they were 13 years old (Kramer & Kowal, 2005). Extending this work, our own findings with the Cambridge Toddlers Up sample confirm the stability of questionnaire measures of relationship quality over a similar time period but highlight differential stability in positive versus negative aspects of behaviour. Specifically, while reports of sibling positivity and negativity showed substantial stability over a nine-year period beginning when the younger child was three years old, stability was higher for negative behaviour (White, 2014). This contrast fits with previous research suggesting greater consistency across contexts in negative than in positive behaviour, perhaps because negative behaviours reflect a gap between the demands of a situation and the child's competence (e.g., Mischel, 1984).

The stability of individual differences in sibling relationship quality is all the more remarkable given that there are substantial developmental changes occurring across middle childhood. Children have increased opportunities for developing friendships outside the home after starting school, and these friendships may take precedence over family relationships, such that siblings spend much less time together (Kramer & Kowal, 2005). At the same time, the gap between the two children's ability levels is also likely to decline resulting in a more even balance of power (Buhrmester & Furman, 1990). Despite these changes, many characteristics of the sibling relationships discussed in relation to early childhood, such as sibling teaching and conflict, remain prominent in middle childhood.

The changes in sibling relationships discussed above may help to explain mean-level differences in sibling relationship quality over middle childhood. Using data from a subsample of the Avon Longitudinal Study of Parents and Children (ALSPAC), Jenkins and colleagues (2005) showed that maternal perceptions of sibling negativity decreased over a two-year period from when the younger child was five years old. In contrast, in a longitudinal study spanning middle childhood to early adolescence, Brody et al. (1994b) showed that the elder, but not the younger sibling within a dyad reported an increase in negative relationship quality and a decrease in positive relationship quality over the study period. Buhrmester (1992) observed similar findings of a decrease in reports of positive relationship quality, but no change in perceived conflict, from middle childhood to adolescence. In contrast, in a study comparing both children's perceptions of their sibling relationship, Slomkowski and Manke (2004) suggested a drop in intensity through late childhood: that is, children's reports showed decreases in both conflict and warmth over a two-year period.

Using data from the Cambridge Toddlers Up study, we extended the developmental scope of Slomkowski and Manke's (2004) work by examining children's older siblings' and mothers' ratings of the relationship over a two-year period beginning when the younger child was ten years old (White, 2014). Consistent with the findings from this earlier study, children's and siblings' ratings showed a drop in the intensity and involvement of sibling relationships, indicating reduced companionship, intimate disclosure, affection, reassurance of worth (i.e., the extent to which the other child made them feel respected) and conflict. In contrast, mothers' reports of the sibling relationship only showed decreases in companionship and intimate disclosure. These findings suggest that those in the sibling relationship (e.g., children and their siblings) have different perspectives of the quality of interactions from those outside of the relationship (e.g., parents; Olson, 1977), such that outsiders may be unaware of more subtle changes in the subjective quality of the relationship. This finding illustrates the importance of gaining children's perspectives of their own relationships, particularly when considering subjective aspects of relationships.

Adolescence. By adolescence sibling relationships appear even more egalitarian, as evidenced by studies indicating equivalent reports of nurturance and dominance from older and younger siblings (Buhrmester, 1992). As the younger child reaches an age at which they no longer require constant supervision, older siblings may no longer be asked by parents to "keep an eye on" their siblings (Buhrmester, 1992). This change may reduce the frequency of conflictual interactions, for example situations where the younger sibling feels resentful that the older sibling is "in charge". In support of this view, one study of 15-year-olds and their younger siblings reported a decrease in sibling conflict and an increase in sibling intimacy over a two-year period (Feinberg, McHale, Crouter, & Cumsille, 2003). Conversely, increased independence is also likely to reduce opportunities for sibling interactions as both children have more freedom to spend time with friends outside the home. Indeed, observational work suggests that by adolescence siblings spend only a very small proportion of their time in direct interactions (Raffaelli & Larson, 1987).

That is not to say that siblings are no longer important fixtures in adolescents' lives. Adolescents rate their siblings as important sources of support, on a par with their parents (Furman & Buhrmester, 1992), and this support appears to continue into late adolescence. For example, using latent growth modelling to track perceived sibling support over a four-year period beginning when younger siblings were 11 years old and older siblings were 13 years old, Branje, van Lieshout, van Aken and Haselager (2004) demonstrated that younger siblings' perceived support from an older sibling increased until age 13 before levelling off. In contrast, older siblings' perceived support from a younger sibling remained stable throughout adolescence. Moreover, although overall closeness with siblings appears to decrease over adolescence, decreases in intimate disclosure and affection are more modest (Buhrmester, 1992). In fact, personal disclosure to siblings may increase over adolescence, at least when considered relative to disclosure to parents (Campione-Barr, Lindell, Giron, Killoren & Greer, 2015). Furthermore, although sibling relationships in adolescence may be less conflictual than earlier in childhood, ratings of sibling conflict remain high relative to other close relationships (Furman & Buhrmester, 1992), with arguments typically centring on issues of fairness (e.g., whose turn it is to choose the TV programme) and invasion of the personal domain (e.g., borrowing clothes, spending time with the adolescent's friends; Campione-Barr & Smetana, 2010).

Adulthood. Early adulthood has been described as a period of self-exploration in which individuals begin to take responsibility for themselves and become independent from their parents (Arnett, 2004). This period is accompanied by a number of structural changes as individuals leave the parental home, start university or employment and begin to establish families of their own. In describing changes in sibling relationships over the transition to adulthood, Conger and Little (2010) advocate a "dynamic recentring" approach: alongside new roles and responsibilities in new contexts, young adults incorporate new social relationships into their social networks, which have more everyday importance than family relationships. Consistent with this perspective, Scharf, Shulman and Avigad-Spitz (2005) found that emerging adults reported spending less time with their siblings than did adolescents. However, emerging adults also reported warmer and less conflictual sibling relationships than adolescents, suggesting that the adage that "absence makes the heart grow fonder" may hold true for some siblings. Qualitative analysis of interviews conducted with American university undergraduates echoed this theme with many students reporting that distance and their new experiences had strengthened the sibling bond (Milevsky & Heerwagen, 2013). These reports also emphasised variation in sibling relationship quality based on age, gender and family type, as well as changes in parental interventions in sibling conflicts.

Research on siblings in middle adulthood is very sparse. In Western cultures at least, sibling relationships become increasingly voluntary as adults establish their own lives and families away from the parental home. However, sibling relationships are still likely to continue to evolve through adulthood, as significant life events place new demands on the sibling relationship. For example, siblings may be drawn together to provide care for their ageing parents, an experience that may have a positive effect on the sibling relationship, but may also produce tension due to imbalances in the sharing of caregiving and decision-making (Lashewicz, 2014; Lashewicz & Keating, 2009). Parental death may also have an impact on sibling relationships, but again the nature of this impact appears to vary between families. Siblings may become more distant due to the absence of a parent to unite the family for special occasions, or the resurfacing of old resentments (Khodyakov & Carr, 2009; Merrill, 1996; Rosenthal, 1985). Conversely, siblings may become closer as rivalries for parental attention are eliminated (Stocker, Lanthier, & Furman, 1997; White & Riedmann, 1992).

In later life, sibling relationships may remain important sources of support (e.g., Cicirelli, 1989), particularly for individuals without children (Pinquart, 2003). Analyses of data from nearly 9,000 adults aged 18–85 years interviewed twice over a period of 4–7 years showed that contact and proximity between siblings decreased somewhat over early adulthood before stabilising in middle age (White, 2001). In contrast, although support between siblings also decreased non-linearly across early and middle adulthood, there was an increase in sibling support in older age and this increase was particularly marked for siblings who lived near to each other. These findings may indicate that older adults increasingly turn to their siblings for support following the loss of other members of their support network. Alternatively, as adults reach the end of their lives they may increasingly relish opportunities to reminisce about their earlier life with those with whom they share these early memories. By either account, these results highlight the need to fully understand the role of siblings in adults', and particularly older adults', support networks.

Taken together, these findings across the lifespan point to both continuity and change in the sibling relationship. Although the nature of sibling relationship quality changes at different life stages, there is considerable stability in individual differences in relationship quality. This stability is particularly notable because it occurs over extended periods that include times of considerable change in the nature of sibling relationships, and in children's social and cognitive development. Second, sibling relationships are dynamic. Over the first years of life children gradually become more able and involved playmates for their older siblings. After children start school, and through middle childhood, sibling relationships may become less involved as children have more opportunities to socialise outside of the home. In adolescence, however, sibling relationship quality may increase again as children confide in their siblings about things they do not feel comfortable discussing with their parents. Sibling relationships may become more peripheral in adults' social networks as individuals establish their own lives away from the family home. However, brothers and sisters are likely to share in care for elderly parents, and so may become important sources of support in later life. Age, therefore, seems to be a significant factor in the quality of sibling relationships.

An ecological perspective on sibling relationships

What other factors may influence sibling relationship quality? Bronfenbrenner's (1979) ecological model highlights the role of different levels of the environment in shaping behaviour. According to this model, behaviour is influenced by characteristics of the child, their relationships with others, the properties of the environments they live in and broader societal factors. These broader influences on sibling relationship quality will be discussed in later chapters: here we consider how three characteristics of the dyad (so-called "sibling constellation" variables) or child, gender, age gap and temperament, contribute to sibling relationships.

Gender. Children's peer relationships and friendships are characterised by a number of gender differences (e.g., Ensor, Hart, Jacobs, & Hughes, 2011; Mathieson & Banerjee, 2011), but are similar contrasts found in children's interactions with a sibling? Early observational studies examining gender differences in individual children's behaviour during sibling interactions suggested that in early childhood, girls typically show more prosocial behaviour towards siblings than boys (e.g., Abramovitch, Corter, & Lando, 1979; Abramovitch et al., 1986; Pepler et al., 1981). Older sisters were noted to be particularly prosocial, taking on a mothering role towards their younger siblings (e.g., Cicirelli, 1975; Lamb, 1978a; Sutton-Smith & Rosenberg, 1970). By contrast, boys may engage in more negative sibling behaviour. An early study found that older brothers were more likely to use physical power to influence their younger siblings' behaviour, while older sisters used more prosocial means to achieve their goals (Sutton-Smith & Rosenberg, 1970). Similarly, preschool- but not school-aged brothers showed more negative behaviour (e.g., physical aggression, arguing, teasing) than sisters (Brody, Stoneman, MacKinnon, & MacKinnon, 1985).

Other researchers have taken a dyadic perspective by comparing same-sex siblings with opposite-sex siblings, or brother pairs with sister pairs. Using this approach, Dunn and Kendrick (1981, 1982) found that in early childhood same-sex siblings exhibit more prosocial behaviour than opposite-sex dyads, and this might be especially true for sisters (Brody et al., 1985; Kier & Lewis, 1998). In contrast, pairs of brothers may show particularly high levels of negative behaviour.

In the Cambridge Toddlers Up sample there were no effects of the child or the sibling's gender on children's antisocial behaviour (refusing to share/interact, bullying, harming) towards a sibling at age three, but there was a significant dyadic effect such that pairs of brothers showed higher initial levels of antisocial behaviour and a greater increase in antisocial behaviour over a three-year period than all other sibling dyads (Ensor, Marks, Jacobs, & Hughes, 2010). These dyadic gender effects in sibling interactions mirrored those observed in children's interactions with friends (Ensor et al., 2011). Other studies have shown that the gender composition of the sibling dyad predicts change in behaviour over time. For example, in a six-month study of two-year-olds and their infant siblings Dunn and Kendrick (1982) found that friendly behaviour increased over time for same-sex dyads, but decreased for opposite-sex dyads. Moreover, Abramovitch and colleagues (1980) reported an increase in negative behaviours (e.g., teasing, physical aggression, snatching), and a decrease in imitation across early childhood for opposite-sex dyads, alongside increases in prosocial behaviour for all dyads.

Do gender differences in sibling interactions persist into middle childhood and adolescence? In a study of school-aged children and adolescents' perceptions of their close relationships, Furman and Buhrmester (1992) found that girls reported more positive sibling relationships but less power in their relationships than boys. However, other studies using similar measures have suggested that gender differences in negative sibling behaviour may not persist beyond early childhood. For example, in middle and late childhood, boys and girls typically report similar levels of conflict (Buhrmester & Furman, 1990; Furman & Buhrmester, 1985), perhaps reflecting the focus on verbal conflict rather than more physical forms of aggression in studies of school-age children versus preschoolers. Dyadic gender differences are also evident in middle to late childhood. For example, same-sex siblings report more positive relationships than opposite-sex siblings (Furman & Buhrmester, 1985), and this effect is stronger for girls (Buhrmester & Furman, 1990). In adolescence, too, pairs of sisters may have particularly positive relationships: a study of sibling attachment from 11 to 17 years old showed that attachment was consistently higher for sisters than for brothers, or mixed-sex dyads (Buist, Deković, Meeus, & Van Aken, 2002). Similar gender differences in closeness and support have also been reported among adults (Cicirelli, 1989; Miner & Uhlenberg, 1997).

The research described above provides quantitative evidence of gender differences in sibling relationships based on questionnaire ratings or frequencies of observed behaviours. However, qualitative research also provides interesting insights into sibling gender differences. Using interviews with eight- to 12-year-olds living in the United Kingdom, Edwards, Mauthner and Hadfield (2005) showed that girls typically reported talking as an important means of establishing and maintaining closeness with their sisters, while shared activities fulfilled a similar role for brothers. Interestingly, in brother-sister dyads children typically emphasised shared activities as a core aspect of their relationship, suggesting the presence of gendered power relations. Furthermore, the gendered nature of sibling relationships had implications for the stability of sibling closeness over time: since sisters emphasised talk as a means of connection, sister–sister relationships could more easily be maintained when an older sibling moved away than brother–brother relationships that focused on shared activities. Finally, it is important to note that while gender can account for individual differences in sibling relationships, sibling relationships also play an important role in children's constructions of gender (e.g., Edwards & Weller, 2014). We will return to this theme in Chapter 5.

Age gap. A common question on parenting forums regards the "best" age spacing between children. Answers to this question may consider a range of factors, including the consequences of age spacing on parents' physical and mental health, the firstborn's ability to adjust to a new baby, and the effects upon the children's relationship. In the previous chapter we discussed evidence that suggested that children are more likely to struggle during the transition to siblinghood when the age gap is small. Here, we consider how age spacing may influence the quality of sibling relationships in childhood. In an early observational study Cicirelli (1973) showed that children were more likely to accept help from an older sibling when there was a large age gap, presumably because the sibling is perceived as more knowledgeable or skilled. Similarly, studies of children's perceptions of their relationship suggest that older siblings with a wide age gap show more nurturance of younger siblings in middle childhood and adolescence (Buhrmester & Furman, 1990). Conversely, in middle childhood and adolescence sibling dyads who are close in age show higher levels of conflict, competition and dominance (Buhrmester & Furman, 1990; Furman & Buhrmester, 1985; Kramer & Kowal, 2005), perhaps because when a sibling is similar in age there is a greater need to mark out differences. Age gap effects on warmth and closeness may be more complex and are likely to depend on the specific aspect of the relationship being considered. In one cross-sectional study, children from middle childhood to adolescence reported more intimacy with a close-in-age older sibling but more affection and admiration for siblings who were older (Buhrmester & Furman, 1990).

Overall, these findings suggest that relationships between siblings with a wide age gap show more of the complementarity characteristic of parent–child relationships, where the older child helps and supports the younger child. In contrast, relationships between closely spaced siblings may be involved and more ambivalent, featuring higher levels of both warmth and conflict. Findings from the Cambridge Toddlers Up sample when the younger child was 10 and 12 years old provide partial support for this view. Age gap was negatively correlated with companionship and intimate disclosure, especially for dyads with an older sister versus an older brother, but unrelated to subjective measures of sibling relationship quality (e.g., affection, reassurance of worth, satisfaction; White, 2014). In other words, compared with siblings with a wide age gap, siblings with a close age gap spent more time together and shared more of their thoughts and feelings, but did not report feeling closer to their siblings. In contrast with previous studies, conflict was also largely unrelated to sibling age gap (although there was, for younger sister/older brother dyads, a negative association between age gap and conflict at age 12).

Returning to our original question, it becomes clear that, in terms of sibling relationship quality, there is no optimal age spacing between children. That said, the nature of the sibling relationship may well differ depending on the age gap. Closely spaced siblings are more likely to have similar interests and spend more time together but these children are also more likely to be competing directly for parental attention, resulting in a greater likelihood of conflict. In contrast, in widely spaced dyads contrasts in skills and abilities are more evident and so older siblings are more likely to take on a teaching or caregiving role. As we have seen, the extent to which age gap effects are observed also depend on other characteristics of the two children, including their gender and temperament.

Temperament. A growing body of research shows that specific temperamental traits are associated with a range of outcomes including children's psychopathology (e.g., Caspi, Henry, McGee, Moffitt, & Silva, 1995; Eisenberg et al., 2001), social skills (e.g., Eisenberg et al., 1993) and relationships with parents (e.g., Kochanska, Friesenborg, Lange, & Martel, 2004). Temperament can be conceptualised in a number of ways but sibling studies have typically focused on how sibling relationships vary with children's levels of negative emotionality and activity. A common finding is that sibling relationships are less positive and/or more negative and conflictual for children with higher levels of emotionality and/or activity. Adding more detail to this picture, at least two studies have reported contrasts between older and younger siblings in the association between temperament and sibling relationship quality. For example, among preschool children and their school-aged siblings, older siblings' emotionality was associated with mothers' reports of sibling negative behaviour, and less positive interactions, while younger siblings' emotionality and activity were related to competition, control and mothers' reports of negativity (Stocker, Dunn, & Plomin, 1989). Similarly, in a study of infants and their older siblings, Volling, McElwain and Miller (2002) showed that the emotionality of infant siblings, but not their older (preschool-aged) siblings, was related to the frequency of displays of jealousy in triadic interactions with their mothers. Moreover, a recent study showed that different aspects of older and younger children's temperaments predicted the frequency of joint attention in young siblings' interactions (Benigno & Farrar, 2012).

Associations between temperament and relationship quality may also differ by gender: one study of school-aged sibling dyads found that the expected links between negative sibling behaviour and emotionality and activity only held true for sisters (Brody, Stoneman, & Burke, 1987). Among brothers, older siblings' activity was unrelated to sibling behaviour, while younger siblings' activity was associated not only with both children's antisocial behaviour, but also with talk, and younger children's prosocial behaviour. This suggests that for brothers, high levels of activity in the younger child may predict engagement in sibling interactions, and highlights the importance of considering the cumulative impact of child characteristics on children's sibling relationship quality.

Emotionality and activity levels do not always have a negative impact on sibling relationships. For example, in a study of adolescent twins, Pike and Atzaba-Poria (2003) found that twins with high levels of activity showed greater affection towards each other. This result could, of course, reflect differential associations between temperament and sibling relations for twins and non-twin siblings. Other evidence suggests that high emotionality may buffer children from the adverse effects of family stress on sibling relationships. In a study of socially disadvantaged preschoolers and their older siblings, Stoneman, Brody, Churchill and Winn (1999) found that children's emotionality attenuated links between residential instability, or conflict between caregivers, and sibling conflict. In other words, while emotionality may be associated with sibling conflict in normal circumstances, under conditions of stress links between temperament and sibling relationship quality may be very different.

Other aspects of temperament also appear to be linked to sibling relationship quality. In their study of preschoolers and school-aged older siblings, Stocker and colleagues (1989) reported that shyness in older siblings was associated with less competition and control in structured sibling interactions, while younger siblings' sociability was linked with less cooperation in task-oriented interactions, but more positive behaviour in unstructured interactions. Similarly, Pike and Atzaba-Poria's (2003) twin study demonstrated links between early adolescents' sociability and sibling affection. Furthermore, low levels of persistence have been linked with antisocial behaviour between siblings in same-sex dyads (Brody et al., 1987), and with negative behaviour and less satisfaction in children's relationships with a sibling with autism spectrum disorder (Rivers & Stoneman, 2008; see Chapter 8 for a more in-depth discussion of how child characteristics may predict sibling relationship quality in the context of disability).

Rather than looking at different aspects of temperament separately, some researchers have considered the effects of constellations of traits. In particular, the term "difficult" temperament is used to describe the combination of high emotionality, high activity and low persistence or ease of management. In a longitudinal study beginning when children were on average seven and nine years old, Brody and colleagues (1994a; 1994b) reported that older and younger siblings with difficult temperaments predicted more negative and less positive sibling relationships five years later. These findings have been replicated in a cross-sectional study of adolescents (McCoy, Brody, & Stoneman, 2002). Moreover, temperament can influence the strength of links between family relationships, such that sibling and parent-child relationship quality are particularly closely intertwined for children with a difficult temperament (Brody, Stoneman, & Gauger, 1996).

Another way of thinking about temperament within a relationship is to consider the "goodness of fit" between the temperaments of the children involved (e.g., Thomas & Chess, 1977). That is, the specific temperament of each sibling may be less important than whether these two temperaments are compatible with each other. For example, Stoneman and Brody (1993) reported that, individually, children's activity levels did not influence sibling positive behaviour, but that sibling positivity was highest when both children had similar activity levels. In the same study, the authors also reported that siblings showed more social engagement when the older child was rated as higher in adaptability than their younger sibling.

Similarly, as discussed further in Chapter 8, among children with autism spectrum disorder and their typically developing siblings, sibling relationships were less positive when both children were low in persistence (Rivers & Stoneman, 2008).

The findings reviewed in the second half of this chapter demonstrate that the links between sibling relationship quality and gender, age gap and temperament are far from simple. In particular, as shown by the effect of gender on the link between age gap and sibling relationship quality, child and dyadic characteristics interact to predict relationship quality. It is also worth noting that these links are not necessarily unidirectional. For example, while we have largely considered child factors as predictors of sibling relationship quality, siblings are likely to play a role in the development of gender roles. For example, as discussed in more detail in Chapter 5, the gender of a child's older sibling appears to influence the child's gender role behaviour (Rust, Golombok, Hines, Johnston, & Golding, 2000). A modelling perspective might suggest that this influence is likely to be especially strong for children who have a close relationship with their sibling.

Take-home messages

1. There is dramatic variation in the quality of children's sibling relationships.
2. In early and middle childhood sibling relationships are characterised by ambivalence – that is, high levels of positive and negative behaviours. During this time, older siblings typically take the lead in instigating positive interaction, such as teaching or play, but also in initiating conflict.
3. Later in childhood and adolescence, sibling relationships may become less involved as children develop friendships outside the home, and siblings become more equal relationship partners. However, despite a reduction in time spent together, siblings remain an important part of young people's lives, as confidants and sources of support.
4. In adulthood, siblings may be less involved in adults' day-to-day lives particularly if they do not live close by, but still remain important sources of support and may work together to care for elderly parents.
5. Even over extended periods that include major developmental milestones there is considerable stability in individual differences in the quality of children's sibling relationships. This stability is described as "heterotypic": siblings who get along well in the early years are likely to get along well later in life, but the way in which this relationship quality is evident changes as children grow up.
6. In early childhood, sisters show more prosocial behaviours and fewer aggressive behaviours than brothers; in middle childhood and adolescence, sisters report more positive sibling relationships than brothers. Relationships between siblings of the same sex tend to be more positive than those of opposite-sex dyads, perhaps because they are more likely to have common interests.
7. Interviews with children suggest that sisters predominantly use talk as a way to maintain closeness in their relationship, while among brothers shared activities play a similar role. This focus on talk rather than activities may make it easier

for sisters than brothers to maintain their relationship when one sibling leaves home.

8. The age spacing between siblings is also related to contrasts in relationship quality. Siblings with a small age gap often have involved relationships that feature high levels of companionship but also some conflict. Siblings with a wider age gap may show less conflict but spend less time together because of their different abilities and interests.

9. A child's temperament contributes to the quality of their sibling relationships. Children who show characteristics of a "difficult" temperament (e.g., high levels of negative emotionality or activity, or low levels of persistence) tend to have poorer quality sibling relationships than children with "easier" temperaments.

10. The fit between the two siblings' temperaments also seems to be important. For example, children may show the highest levels of sibling positivity when their activity levels are similar.

References

Abramovitch, R., Corter, C., & Lando, B. (1979). Sibling interaction in the home. *Child Development, 50,* 997–1003. doi:10.2307/1129325.

Abramovitch, R., Corter, C., & Pepler, D. (1980). Observations of mixed-sex sibling dyads. *Child Development, 51,* 1268–1271. doi:10.2307/1129570.

Abramovitch, R., Corter, C., Pepler, D., & Stanhope, L. (1986). Sibling and peer interaction: A final follow-up and a comparison. *Child Development, 57,* 217–229. doi:10.2307/1130653.

Arnett, J. J. (2004). *Emerging adulthood: The winding road from late teens through the twenties.* New York: Oxford University Press.

Benigno, J. P., & Farrar, M. J. (2012). Determinants of joint attention in young siblings' play. *Infant and Child Development, 21,* 160–174. doi: 10.1002/icd.743.

Branje, S., van Lieshout, C., van Aken, M., & Haselager, G. (2004). Perceived support in sibling relationships and adolescent adjustment. *Journal of Child Psychology and Psychiatry, 45,* 1385–1396. doi:10.1111/j.1469-7610.2004.00332.x.

Brody, G. H., Stoneman, Z., & Burke, M. (1987). Child temperaments, maternal differential behavior, and sibling relationships. *Developmental Psychology, 23,* 354–362. doi:10.1037/0012-1649.23.3.354.

Brody, G. H., Stoneman, Z., & Gauger, K. (1996). Parent-child relationships, family problem-solving behavior, and sibling relationship quality: The moderating role of sibling temperaments. *Child Development, 67,* 1289–1300. doi:10.1111/j.1467-8624.1996.tb01796.x.

Brody, G. H., Stoneman, Z., MacKinnon, C., & MacKinnon, R. (1985). Role relationships and behavior among preschool-aged and school-aged sibling pairs. *Developmental Psychology, 21,* 124–129. doi:10.1037/0012-1649.21.1.124.

Brody, G. H., Stoneman, Z., & McCoy, J. (1994a). Contributions of family relationships and child temperaments to longitudinal variations in sibling relationship quality and sibling relationship styles. *Journal of Family Psychology, 8,* 274–286. doi:10.1037/0893-3200.8.3.274.

Brody, G. H., Stoneman, Z., & McCoy, J. (1994b). Forecasting sibling relationships in early adolescence from child temperaments and family processes in middle childhood. *Child Development, 65,* 771–784. doi:10.1111/j.1467-8624.1994.tb00782.x.

Bronfenbrenner, U. (1979). *The ecology of human development: Experiments by nature and design.* Cambridge, MA: Harvard University Press.

Buhrmester, D. (1992). The developmental courses of sibling and peer relationships. In F. Boer and J. Dunn (Eds.), *Children's sibling relationships: Developmental and clinical issues* (pp. 19–40). Hillsdale, NJ: Lawrence Erlbaum Associates.

Buhrmester, D., & Furman, W. (1990). Perceptions of sibling relationships during middle childhood and adolescence. *Child Development, 61,* 1387–1398. doi:10.1111/j.1467-8624.1990.tb02869.x.

Buist, K. L., Deković, M., Meeus, W., & Van Aken, M. A. G. (2002). Developmental patterns in adolescent attachment to mother, father and sibling. *Journal of Youth and Adolescence, 31,* 167–176. doi:10.1023/A:1015074701280

Campione-Barr, N., Lindell, A. K., Giron, S. E., Killoren, S. E., & Greer, K. B. (2015). Domain differentiated disclosure to mothers and siblings and associations with sibling relationship quality and youth emotional adjustment. *Developmental Psychology, 51,* 1278–1291. doi:10.1037/dev0000036.

Campione-Barr, N., & Smetana, J. G. (2010). "Who said you could wear my sweater?" Adolescent siblings' conflicts and associations with relationship quality. *Child Development, 81,* 464–471. doi: 10.1111/j.1467-8624.2009.01407.x.

Caspi, A., Henry, B., McGee, R. O., Moffitt, T., & Silva, P. (1995). Temperamental origins of child and adolescent behavior problems: From age three to age fifteen. *Child Development, 66,* 55–68. doi:10.1111/j.1467-8624.1995.tb00855.x.

Cicirelli, V. (1973). Effects of sibling structure and interaction on children's categorization style. *Developmental Psychology, 9,* 132–139. doi: 10.1037/h0035061.

Cicirelli, V. (1975). Effects of mother and older sibling on the problem-solving behavior of the older child. *Developmental Psychology, 11,* 749–756. doi:10.1037/0012-1649.11.6.749.

Cicirelli, V. (1989). Feelings of attachment to siblings and well-being in later life. *Psychology and Aging, 4,* 211–216. doi:10.1037/0882-7974.4.2.211.

Conger, K. J., & Little, W. M. (2010). Sibling relationships during the transition to adulthood. *Child Development Perspectives, 4,* 87–94. doi:10.1111/j.1750-8606.2010.00123.x.

Dunn, J., & Kendrick, C. (1981). Social behavior of young siblings in the family context: Differences between same-sex and different-sex dyads. *Child Development, 52,* 1265–1273. doi:10.2307/1129515.

Dunn, J., & Kendrick, C. (1982). *Siblings: Love, envy, and understanding.* London: Grant McIntyre Ltd.

Dunn, J., & Munn, P. (1986a). Sibling quarrels and maternal intervention: Individual differences in understanding and aggression. *Journal of Child Psychology and Psychiatry, 27,* 583–595. doi:10.1111/j.1469-7610.1986.tb00184.x.

Dunn, J., & Munn, P. (1986b). Siblings and the development of prosocial behaviour. *International Journal of Behavioral Development, 9,* 265–284. doi:10.1177/016502548600900301.

Dunn, J., Slomkowski, C., & Beardsall, L. (1994). Sibling relationships from the preschool period through middle childhood and early adolescence. *Developmental Psychology, 30,* 315–324. doi:10.1037/0012-1649.30.3.315.

Edwards, R., Mauthner, M., & Hadfield, L. (2005). Children's sibling relationships and gendered practices: Talk, activity and dealing with change. *Gender and Education, 17,* 499–513. doi: 10.1080/09540250500192678.

Edwards, R., & Weller, S. (2014). Sibling relationships and the construction of young people's gendered identities over time and in different spaces. *Families, Relationships and Societies, 3,* 185–199. doi: 10.1332/204674314X13951457865780.

Eisenberg, N., Cumberland, A., Spinrad, T., Fabes, R., Shepard, S. A., Reiser, M., Murphy, B. C., Losoya, S. H., & Guthrie, I. (2001). The relations of regulation and emotionality to children's externalizing and internalizing problem behavior. *Child Development, 72,* 1112–1134. doi: 10.1111/1467-8624.00337.

Eisenberg, N., Fabes, R., Bernzweig, J., Karbon, M., Poulon, R., & Hanish, L. (1993). The relations of emotionality and regulation to preschoolers' social skills and sociometric status. *Child Development, 64,* 1418–1438. doi: 10.1111/j.1467-8624.1993.tb02961.x.

Ensor, R., Hart, M., Jacobs, L., & Hughes, C. (2011). Gender differences in children's problem behaviour in competitive play with friends. *British Journal of Developmental Psychology, 29,* 176–187. doi: 10.1111/j.2044-835X.2010.02016.x.

Ensor, R., Marks, A., Jacobs, L., & Hughes, C. (2010). Trajectories of antisocial behaviour towards siblings predict antisocial behaviour towards peers. *Journal of Child Psychology and Psychiatry, 51,* 1208–1216. doi:10.1111/j.1469-7610.2010.02276.x.

Feinberg, M. E., McHale, S. M., Crouter, A. C., & Cumsille, P. (2003). Sibling differentiation: Sibling and parent relationship trajectories in adolescence. *Child Development, 74,* 1261–1274. doi:10.1111/1467-8624.00606

Furman, W., & Buhrmester, D. (1985). Children's perceptions of the qualities of sibling relationships. *Child Development, 56,* 448–461. doi: 10.2307/1129733.

Furman, W., & Buhrmester, D. (1992). Age and sex differences in perceptions of networks of personal relationships. *Child Development, 63,* 103–115. doi:10.1111/j.1467-8624.1992.tb03599.x.

Howe, N., Brody, M. H., & Recchia, H. (2006). Effects of task difficulty on sibling teaching in middle childhood. *Infant and Child Development, 15,* 455–470. doi:10.1002/icd.470.

Howe, N., Ross, H. S., & Recchia, H. (2011). Sibling relations in early and middle childhood. In P. K. Smith and C. H. Hart (Eds.), *The Wiley-Blackwell handbook of childhood social development* (2nd ed., pp. 356–372). New York: Wiley.

Hughes, C. (2011). *Social understanding and social lives: From toddlerhood through to the transition to school.* London: Psychology Press.

Jenkins, J., O'Connor, T., Dunn, J., Rasbash, J., & Behnke, P. (2005). Change in maternal perception of sibling negativity: Within- and between-family influences. *Journal of Family Psychology, 19,* 533–541. doi: 10.1037/0893-3200.19.4.533.

Khodyakov, D., & Carr, D. (2009). The impact of late-life parental death on adult sibling relationships. *Research on Aging, 31,* 495–519.

Kier, C., & Lewis, C. (1998). Preschool sibling interaction in separated and married families: Are same-sex pairs or older sisters more sociable? *Journal of Child Psychology and Psychiatry, 39,* 191–201. doi:10.1111/1469-7610.00313.

Kochanska, G., Friesenborg, A., Lange, L., & Martel, M. (2004). Parents' personality and infants' temperament as contributors to their emerging relationship. *Journal of Personality and Social Psychology, 86,* 744–759. doi: 10.1037/0022-3514.86.5.744.

Kramer, L., & Kowal, A. (2005). Sibling relationship quality from birth to adolescence: The enduring contributions of friends. *Journal of Family Psychology, 19,* 503–511. doi:10.1037/0893-3200.19.4.503.

Lamb, M. E. (1978a). The development of sibling relationships in infancy: A short-term longitudinal study. *Child Development, 49,* 1189–1196. doi:10.2307/1128759.

Lamb, M. E. (1978b). Interactions between 18-month-olds and their preschool-aged siblings. *Child Development, 49,* 51–59. doi:10.2307/1128592.

Lashewicz, B. (2014). Sibling resentments and alliances during the parent care years: Implications for social work practice. *Journal of Evidence-Based Social Work, 11,* 460–467. doi:10.1080/15433714.2013.764834.

Lashewicz, B., & Keating, N. (2009). Tensions among siblings in parent care. *European Journal of Ageing, 6,* 127–135. doi: 10.1007/s10433-009-0109-9.

Lawson, A., & Ingleby, J. (1974). Daily routines of pre-school children: Effects of age, birth order, sex and social class, and developmental correlates. *Psychological Medicine, 4*, 399–415. doi:10.1017/S0033291700045852.

McCoy, J., Brody, G. H., & Stoneman, Z. (2002). Temperament and the quality of best friendships: Effect of same-sex sibling relationships. *Family Relations, 51*, 248–255. doi:10.1111/j.1741-3729.2002.00248.x.

Mathieson, K., & Banerjee, R. (2011). Peer play, emotion understanding, and socio-moral explanation: The role of gender. *British Journal of Developmental Psychology, 29*, 188–196. doi:10.1111/j.2044-835X.2010.02020.x.

Merrill, D. M. (1996). Conflict and cooperation among adult siblings during the transition to the role of filial caregiver. *Journal of Social and Personal Relationships, 13*, 399–413. doi: 10.1177/0265407596133006.

Milevsky, A., & Heerwagen, M. (2013). A phenomenological examination of sibling relationships in emerging adulthood. *Marriage and Family Review, 49*, 251–263. doi:10.1080/01494929.2012.762444.

Miner, S., & Uhlenberg, P. (1997). Intragenerational proximity and the social role of sibling neighbors after midlife. *Family Relations, 46*, 145–153. doi: 10.2307/585038.

Mischel, W. (1984). Convergences and challenges in the search for consistency. *American Psychologist., 39*, 351–364. doi:10.1037/0003-066X.39.4.351

Olson, P. H. (1977). Insiders' and outsiders' views of relationships: Research studies. In G. Levinger and H. Raush (Eds.), *Close relationships: Perspectives on the meaning of intimacy.* (pp. 115–135) Amherst, MA: University of Massachusetts Press.

Pepler, D., Abramovitch, R., & Corter, C. (1981). Sibling interaction in the home: A longitudinal study. *Child Development, 52*, 1344–1347. doi:10.2307/1129530.

Perlman, M., & Ross, H. S. (2005). If-then contingencies in children's sibling conflicts. *Merrill-Palmer Quarterly, 51*, 42–66. doi: 10.1353/mpq.2005.0007.

Pike, A., & Atzaba-Poria, N. (2003). Do sibling and friend relationships share the same temperamental origins? A twin study. *Journal of Child Psychology and Psychiatry and Allied Disciplines, 44*, 598–611. doi:10.1111/1469-7610.00148.

Pinquart, M. (2003). Loneliness in married, widowed, divorced, and never-married older adults. *Journal of Social and Personal Relationships, 20*, 31–53. doi:10.1177/02654075030201002.

Raffaelli, M., & Larson, R. (1987). *Sibling interactions in late childhood and early adolescence.* Paper presented at the Biennial Meeting of the Society for Research in Child Development, Baltimore, MD.

Rivers, J. W., & Stoneman, Z. (2008). Child temperaments, differential parenting, and the sibling relationships of children with autism spectrum disorder. *Journal of Autism and Developmental Disorders, 38*, 1740–1750. doi:10.1007/s10803-008-0560-z.

Rosenthal, C. J. (1985). Kinkeeping in the familial division of labor. *Journal of Marriage and Family, 47*, 965–974. doi:10.2307/352340.

Rust, J., Golombok, S., Hines, M., Johnston, K., & Golding, J. (2000). The role of brothers and sisters in the gender development of preschool children. *Journal of Experimental Child Psychology, 77*, 292–303. doi:10.1006/jecp.2000.2596.

Scharf, M., Shulman, S., & Avigad-Spitz, L. (2005). Sibling relationships in emerging adulthood and in adolescence. *Journal of Adolescent Research, 20*, 64–90.

Slomkowski, C., & Manke, B. (2004). Sibling relationships during childhood: Multiple perceptions from multiple perspectives. In R. Conger, F. Lorenz & K. Wickrama (Eds.), *Continuity and change in family relations: Theory, methods, and empirical findings* (pp. 293–317). Mahwah, NJ: Lawrence Erlbaum Associates.

Stillwell, R., & Dunn, J. (1985). Continuities in sibling relationships: Patterns of aggression and friendliness. *Journal of Child Psychology and Psychiatry, 26*, 627–637. doi:10.1111/j.1469-7610.1985.tb01645.x.

Stocker, C., Dunn, J., & Plomin, R. (1989). Sibling relationships: Links with child temperament, maternal behavior, and family structure. *Child Development, 60*, 715–727. doi:10.2307/1130737.

Stocker, C., Lanthier, R. P., & Furman, W. (1997). Sibling relationships in early adulthood. *Journal of Family Psychology, 11*, 210–221. doi:10.1037/0893-3200.11.2.210.

Stoneman, Z., & Brody, G. H. (1993). Sibling temperaments, conflict, warmth, and role asymmetry. *Child Development, 64*, 1786–1800. doi:10.1111/j.1467-8624.1993.tb04213.x.

Stoneman, Z., Brody, G. H., Churchill, S. L., & Winn, L. L. (1999). Effects of residential instability on Head Start children and their relationships with older siblings: Influences of child emotionality and conflict between family caregivers. *Child Development, 70*, 1246–1262. doi:10.1111/1467-8624.00090.

Sutton-Smith, B., & Rosenberg, B. (1970). *The sibling.* New York: Holt, Rinehart and Winston.

Thomas, A., & Chess, S. (1977). *Temperament and development.* Oxford, England: Brunner/Mazel.

Volling, B. L., McElwain, N. L., & Miller, A. L. (2002). Emotion regulation in context: The jealousy complex between young siblings and its relations with child and family characteristics. *Child Development, 73*, 581–600. doi:10.1111/1467-8624.00425.

White, L. (2001). Sibling relationships over the life course: A panel analysis. *Journal of Marriage and Family, 63*, 555–568.

White, L. K., & Riedmann, A. (1992). Ties among adult siblings. *Social Forces, 71*, 85–102. doi:10.1093/sf/71.1.85.

White, N. (2014). *Sibling relationships from preschool to pre-adolescence: Change, correlates, and consequences.* (Unpublished doctoral dissertation). University of Cambridge. Cambridge, UK.

4

SIBLING RELATIONSHIPS IN THE FAMILY CONTEXT

Parents with more than one child are often surprised that their children are "like chalk and cheese" in terms of their behaviour, interests and abilities. Despite anecdotal evidence of large differences between siblings, psychologists have traditionally focused on differences *between* rather than *within* families to explain children's developmental outcomes. As a result, shared genes and shared environmental influences are often assumed to lead to similarities across children within the same family. A clear example of this between-family perspective comes from sibling case-control studies, in which a cohort of individuals with a certain condition, or exhibiting a certain behaviour, are followed and their siblings treated as a comparison control group. In this design, siblings are assumed to match the target individual on most variables except the variable of interest.

Crucially the sibling case-control design assumes that effects of family environment are similar for all children within each family, a view that has been challenged by the emergence of behavioural genetics. In their seminal book, *Separate Lives: Why Siblings are So Different*, Dunn and Plomin (1990) examined the origins of differences between siblings in temperament and adjustment, and concluded that most of the similarity between family members can be explained by genetics and that shared environmental influences are typically weaker than *non-shared* environmental influences. That is, while family environments may seem similar for each child, they are perceived and experienced very differently by each sibling. Non-shared environmental influences come from a variety of sources, including one-off events, such as accidents or illness, that occur to only one child, and more systematic non-shared environmental influences such as differences related to birth order, gender differences and differential experiences with parents, peers and teachers (Plomin & Daniels, 1987).

These findings highlight the distinction between *within-* and *between-*family variance: that is, differences *within* families (e.g., birth order, differential exposure to adverse events, differential parental treatment) and differences *between* families (e.g., in socioeconomic status, ethnicity, genetic risk) each help to explain individual differences in characteristics or outcomes (e.g., personality, adjustment, relationship quality). This distinction is illustrated by a study by Jenkins, Rasbash, Leckie, Gass and Dunn (2012) that was unusual in examining the quality of multiple sibling relationships within a family. Specifically, sibling relationship quality, maternal depression and parenting variables were examined in a sample that included families with three or more children, followed from when the target children were five years old. Importantly, patterns of change in sibling affection and hostility over the two-year study period clustered within families, and this clustering effect could be explained by maternal mental health and mother-child relationship quality. At the same time, there was also significant variation in the quality of the relationships between sibling pairs within the same family (Jenkins et al., 2012; Pike, 2012).

These findings emphasise the need to shift from considering the family as a homogenous whole to examine processes within a family and the way in which different family relationships interact with each other. This idea aligns with family systems perspectives (e.g., Cox & Paley, 1997; Hinde & Stevenson-Hinde, 1987; Minuchin, 1988), which view the family as a large system made up of smaller subsystems of dyadic and triadic relationships. For example, a traditional two-parent, two-child family is made up of a couple subsystem, a sibling subsystem and parent-child subsystems, as well as larger units reflecting triadic relationships. Crucially, family systems theory emphasises the inter-relatedness of family relationships, such that a given family relationship cannot be fully understood without consideration of other components of the family system (Cox & Paley, 1997; Minuchin, 1985, 1988). A widely used metaphor here is that of an engine, which malfunctions when any one part breaks down.

In this chapter, we adopt three different approaches to explore the interdependence of family relationships. First, we consider the convergence between different family members' perspectives of the sibling relationship. For example, does each sibling see their relationship in the same light, and do parents see their children's relationship in the same way as their children? Next, we apply the lens of spillover and compensatory processes to consider the interplay between the quality of sibling relationships and the quality of parent-child relationships. Finally, we examine links between parental differential treatment and sibling relationship quality to consider how two parent-child subsystems can interact with the sibling subsystem.

Differing perspectives on sibling relationships

How similar are different family members' views of the sibling relationship? This is an important question for several reasons. From a methodological perspective, to integrate findings from research studies using different informants, researchers need to know whether parents', older siblings' and younger siblings' reports or ratings of the sibling relationship are interchangeable. Moreover, informants' views of the sibling relationship may show different associations with children's adjustment. For example, we might expect that children's own views of relationships might be especially strong predictors of behavioural and social outcomes. In support of this idea, previous family research has highlighted the importance of children's perceptions: for example, in a longitudinal study early adolescents' appraisals of blame explained the link between parents' marital conflict and children's poor academic achievement (Harold, Aitken, & Shelton, 2007).

Why might individual family members have different views of a sibling relationship? As direct participants in the relationship versus closely connected observers, children might be expected to have a different view of their sibling relationship than their parents due to their history with the relationship and their understanding of the meaning of specific behaviours within sibling interactions. Two siblings may also have very different perspectives of their relationship from each other. Over four decades ago, Bernard (1972) discussed the idea of "his" and "her" marriage, that is, that husbands and wives may have very different views of their marriage, due to gender inequalities in relationships and in society more generally. In the case of siblings, differing perspectives might reflect contrasts in age, gender and power within the relationship.

To examine the convergence between different family members' views of the sibling relationship, researchers typically calculate correlations between different family members' ratings of the relationship, often during middle childhood. Using this approach, Furman and colleagues (1989) found moderate to strong associations (mean $r = .53$) between mothers', fathers' and both siblings' ratings of warmth/closeness, conflict and relative status/power in a sample of ten- to 12-year-olds. In contrast, informants' reports of sibling rivalry were uncorrelated. Other studies in middle childhood have revealed similar findings (e.g., Rinaldi & Howe, 1998; White, 2014), although many studies suggest that family members' views may be more similar for positive than negative aspects of the sibling relationship (Dunn, Slomkowski, & Beardsall, 1994; Howe, Karos, & Aquan-Assee, 2011; Slomkowski & Manke, 2004; Stocker & McHale, 1992), particularly when comparing parents' and children's views of the relationship (e.g., Rinaldi & Howe, 2003). In contrast, Lecce and colleagues (2009) used both a questionnaire measure and a drawing task and found no agreement between six- to 11-year-old younger and older siblings' reports of their relationship. Other researchers have also reported a lack of correspondence between siblings' reports of sources of conflict and methods of conflict resolution (McGuire, Manke, Eftekhari, & Dunn, 2000).

The convergence of siblings' perceptions of their relationship may vary across childhood. While most of the findings above relate to middle childhood, Pike, Coldwell and Dunn (2005) applied a puppet methodology to interview sibling dyads aged four to eight years old and showed that views of the sibling relationship were quite similar for younger and older siblings. Similarly, in a study of adolescents, growth model slopes of siblings' perceptions of intimacy and conflict were significantly associated, suggesting a similar pattern of change over time for both children in the sibling dyad (Feinberg, McHale, Crouter, & Cumsille, 2003).

Studies that examine the congruence in siblings' ratings of their relationship have typically examined the consistency of individual differences in relationship quality between informants. Another way to investigate differences between informants is to examine mean-level differences in ratings, to see if, on average, one informant tends to rate the relationship higher or lower on a given quality. Note also that because correlations assess the linear association between ratings (rather than agreement), ratings from two informants could be perfectly correlated but show large mean differences. Examining mean differences in reports from nine- to 11-year-olds and their younger siblings, Stocker and McHale (1992) found similarity between the two children's reports of affection, conflict and rivalry in their relationship. In contrast, Buhrmester and Furman (1990) reported a discrepancy between older and younger siblings' perceptions of conflict over time. Specifically, younger children reported a decrease in sibling conflict from middle childhood into adolescence, whereas older siblings' reports of conflict remained stable.

The Cambridge Toddlers Up study provided the opportunity to expand previous investigations by comparing mothers' reports of the quality of their children's sibling relationship to reports from the two children. All three informants completed six subscales of the Network of Relationships Inventory (Furman & Buhrmester, 1985), measuring companionship, intimate disclosure, affection, reassurance of worth (i.e., how much the child feels admired by their sibling) at two time points, when the younger sibling was 10 and 12 years old. At each time point, observed inter-informant differences typically occurred between the mother and one of the children. At age 10, younger and older siblings each reported more companionship than mothers, and older siblings also reported more sibling conflict than their mothers. A different pattern of results emerged at age 12: compared with the siblings themselves, mothers reported more affection and reassurance of worth between their children. In addition, compared with younger siblings and mothers, older siblings reported less satisfaction with the sibling relationship.

In sum, inter-informant correlations indicate that family members' views of the sibling relationship are generally convergent, particularly for positive aspects of the sibling relationship. At the same time, there do appear to be some small differences in informants' ratings of more subjective aspects of the relationship, particularly when comparing children's views with those from their parents. It is interesting to note, too, that mothers appeared to have a particularly rose-tinted view of their children's relationship in early adolescence relative to the children themselves, perhaps highlighting the importance of obtaining children's views of their relationships. Of course, from the studies reported here it is not possible to determine what the implications of these different views are for children's adjustment. For example, are children's reports of the sibling relationship better predictors of adjustment than parents' reports? Future research should examine the predictive power of different informants' ratings of sibling relationships for developmental outcomes. That said, a recent set of meta-analyses of links between sibling relationship quality and children's internalising and externalising behaviour showed that the strength of these associations did not vary with informant (Buist, Deković, & Prinzie, 2013).

Sibling and parent-child relationships

The main tenet of family systems theory is that subsystems or relationships within a family are interdependent, such that functioning within one relationship should be associated with functioning within another relationship, and changes in one relationship will have a knock-on effect on other relationships (e.g., Cox & Paley, 1997). This interdependence can be viewed in two ways. Many researchers advocate a "spillover" hypothesis in which family relationships show similarities because behaviour and emotion spill over from one relationship to another. For example, consistent with a social learning or attachment theory perspective (e.g., Bretherton, 1985; Parke, MacDonald, Beitel, & Bhavnagri, 1988), parents who have warm and supportive relationships with their children may provide a model of warm and supportive relationships that is emulated in sibling interactions. A spillover perspective also fits with personality theory (e.g., Caspi & Elder, 1988), which suggests that an individual's temperament evokes similar responses from different interactional partners, such that a sibling may react towards a child's behaviour in a similar way to other family members.

An alternative perspective to spillover, the "compensatory" hypothesis (e.g., Erel & Burman, 1995), suggests that adverse effects of a negative family relationship are reduced in the context of a positive relationship with another family member. In this view, children who have a negative relationship with a parent may turn to their sibling for support. While, like most research on family influences on sibling interaction, we will focus on the interplay between parent-child and sibling relationships in this section, note that several studies have indicated that unhappiness and conflict within the couple relationship is also linked to poorer sibling relationships (e.g., Brody, Stoneman, & Burke, 1987b; Brody, Stoneman, & McCoy, 1994a; Brody, Stoneman, McCoy, & Forehand, 1992).

Overall, most empirical findings appear to support a spillover hypothesis of the interplay between parent-child and sibling relationships. In a study of four- to eight-year-olds, Kretschmer and Pike (2009) showed that sibling relationship quality was positively associated with parental warmth, and negatively associated with parental harsh discipline. These associations also explained the link between household chaos and lower sibling relationship quality. Moreover, in a study of five-year-olds and their older siblings, maternal positivity predicted change in sibling affection, and maternal negativity predicted change in sibling negativity over a two-year period (Jenkins, O'Connor, Dunn, Rasbash, & Behnke, 2005; Jenkins et al., 2012). Similar associations have been reported in the preschool years (Stocker, Dunn, & Plomin, 1989), middle childhood (Brody, Stoneman, & Gauger, 1996; Brody, Stoneman, & McCoy, 1994b; Rinaldi & Howe, 2003) and adolescence (Derkman, Engels, Kuntsche, van der Vorst, & Scholte, 2011; McHale, Whiteman, Kim, & Crouter, 2007). Spillover processes may also account for negative associations between marital conflict and sibling relationship quality. In middle childhood, Stocker and Youngblade (1999) found that mothers' and fathers' hostility towards their children explained the relationship between marital conflict and sibling relationship quality. That is, spillover of conflict from the couple relationship into parent-child relationships could explain the association between marital conflict and sibling relationship quality.

Other studies in late childhood have found evidence for both spillover and compensatory processes. In one study of eight- to 12-year-olds and their younger siblings, maternal and paternal acceptance were associated with sibling affection, and mother-child conflict was associated with sibling quarrelling (Hakvoort, Bos, Van Balen, & Hermanns, 2010). However, higher levels of father-child conflict were linked to lower levels of sibling quarrelling, suggesting that mother-child and father-child relationships may have somewhat different influences on sibling relationships. Similarly, in a longitudinal study spanning six years, Kim, McHale, Osgood and Crouter (2006) reported the expected spillover associations between father-child conflict and sibling conflict, and between maternal acceptance and sibling intimacy, but fathers' love was negatively correlated with sibling intimacy. Note that these findings of compensation between parent-child and sibling relationships all concerned father-child relationships, and may reflect differences in fathers' versus mothers' roles in the family. For example, Bhavnagri and Parke (1991) suggested that fathers typically assume a playmate role with children, while mothers engage in more instruction and supervision. If this is the case, then compensatory processes between sibling and father-child relationships might represent competition between fathers and siblings to fulfil similar playmate roles.

Links between parent-child and sibling relationships may also vary for younger versus older siblings. Using data from a sample of 246 Mexican-origin families followed over a five-year period from when the younger sibling was 12 years old, Killoren, Wheeler, Updegraff, Rodriguez de Jesús and McHale, (2015) examined associations between mother-child and father-child acceptance and sibling intimacy five years later, while controlling for changes in sibling intimacy over the period. Their findings showed that parent-child acceptance predicted sibling intimacy five years later, but only for older siblings. The authors suggest that this finding may reflect the hierarchical nature of family relationships in Mexican-origin families, whereby older siblings view their parents as role models, while younger siblings look up to their older siblings, highlighting the role of birth order in family experiences. From a family systems perspective, these findings show that the interplay between sibling and other family relationships may differ even when relationships appear functionally similar (as in the case of mother-child and father-child relationships, or parent-older sibling and parent-younger sibling relationships), thus highlighting the need to understand interactions between all components within the family system.

Parental differential treatment and sibling relationships

Alongside links between individual relationships, sibling interactions may also be affected by contrasts in the relationships between a parent and both children (Cox & Paley, 1997). Differential parental treatment is commonplace, and may reflect sensitive parenting if parents adapt their parenting to each child's temperament and individual needs. However, many parents will know from experience that children can be extremely sensitive to perceived unfairness in treatment from parents, and large disparities in parental treatment to each child have been linked to poorer child adjustment (e.g., Buist et al., 2013). Although researchers typically measure differential treatment with respect to a moment in time, equal treatment may not necessarily reflect consistent parenting because of age differences between siblings. For example, in the Cambridge Toddlers Up study, when asked as part of a study activity to identify an issue that he and his mother disagreed about, one older sibling described how unfair it was that his younger sibling had the same bedtime as him during the holidays, because this bedtime was later than he had experienced at the same age.

There are several methodological challenges when studying differential treatment. First, differential parenting can be conceptualised in terms of either the magnitude of or the direction of unequal treatment. Second, the methods to examine differential treatment vary across studies and include direct observations of parents' behaviour in triadic interactions, children's ratings of perceptions of differential treatment, or measures of the disparities between ratings of the parent-child relationship with each child. In the latter case difference scores indexing differential treatment can be calculated from each child's rating of the parent-child relationship, or from the parent's rating of their relationship with each child. Importantly, different measures of differential treatment appear to be relatively independent, and differences between children's reports of parent-child relationship quality are typically larger than those reported by parents (e.g., Daniels, Dunn, Furstenberg, & Plomin, 1985; White, 2014). This may suggest that children are particularly sensitive to differences in parenting, but could also reflect increased measurement error in difference scores from children because these are calculated from ratings from two separate individuals.

Early observational studies showed that disparities in mothers' behaviour were associated with observers' and mothers' reports of sibling negativity in early and middle childhood, both concurrently and one year later (Brody, Stoneman, & McCoy, 1992a; Stocker et al., 1989). Findings from the Cambridge Toddlers Up study in pre-adolescence also point to the negative consequences of differential treatment. However, in contrast to previous findings linking differential treatment to increased sibling conflict, unequal treatment was associated with lower levels of sibling positivity both concurrently and two years later, suggesting that children might disengage from sibling relationships as a result of differential parental treatment. Interestingly, in this study, mothers' but not children's reports of differential treatment were associated with sibling relationship quality. This may reflect the reduced salience of differential treatment to parents versus children, such that parents' reports of differential treatment represent inequalities large enough to have implications for sibling relationships. While we tend to think of differential parental treatment as a feature of childhood, it is important to note that unequal treatment continues to be linked with sibling relationship quality in adulthood even when siblings no longer live together (Boll, Ferring, & Filipp, 2003; Jensen, Whiteman, Fingerman, & Birditt, 2013). For example, in middle adulthood, differences in responsibility for the care of elderly parents may cause resentment between siblings.

Studies examining the direction of differential treatment have reported negative consequences for sibling behaviour for both the favoured and disfavoured child. In a sample of school-aged children, Brody, Stoneman and Burke (1987a) reported that the degree of maternal favouritism towards the younger child was associated with lower levels of verbal interaction and prosocial behaviour for both children. Similarly, among young adult siblings, fathers' favouritism interacted with the magnitude of differential treatment, such that children who were substantially less favoured reported lower levels of sibling intimacy (Jensen et al., 2013).

Links between differential treatment and sibling relationship quality may also depend on children's appraisals of the reasons for, and fairness of differential treatment. For example, McHale and Pawletko (1992) showed that links with sibling relationship quality were weaker for families with a disabled child than for families with two non-disabled children, even though the magnitude of differential treatment was greater in these families (see Chapter 8). Expanding on these findings, Kowal and Kramer (1997) showed that when adolescents attributed parental differential treatment to their siblings' needs, differential treatment was actually linked with more positive sibling relationships. Similarly, McHale, Updegraff, Jackson-Newsom, Tucker and Crouter (2000) reported that in middle childhood and adolescence children's ratings of the fairness of parental treatment were more consistently linked with sibling relationship quality than were their perceptions of differential treatment per se. In contrast, Shanahan, McHale, Crouter and Osgood (2008) found that, even with parent-child relationship quality and evaluations of fairness controlled, maternal and paternal favouritism predicted unique variance in both concurrent and later sibling warmth and conflict.

Findings from the Cambridge Toddlers Up study offered partial support for a link between unfair differential treatment and sibling relationship quality, but these associations differed by informant (White, 2014). Specifically, children's ratings of unfair differential affection, and siblings' ratings of unfair differential control (e.g., differential discipline) predicted higher levels of sibling conflict. These findings suggest a contrast between the salience of differential affection and control for younger and older siblings, perhaps due to differences in the direction of differential treatment, or in children's perceptions of responsibility for unequal treatment. For example, unfair differential treatment may cause difficulties in the parent-child relationship if the parent is viewed as responsible, but difficulties in the sibling relationship if the sibling is considered to be to blame (e.g., Kowal & Kramer, 1997).

A final factor to consider when examining links between differential treatment and sibling relationship quality concerns the agreement between family members about unequal treatment. Previous research has indicated that family relationships are more positive and less conflictual when members of the family agree on key beliefs and processes, (e.g., Alessandri & Wozniak, 1987; Carlson, Cooper, & Spradling, 1991; McCubbin & Patterson, 1983), suggesting that agreement about differential treatment may attenuate its negative consequences for sibling relationships. Examining this premise, Kowal, Krull and Kramer (2006) showed that siblings' agreement about the magnitude and direction of mothers' and fathers' differential affection (but not differential control) predicted more warmth and less negativity and rivalry between siblings. Agreement between siblings about the *fairness* of mothers' but not fathers' differential treatment was also associated with less sibling negativity and rivalry, and more sibling warmth. In contrast, agreement between parents and each child showed few associations with sibling relationship quality.

Results from the Cambridge Toddlers Up study also showed some evidence of the importance of agreement about differential treatment for sibling relationship quality (White, 2014). Specifically, agreement between siblings in ratings of the degree and the fairness of differential affection were linked to lower levels of sibling conflict, but these associations did not hold for differential control. Moreover, in contrast with Kowal, Krull and Kramer (2006), there were no links between siblings' agreement and sibling positivity. Similar findings were observed when the agreement between discrepancy scores from mothers' ratings of the parent-child relationship and discrepancy scores from the child and sibling's ratings of the parent-child relationship was examined. When mothers and children agreed about differential positivity, sibling relationships were more positive; in contrast, agreement about differential conflict was not related to sibling relationship quality.

Taken together, these findings indicate that while differential treatment can be associated with poorer sibling interactions, children's perceptions of the reasons for this unequal treatment, and shared understanding between family members about differential treatment can attenuate this link. Moreover, in contrast with the convergence between perceptions of the sibling relationship discussed earlier, family members may have different views of parental differential treatment and these different perspectives may have unique implications for children's sibling relationships. These findings highlight that as well as examining relationship quality per se, family systems perspectives should include measures of family members' perceptions of, and agreement about the reasons for family processes, as these may play an important role in determining family functioning.

Take-home messages

1. Both within- and between-family contrasts contribute to individual differences in children's developmental outcomes.
2. In family systems perspectives, the family is viewed as a system made up of component subsystems reflecting dyadic relationships and larger units.
3. Several studies report considerable convergence between different family members' views of the sibling relationship, particularly when considering positive aspects of relationship quality.
4. At the same time, there appear to be some mean-level differences between different informants' ratings of sibling relationship quality. In particular, mothers may provide more positive ratings of subjective qualities of the relationship than their children.
5. Spillover and compensatory processes help explain the interplay between family relationships.
6. Reflecting differences in parental roles within the family, the relative salience of spillover and compensatory processes for sibling relationship quality differs for mothers and fathers (typically mother-child relationships show spillover while father-child relationships may play a compensatory role).

7. Differential parental treatment is common, and may reflect sensitive parenting. However, large disparities in parenting may be detrimental to children's adjustment.

8. Parental differential treatment appears especially linked to poorer sibling relationship quality when mothers' ratings of parent-child relationship quality are used to index differential parenting.

9. Children's perceptions of the fairness of differential treatment matter. Differential treatment is more strongly related to poorer relationship quality when this treatment is considered to be unfair, particularly if the sibling is perceived to be to blame.

10. Even when differential treatment does occur, agreement between family members about differential treatment is associated with reduced levels of sibling conflict and increased positivity, presumably because children feel their views are understood.

References

Alessandri, S. M., & Wozniak, R. H. (1987). The child's awareness of parental beliefs concerning the child: A developmental study. *Child Development, 58*, 316–323. doi: 10.2307/1130509.

Bernard, J. (1972). *The future of marriage*. New Haven: Yale University Press.

Bhavnagri, N., & Parke, R. (1991). Parents as direct facilitators of children's peer relationships: Effects of age of child and sex of parent. *Journal of Social and Personal Relationships, 8*, 423–440. doi: 10.1177/0265407591083007.

Boll, T., Ferring, D., & Filipp, S. H. (2003). Perceived parental differential treatment in middle adulthood: Curvilinear relations with individuals' experienced relationship quality to sibling and parents. *Journal of Family Psychology, 17*, 472–487. doi: 10.1037/0893-3200.17.4.472.

Bretherton, I. (1985). Attachment theory: Retrospect and prospect. In I. Bretherton and E. Waters (Eds.), *Monographs of the Society for Research in Child Development* (Vol. 50 Serial No. 209 (1–2), 3–35).

Brody, G. H., Stoneman, Z., & Burke, M. (1987a). Child temperaments, maternal differential behavior, and sibling relationships. *Developmental Psychology, 23*, 354–362. doi:10.1037/0012-1649.23.3.354.

Brody, G. H., Stoneman, Z., & Burke, M. (1987b). Family systems and individual child correlates of sibling behavior. *American Journal of Orthopsychiatry, 57*, 561–569. doi:10.1111/j.1939-0025.1987.tb03571.x.

Brody, G. H., Stoneman, Z., & Gauger, K. (1996). Parent-child relationships, family problem-solving behavior, and sibling relationship quality: The moderating role of sibling temperaments. *Child Development, 67*, 1289–1300. doi:10.1111/j.1467-8624.1996.tb01796.x.

Brody, G. H., Stoneman, Z., & McCoy, J. (1992). Associations of maternal and paternal direct and differential behavior with sibling relationships: Contemporaneous and longitudinal analyses. *Child Development, 63*, 82–92. doi:10.1111/j.1467-8624.1992.tb03597.x.

Brody, G. H., Stoneman, Z., & McCoy, J. (1994a). Contributions of family relationships and child temperaments to longitudinal variations in sibling relationship quality and sibling relationship styles. *Journal of Family Psychology, 8*, 274–286. doi:10.1037/0893-3200.8.3.274.

Brody, G. H., Stoneman, Z., & McCoy, J. (1994b). Forecasting sibling relationships in early adolescence from child temperaments and family processes in middle childhood. *Child Development*, *65*, 771–784. doi:10.1111/j.1467-8624.1994.tb00782.x.

Brody, G. H., Stoneman, Z., McCoy, J., & Forehand, R. (1992). Contemporaneous and longitudinal associations of sibling conflict with family relationship assessments and family discussions about sibling problems. *Child Development*, *63*, 391–400. doi:10.1111/j.1467-8624.1992.tb01635.x.

Buhrmester, D., & Furman, W. (1990). Perceptions of sibling relationships during middle childhood and adolescence. *Child Development*, *61*, 1387–1398. doi:10.1111/j. 1467-8624.1990.tb02869.x.

Buist, K. L., Deković, M., & Prinzie, P. (2013). Sibling relationship quality and psycho-pathology of children and adolescents: A meta-analysis. *Clinical Psychology Review*, *33*, 97–106. doi:10.1016/j.cpr.2012.10.007.

Carlson, C. I., Cooper, C. R., & Spradling, V. Y. (1991). Developmental implications of shared versus distinct perceptions of the family in early adolescence. *New Directions in Child Development*, *51*, 13–31. doi:10.1002/cd.23219915103.

Caspi, A., & Elder, G. (1988). Emergent family patterns: The intergenerational construction of problem behavior and relationships. In R. Hinde and J. Stevenson-Hinde (Eds.), *Relationships within families* (pp. 218–240). Oxford, UK: Oxford University Press.

Cox, M. J., & Paley, B. (1997). Families as systems. *Annual Review of Psychology*, *48*, 243–267. doi:10.1146/annurev.psych.48.1.243.

Daniels, D., Dunn, J., Furstenberg, F., & Plomin, R. (1985). Environmental differences within the family and adjustment differences within pairs of adolescent siblings. *Child Development*, *56*, 764–774. doi:10.2307/1129765.

Derkman, M. M. S., Engels, R. C. M. E., Kuntsche, E., van der Vorst, H., & Scholte, R. H. J. (2011). Bidirectional associations between sibling relationships and parental support during adolescence. *Journal of Youth and Adolescence*, *40*, 490–501. doi:10.1007/s10964-010-9576-8.

Dunn, J., & Plomin, R. (1990). *Separate lives: Why siblings are so different*. New York: Basic Books.

Dunn, J., Slomkowski, C., & Beardsall, L. (1994). Sibling relationships from the preschool period through middle childhood and early adolescence. *Developmental Psychology*, *30*, 315–324. doi:10.1037/0012-1649.30.3.315.

Erel, O., & Burman, B. (1995). Inter-relatedness of marital relations and parent-child relations: A meta-analytic review. *Psychological Bulletin*, *118*, 108–132. doi:10.1037/0033-2909.118.1.108.

Feinberg, M. E., McHale, S. M., Crouter, A. C., & Cumsille, P. (2003). Sibling differentiation: Sibling and parent relationship trajectories in adolescence. *Child Development*, *74*, 1261–1274. doi:10.1111/1467-8624.00606.

Furman, W., & Buhrmester, D. (1985). Children's perceptions of the personal relationships in their social networks. *Developmental Psychology*, *21*, 1016–1024. doi: 10.1037/0012-1649.21.6.1016.

Furman, W., Jones, L., Buhrmester, D., & Adler, T. (1989). Children's, parents' and observers' perspectives on sibling relationships. In P. Zukow (Ed.), *Sibling interaction across cultures: Theoretical and methodological issues* (pp. 165–183). New York: Springer-Verlag.

Hakvoort, E. M., Bos, H. M. W., Van Balen, F., & Hermanns, J. M. A. (2010). Family relationships and the psychosocial adjustment of school-aged children in intact families. *Journal of Genetic Psychology*, *171*, 182–201. doi:10.1080/00221321003657445.

Harold, G., Aitken, J., & Shelton, K. (2007). Inter-parental conflict and children's academic attainment: a longitudinal analysis. *Journal of Child Psychology and Psychiatry*, *48*, 1223–1232. doi: 10.1111/j.1469-7610.2007.01793.x.

Hinde, R.A., & Stevenson-Hinde, J. (1987). Interpersonal relationships and child development. *Developmental Review, 7*, 1–21. doi:10.1016/0273-2297(87)90002-5.

Howe, N., Karos, L., & Aquan-Assee, J. (2011). Sibling relationship quality in early adolescence: Child and maternal perceptions and daily interactions. *Infant and Child Development, 20*, 227–245. doi:10.1002/icd.694.

Jenkins, J., O'Connor, T., Dunn, J., Rasbash, J., & Behnke, P. (2005). Change in maternal perception of sibling negativity: Within- and between-family influences. *Journal of Family Psychology, 19*, 533–541. doi: 10.1037/0893-3200.19.4.533.

Jenkins, J., Rasbash, J., Leckie, G., Gass, K., & Dunn, J. (2012). The role of maternal factors in sibling relationship quality: A multilevel study of multiple dyads per family. *Journal of Child Psychology and Psychiatry, 53*, 622–629. doi:10.1111/j.1469-7610.2011.02484.x.

Jensen, A. C., Whiteman, S. D., Fingerman, K. L., & Birditt, K. S. (2013). "Life still isn't fair": Parental differential treatment of young adult siblings. *Journal of Marriage and Family, 75*, 438–452. doi: 10.1111/jomf.12002.

Killoren, S. E., Wheeler, L. A., Updegraff, K. A., Rodríguez de Jésus, S. A., & McHale, S. M. (2015). Longitudinal associations among parental acceptance, familism values, and sibling intimacy in Mexican-origin families. *Family Process, 54*, 217–231. doi:10.1111/famp.12126.

Kim, J.Y., McHale, S. M., Osgood, D. W., & Crouter, A. C. (2006). Longitudinal course and family correlates of sibling relationships from childhood through adolescence. *Child Development, 77*, 1746–1761. doi:10.1111/j.1467-8624.2006.00971.x.

Kowal, A., & Kramer, L. (1997). Children's understanding of parental differential treatment. *Child Development, 68*, 113–126. doi: 10.2307/1131929.

Kowal, A. K., Krull, J. L., & Krumer, L. (2006). Shared understanding of parental differential treatment in families. *Social Development, 15*, 276–295. doi:10.1046/j.1467-9507.2006.00341.x.

Kretschmer, T., & Pike, A. (2009). Young children's sibling relationship quality: Distal and proximal correlates. *Journal of Child Psychology and Psychiatry, 50*, 581–589. doi:10.1111/j.1469-7610.2008.02016.x.

Lecce, S., Pagnin, A., & Pinto, G. (2009). Agreement in children's evaluations of their relationships with siblings and friends. *European Journal of Developmental Psychology, 6*, 153–169. doi: 10.1080/17405620701795536.

McCubbin, H. I., & Patterson, J. (1983). The family stress process: The double ABCX model of family adjustment and adaptation. *Marriage & Family Review, 6*, 7–37. doi:10.1300/J002v06n01_02.

McGuire, S., Manke, B., Eftekhari, A., & Dunn, J. (2000). Children's perceptions of sibling conflict during middle childhood: Issues and sibling (dis)similarity. *Social Development, 9*, 173–190. doi: 10.1111/1467-9507.00118.

McHale, S. M., & Pawletko, T. M. (1992). Differential treatment of siblings in two family contexts. *Child Development, 63*, 68–81. doi:10.1111/j.1467-8624.1992.tb03596.x.

McHale, S. M., Updegraff, K. A., Jackson-Newsom, J., Tucker, C. J., & Crouter, A. C. (2000). When does parents' differential treatment have negative implications for siblings? *Social Development, 9*, 148–172. doi: 10.1111/1467-9507.00117.

McHale, S. M., Whiteman, S. D., Kim, J.-Y., & Crouter, A. C. (2007). Characteristics and correlates of sibling relationships in two-parent African American families. *Journal of Family Psychology, 21*, 227–235. doi:10.1037/0893-3200.21.2.227.

Minuchin, P. (1985). Families and individual development: Provocations from the field of family therapy. *Child Development, 56*, 289–302. doi:10.2307/1129720.

Minuchin, P. (1988). Relationships within the family: A systems perspective on development. In R. Hinde & J. Stevenson-Hinde (Eds.), *Relationships within families: Mutual influences* (pp. 7–26). Oxford, UK: Clarendon.

Parke, R., MacDonald, K., Beitel, A., & Bhavnagri, N. (1988). The role of the family in the development of peer relationships. In R. McMahon & R. Peters (Eds.), *Social learning and systems approaches to marriage and the family* (pp. 17–44). Philadelphia, PA: Brunner/Mazel.

Pike, A. (2012). Commentary: Are siblings birds of a feather? – Reflections on Jenkins et al. (2012). *Journal of Child Psychology and Psychiatry and Allied Disciplines, 53*, 630–631. doi:10.1111/j.1469-7610.2012.02536.x

Pike, A., Coldwell, J., & Dunn, J. (2005). Sibling relationships in early/middle childhood: links with individual adjustment. *Journal of Family Psychology, 19*, 523–532. doi:10.1037/0893-3200.19.4.523.

Plomin, R., & Daniels, D. (1987). Why are children in the same family so different from one another? *Behavioural and Brain Sciences, 10*, 1–60. doi:10.1017/S0140525X00055941.

Rinaldi, C., & Howe, N. (1998). Siblings' reports of conflict and the quality of their relationships. *Merrill-Palmer Quarterly, 44*, 404–422.

Rinaldi, C., & Howe, N. (2003). Perceptions of constructive and destructive conflict within and across family subsystems. *Infant and Child Development, 12*, 441–459. doi:10.1002/icd.324.

Shanahan, L., McHale, S. M., Crouter, A. C., & Osgood, D. W. (2008). Linkages between parents' differential treatment, youth depressive symptoms, and sibling relationships. *Journal of Marriage and Family, 70*, 480–494. doi: 10.1111/j.1741-3737.2008.00495.x.

Slomkowski, C., & Manke, B. (2004). Sibling relationships during childhood: Multiple perceptions from multiple perspectives. In R. Conger, F. Lorenz & K. Wickrama (Eds.), *Continuity and change in family relations: Theory, methods, and empirical findings* (pp. 293–317). Mahwah, NJ: Lawrence Erlbaum Associates.

Stocker, C., Dunn, J., & Plomin, R. (1989). Sibling relationships: Links with child temperament, maternal behavior, and family structure. *Child Development, 60*, 715–727. doi:10.2307/1130737.

Stocker, C., & McHale, S. (1992). The nature and family correlates of preadolescents' perceptions of their sibling relationships. *Journal of Personal and Social Relationships, 9*, 179–195. doi: 10.1177/0265407592092002.

Stocker, C., & Youngblade, L. (1999). Marital conflict and parental hostility: Links with children's sibling and peer relationships. *Journal of Family Psychology, 13*, 598–609. doi: 10.1037/0893-3200.13.4.598.

White, N. (2014). *Sibling relationships from preschool to pre-adolescence: Change, correlates, and consequences.* (Unpublished doctoral dissertation). University of Cambridge. Cambridge, UK.

5

SIBLINGS AS AGENTS FOR SOCIAL DEVELOPMENT

Colloquially, the phrase "blood is thicker than water" is often used to indicate that the ties between family members are stronger than those between friends or acquaintances. Yet, the origins of this phrase are much less clear. Several authors (Jack, 2005; Trumbull, 1893) have argued that the phrase originally meant that the bonds between those who had entered into a blood covenant were stronger than "the waters of the womb" shared between siblings. Similarly, Trumbull (1893) notes that there is an equivalent Arabic expression stating that blood is thicker than milk, meaning that a blood covenant between two individuals (blood-brothers) is stronger than that between brothers who shared their mother's breast (milk-brothers).

The expression "blood is thicker than water" is one of many colloquial sayings and quotations that compare and contrast friendships and family relationships. Such phrases are often contradictory, however. For example, friends are often referred to as siblings (e.g., "she's like a sister to me") to demonstrate their closeness, while other quotes, such as the slightly sappy fridge magnet phrase "friends are the family we choose ourselves", or Euripides' statement that "a loyal friend is worth ten thousand relatives" suggest that friendships can be stronger than family relationships. In this chapter, we explore links between sibling relationships and children's social development in three ways. First, we consider the similarities and differences between children's relationships with siblings and with friends or peers, and examine whether there is convergence in the quality of these relationships. That is, do children with positive sibling relationships also show positive relationships with friends and with peers? Second, taking a broader view of children's social relationships, we examine how the quality of sibling relationships may predict children's social competence and social skills more generally. In particular, we consider whether the contribution of siblings to children's social functioning is independent and distinct from the influence of parent-child relationships. Finally, we consider how siblings may directly influence each other's social behaviour through modelling processes and by providing access to contexts and resources necessary for particular behaviours.

Historically, well-being has been defined in hedonic terms (i.e., in terms of positive mood and the absence of negative mood), but more recent work highlights the value of Aristotle's eudaimonic perspective (e.g., Aristotle, Ross, & Brown, 2009), in which well-being also encompasses flourishing. From this viewpoint, high quality social relationships and social competence are an important part of well-being for children and adults (Lippman, Moore, & McIntosh, 2011; Ryff & Keyes, 1995). Understanding the correlates of social competence during childhood is particularly important because these early skills are associated with a range of outcomes in adulthood, including competence at work, academic achievement and social success (Gest, Sesma, Masten, & Tellegen, 2006; Masten, Desjardins, McCormick, Kuo, & Long, 2010). Conversely, poor peer relationships in childhood have been linked with dropping out of school, and adult criminality and psychopathology (e.g., Bornstein, Hahn, & Haynes, 2010; Parker & Asher, 1987).

There are a number of reasons why sibling relationships in childhood might be an important context for children's social development. Early sibling relationships are relatively involuntary, in the sense that children live together, giving rise to a "no-holds-barred" interaction style that provides an arena for practising and honing social skills without fear of the relationship ending (Howe, Ross, & Recchia, 2011). Young siblings also spend a lot of time together (McHale & Crouter, 1996) and are typically frequent playmates. Play, and particularly shared pretend play are important contexts for children's social development. As well as providing a model of friendly interactions, the negotiations involved in shared pretence provide an important context for children to learn about other people's thoughts and feelings (e.g., Hughes & Dunn, 1997; see Chapter 6), and this social understanding is vital for future interactions with other children. In sibling conflict, too, children are faced with the stark contrast between their own and their siblings' thoughts and desires. As well as contributing to children's growing awareness of others' mental states, the enduring nature of sibling relationships means that children must learn how to manage and resolve sibling conflicts (e.g., Howe et al., 2011), and these conflict management abilities are likely to be crucial to maintaining relationships with peers.

Similar to the family systems perspective discussed in Chapter 4, associations between sibling relationships and friend or peer relationships can be understood in terms of spillover and compensatory processes. However, most theoretical perspectives align with a spillover perspective. For example, attachment theory proposes that early experiences with caregivers provide a blue-print for relationships with others, including siblings and other children (Bretherton, 1985), while personality theory suggests that a child's relatively stable temperament will evoke similar responses from different social partners (Caspi & Elder, 1988). Finally, social learning theory posits a more direct link between family relationships and friendships, whereby children learn behaviours within family interactions and then generalise them to relationships outside the home (Parke, MacDonald, Beitel, & Bhavnagri, 1988). Alternatively, a compensatory view would suggest that high quality relationships with children outside the family may compensate for poor sibling relationships or, conversely, that warm sibling relationships may protect children from the negative consequences of poor peer relationships (Stocker, 1994). Therefore, if compensatory processes were at work we might expect to observe a negative association between the quality of children's relationships with their siblings and their relationships with children outside the family. Note also that contrasting spillover and compensatory processes may be evident among different groups of children, such that, overall, links between sibling and peer relationships or friendships might be rather weak.

Siblings, friends and peers

Early empirical evidence suggested that links between sibling relationships and interactions with children outside the home might not be as straightforward as would be predicted simply by spillover and compensatory processes. In a review of sibling, friend and peer relationships, Dunn and McGuire (1992) noted that there are important differences between these three relationships that may mean that children's patterns of behaviour are relatively distinct in the three different contexts (see also Aldercotte, White, & Hughes, 2016, for a review of the contexts and correlates of sibling and peer relationships in early childhood). While sibling relationships and friendships are both close relationships, friendships are voluntary and usually involve a higher degree of mutual affection and reciprocity. Sibling relationships, on the other hand, tend to be characterised by ambivalence (e.g., Dunn, 1983), that is, high levels of both positive interaction and conflict. Friendships and peer relationships also involve two children from different families and the combination of their differing relationship experiences may produce very different behaviour from that shown within family relationships. In support of this idea, in a study of preschool children observed interacting separately with a friend and an older sibling, McElwain and Volling (2005) showed that friends engaged in more complex social play than siblings, and that friends also showed more conflict but only in a free play context. In contrast, using observational data from the Cambridge Toddlers Up study of two-year-olds playing with their older sibling and an unfamiliar peer, Hughes and Dunn (2007) showed a distinction between ratings of the maximum versus the average level of the sophistication of social play in the two contexts. Specifically, maximum ratings of play were higher for interactions with older siblings than with peers, but the reverse was true for average ratings of play, suggesting that although older siblings may be able to scaffold their younger children's play, much of the time younger siblings may be confined to less active roles in play.

Friend and peer relationships also differ from each other in important ways. Peer relationships are not as close as friendships, and may be relatively involuntary, for example in the case of classmates. These relationship differences may influence the types of behaviour that children typically display with peers and friends. For example, Costin and Jones (1992) showed that four- to six-year-olds exposed to a hypothetical situation involving a friend who needed help were more likely to respond sympathetically and to propose an intervention than children who were told a situation involved an acquaintance. Moreover, the methods used to study peer relationships typically differ from those used to study sibling relationships or friendships.

Measures of friendship quality typically focus on behaviours with a single friend whereas peer relations measures (e.g., sociometric tasks involving peer nominations, teacher ratings of peer behaviour) focus on more generalised behaviour with a number of peers (e.g., all classmates). Supporting this distinction, Mendelson, Aboud and Lanthier (1994) found that among kindergarten children peer-rated popularity (assessed using a sociometric task) was unrelated to friendship quality or observed friendliness. Finally, in addition to possible compensatory processes, behaviours in sibling relationships may have different functions and impacts on development than behaviours in peer or friend interactions (Dunn & McGuire, 1992). For example, sibling conflict may help children develop the social understanding abilities to enable them to maintain positive relationships with friends and peers. In light of these key differences between these two relationships we will explore links between sibling relationships and peer and friend relationships separately.

Sibling relationships and friendships

Studies examining associations between young children's relationships with siblings and with friends have produced relatively mixed findings. At least two studies of preschool or early school-age children have reported associations between friendship closeness and either friendly behaviour towards younger siblings (Kramer & Gottman, 1992) or sibling closeness (Sturgess, Dunn, & Davies, 2001). In contrast, other studies have reported either no consistent patterns of association between children's behaviour with a friend and with a sibling (Abramovitch, Corter, Pepler, & Stanhope, 1986), or no association between the type of conflict strategies (e.g., other-oriented, self-oriented) used in arguments with a sibling and with a friend (Dunn, Slomkowski, Donelan, & Herrera, 1995). Indeed, another study reported that negative aspects of the sibling relationship were related to mothers' reports of positive behaviour, and children's reports of closeness, in friendships, suggesting compensatory processes may be at work (Stocker & Dunn, 1990). These mixed findings may suggest that similarities between sibling relationships and friendships depend on the particular behaviour or aspect of relationship quality that is assessed, or on characteristics of the sample in which associations are assessed. That is, spillover processes may explain associations between sibling and peer relationships in some groups of children or for some behaviours, but compensatory processes may be evident for others.

In adolescence, links between sibling relationships and friendships appear to largely fit with a spillover perspective. For example, Yeh and Lempers (2004) showed that positive sibling relationships predicted early adolescents' friendship quality a year later. These authors also looked at the direction of effect: that is, whether sibling relationships influence friendships, or the reverse. Their findings showed a bidirectional relationship between sibling and friend relationship quality although the sibling to friend association was stronger than the reverse. This result suggests that there is a dynamic interaction between sibling relationship quality and the quality of children's friendships. In support of this idea, a longitudinal study by Kramer and colleagues (Kramer & Gottman, 1992; Kramer & Kowal, 2005) showed that the quality of older siblings' interactions with a best friend before the birth of a younger sibling predicted the subsequent quality of sibling relationships. This effect was enduring – early friend interactions remained a significant predictor of sibling relationship quality over thirteen years later – suggesting that researchers examining the transition to siblinghood should consider the role of children's interactions with peers as well as with other family members when examining individual differences in adjustment over this period (see Chapter 2).

Sibling relationships and peer relationships

Early studies of children's sibling and peer relationships typically suggested that these relationships were fairly distinct. Berndt and Bulleit (1985) found very few associations between children's observed behaviour with siblings and with peers. Similarly, Stocker and Dunn (1990) reported no association between sibling relationship quality and teachers' ratings of children's peer relationships. In contrast, in a study of children in kindergarten, Mendelson and colleagues (1994) showed that children who were popular with their peers reported more positive feelings towards their siblings. A similar association with peer popularity was also found when older siblings' reports of the sibling relationship were considered. The authors also noted that sibling gender composition influenced associations with sibling relationship quality for popularity with peers of the opposite sex but not for popularity with same-sex peers. Specifically, popularity with other-sex peers was only associated with sibling relationship quality for mixed-sex dyads, perhaps suggesting that interactions with a sibling of the opposite gender may provide a model for future mixed-sex peer interactions.

Differences in family composition may also contribute to the early findings regarding links between sibling and peer relationship quality in early childhood. In a recent study spanning the transition to primary school, Harrist, Achacoso, John, Pettit, Bates and Dodge (2014) showed that associations between engagement with peers and reciprocity (i.e., cooperation, shared humour) and complementarity (e.g., teaching, support) in children's sibling interactions varied with family type. Specifically, for children in single-parent families, high reciprocity and low complementarity were linked with higher peer engagement, but for children from two-parent families, low reciprocity between siblings was associated with peer engagement (Harrist et al., 2014). Given that peer interactions are likely to show high levels of reciprocal rather than complementary behaviours, the association for single-parent families suggests that interactions between siblings may be an important model for peer relations. The stronger associations between sibling interaction types and peer engagement for single-parent families suggest that sibling support may be particularly important when parental resources are more limited, and highlights the need to consider how sibling processes may vary in different family forms (see Chapter 10).

Siblings may also play a particularly important role in social development for children who, by temperament, are less sociable. Using data from the first time point of the Cambridge Toddlers Up study, when the children were two years old, Hughes and Dunn (2007) showed that mothers' reports of their child's sociability were linked to more sophisticated social play with unfamiliar peers. However, further analysis of this correlation among groups of children whose mothers reported that they experienced low, medium and high levels of positive sibling interaction showed that the link between sociability and peer play was only significant for children who experienced low levels of positive sibling interaction. This finding suggests that experience of positive interactions with siblings can compensate for low levels of temperamental sociability, presumably by providing a model for positive peer interactions.

Other findings from the Cambridge Toddlers Up study point to contrasting patterns of association with sibling relationships for friend and peer relationships. White, Ensor, Marks, Jacobs and Hughes (2014) examined sharing between siblings at age three as a predictor of sharing with a friend or with two unfamiliar peers at age six. In this study, early sibling sharing was unrelated to sharing with a best friend but did predict sharing with peers three years later, even when concurrent sibling behaviour was controlled. These findings highlight the different contexts of friendships and peer relationships, and taken together with previous findings suggest that similarities in behaviour with siblings, peers and friends may vary depending on the type of behaviour being examined. Prosocial behaviour with unfamiliar peers may reflect children's underlying prosocial tendencies, which are formed through interactions with siblings and other family members. In contrast, interactions with friends may be heavily influenced by relationship quality and past experiences of reciprocity, and thus be relatively independent of sibling prosocial behaviour. Alternatively, uncontrolled factors such as the length of the friendship and its quality may influence the strength of the association between children's sharing with siblings and friends, thus tempering the overall association between behaviour in the two contexts.

Before concluding this section on the congruence between sibling and peer relationships, the emerging literature examining links between sibling relationship quality and adolescents' romantic relationships deserves note. Here, dyadic gender effects are prominent. For example, in a study of pairs of adolescent siblings, perceived competence in romantic relationships increased from age 12 to 20 for adolescents with an opposite-gender sibling but decreased in adolescents with a same-gender sibling (Doughty, Lam, Stanik, & McHale, 2015). Similarly, in another study adolescents with an opposite-gender sibling reported more intimacy in their romantic relationships than those with a same-gender sibling (Doughty, McHale, & Feinberg, 2015). Note, however, that, these studies have only examined pairs of siblings and so it is not clear how having a sister *and* a brother impacts success in romantic relationships. The *quality* of sibling relationships also appears to contribute to adolescents' romantic relationships. In the first of the above two studies, high levels of sibling intimacy and low levels of sibling conflict predicted high levels of romantic competence from adolescence to early adulthood, and increases in sibling intimacy coincided with increases in romantic competence. Similarly, Doughty, McHale and Feinberg (2015) showed that sibling intimacy at age 16 predicted perceived power in romantic relationships two years later, while sibling conflict predicted lower intimacy in romantic relationships, although only for girls. This literature extends earlier research of parental influences on adolescents' romantic relationships (e.g., Conger, Cui, Bryant, & Elder, 2000) to demonstrate the important contribution of sibling relationship quality, and also suggests that the familiarity of interactions with members of the opposite-sex in a family context may promote intimacy in heterosexual romantic relationships.

Parents, siblings and social competence

Having considered similarities and differences between sibling relationships and friend and peer relationships, we turn our attention to the contribution of sibling relationship quality to social competence more broadly. Social competence can be defined as the ability to maintain positive relationships with peers, the exhibition of socially competent behaviour (e.g., prosocial behaviour), and the absence of loneliness or social isolation (e.g., Crick & Dodge, 1994). The role of parents in children's socialisation has long been recognised. For example, children whose parents are warm and responsive (i.e., authoritative) generally show better social skills, more popularity and prosocial behaviour, are more accepted by peers and are less likely to be bullied (e.g., Attili, Vermigli, & Roazzi, 2010; Chen, Dong, & Zhou, 1997; Healy, Sanders, & Iyer, 2013; Healy, Sanders, & Iyer, 2014; Lamborn, Mounts, Steinberg, & Dornbusch 1991). Aspects of parent-child relationship quality, as opposed to parenting behaviours are also associated with children's social competence. For example, Lindsey and colleagues (2010) showed that parents' mutuality in play interactions with their toddler was associated with toddlers' prosocial behaviour. In addition, another study showed that five-year-olds' reports of closeness to their mother were associated with prosocial behaviour and children's closeness to friends (Sturgess et al., 2001). These findings suggest that in addition to direct coaching of positive social behaviours, family influences on children's social behaviour may operate through incidental associations, because children are motivated to engage in prosocial behaviours as a way of sustaining positive interactions with family members (e.g., Brownell, 2016; Paulus, 2014)

McDowell and Parke (2009) have suggested that parents influence children's social abilities in (at least) three separate ways: through parent-child interactions, through direct instruction, and by providing opportunities for children to interact with peers. Siblings are also likely to contribute to social competence through these three processes. Children typically spend more time interacting with their sibling than their parent (e.g., McHale & Crouter, 1996), and thus both the frequency of these interactions and their similarity to peer relationships make them a good model for future peer interactions. In addition, older siblings often take on teaching or care-giving roles in sibling interactions (e.g., Brody, Stoneman, MacKinnon, & MacKinnon, 1985; Bryant, 1989; Lamb, 1978), and may directly teach children about socially competent behaviours. Finally, studies examining sibling influences on substance use and delinquency in adolescence indicate that older siblings can serve as gate-keepers to deviant peer groups for their younger siblings, suggesting that older siblings may provide opportunities for their younger children to interact with peers (e.g., Rowe & Gulley, 1992; Windle, 2000).

Empirical studies indicate links between sibling relationship quality and aspects of social competence throughout childhood. In the Cambridge Toddlers Up study, preschool prosocial behaviour with siblings predicted lower loneliness and social dissatisfaction in the first year of school (Marks, 2010). Moreover, in a study of socially disadvantaged five-year-old boys, Morgan, Shaw and Olino (2012) reported a negative link between sibling conflict and teacher-rated social skills but only among boys who showed high negative emotionality. In the primary school years, Stocker (1994) showed that seven- and eight-year-olds' reports of warmth in relationships with both their mother and siblings were associated with lower levels of loneliness, whereas high sibling conflict was linked to increased loneliness. Similarly, Stormshak and colleagues (1996) demonstrated that children who had involved (i.e., moderate levels of warmth and conflict) sibling relationships exhibited higher levels of social competence, attention and emotional control, and were less likely to be disliked by peers than children with conflictual (i.e., low warmth, high conflict) sibling relationships. Note, however, that among similar-aged children, Hakvoort and colleagues (2010) found no associations between parent-child, marital or sibling relationships and children's self-reported social acceptance, even though these variables were linked to other psychosocial outcomes. Among young adults too, high levels of sibling support, closeness and rivalry and low levels of conflict are linked to decreased loneliness (Milevsky, 2005; Ponzetti & James, 1997; Sherman, Lansford, & Volling, 2006), results that resonate with the finding that adults with developmental disabilities desire more contact with their siblings (Burbidge & Minnes, 2014, see Chapter 8).

In light of Chapter 4's discussion of the clustering of relationship quality within families, the sceptical reader might ask to what extent links between sibling relationship quality and social competence reflect a more general influence of family climate, or the indirect influence of parent-child relationship quality on socialisation. Studies that examine the contribution of both relationships to social competence are relatively scarce, but point to both independent and interactive effects of parent-child and sibling relationship quality. For example, in a study of four- to eight-year-olds, Pike, Coldwell, and Dunn (2005) showed that, over and above the contribution of parent-child relationships, the quality of sibling relationships (as reported by the children themselves or by parents) predicted a small but significant portion of variance in older siblings' prosocial behaviour. Similarly, in a study of young adults, closeness in mother-child, father-child and sibling relationships was differentially and independently associated with social competence, but these associations varied by gender (Bell, Avery, Jenkins, Feld, & Schoenrock, 1985). Specifically, among men, most indices of social competence were linked to father-child or sibling relationship quality, whereas among women more general family factors (such as contentment at home) were stronger predictors of most indices of social competence, although sibling relationship quality predicted the frequency of interactions with close friends. In addition, in a study of boys' conflict with teachers and peers over the transition to school, Ingoldsby, Shaw and Garcia (2001) showed both an independent effect of mother-child conflict and interactive effects of marital and sibling conflict. As a result, teacher conflict was lowest in the context of lower levels of sibling and marital conflict. Likewise, in a study of loneliness among young adults, Milevsky (2005) has reported that sibling support compensates for the effects of low paternal support.

These studies have examined the contribution of parent and sibling influences at a single point in time, yet the relative influence of parents and siblings on children's social competence is likely to change during childhood. For example, studies examining individuals' networks of relationships report that the salience of close relationships changes over the life course, and in particular, that primary sources of support change through childhood and adolescence (e.g., Furman & Buhrmester, 1992). Support from parents is particularly prominent in childhood, but support from peers and then romantic partners become more important in adolescence and beyond, as children's social spheres move beyond the nuclear family (e.g., Furman & Buhrmester, 1992). For example, life satisfaction among undergraduate students is linked with relationship quality with a partner but not with family members (Chow, 2010).

To examine how the relative contributions of parent-child and sibling relationships to children's social competence might change over childhood we used data from the Cambridge Toddlers Up study to examine associations between family relationships and social competence at four time points over a period of nine years (White, 2014). This period of time spanned two important transitions for the target children: starting primary school, and moving up to secondary school. While previous studies have tended to look at specific aspects of social competence such as prosocial behaviour or social skills, we took advantage of the rich data available from study families to create a multi-faceted, multi-informant aggregate of social competence. Specifically, our measure included parents' reports of prosocial behaviour and peer problems, and from age six onwards children's reports of peer acceptance, loneliness and social dissatisfaction.

To examine the relative contribution of parent-child and sibling relationships we conducted a series of hierarchical regression analyses predicting social competence, at age three, six, 10 and 12, from mothers' reports of the mother-child relationship and mothers' (age three and six) and children's (age 10 and 12) ratings of sibling relationship quality collected at the same time point, and the previous time point. Specifically, at each time point ratings of mother-child and sibling positivity and conflict were included in the regression model. At age three, after controlling for verbal ability, the only family relationship variable to predict social competence was mother-child positivity. Similar results were found at age six: after controlling for earlier levels of social competence, only mother-child positivity predicted unique variance in social competence. However, in the pre-adolescent time points of the study, a different pattern of results emerged. At age 10, sibling (but not mother-child) positivity predicted higher levels of social competence, and sibling conflict predicted lower levels of social competence but only in the context of high levels of mother-child conflict. Similarly, at age 12, children with more positive sibling relationships again showed higher levels of social competence, although mother-child positivity was also a marginally significant predictor.

Two important points arise from these results. First, the findings point to a developmental shift in the contribution of mother-child and sibling relationship quality to children's social competence. In the early phases of the study only individual differences in the mother-child relationship predicted unique variance in children's social competence, whereas in the later two time points, the quality of sibling relationships became an important predictor. Thus, the influence of the sibling versus the mother-child relationship appeared to increase as children reached middle childhood. This finding fits with research suggesting that as children approach adolescence peers have a stronger influence on children's development (e.g., Furman & Buhrmester, 1992). That is, as children gain independence and begin to spend more time away from the home, at school and with peers, they may rely less and less on parents. In contrast, siblings may be viewed as a bridge between their home and outside lives and increasingly become important sources of support. A second interesting point was that, at all ages, social competence was more strongly related to family positivity than to family conflict, suggesting that positive behaviours learned in family relationships act as a model for friendly interactions with peers and friends.

In contrast, our findings suggest that family conflict may have little impact on social competence. This may be because conflict in family relationships is relatively normative and thus may not be detrimental to social competence except at very high levels. That said, other research shows that high levels of family conflict are strongly related to antisocial behaviour in peer relationships (e.g., Buist, Deković, & Prinzie, 2013; Garcia, Shaw, Winslow, & Yaggi, 2000; Ingoldsby et al., 2001; Kim, Hetherington, & Reiss, 1999; Patterson, 1986). These findings highlight the idea of "ambivalence", where positive interactions and conflict are separate aspects of sibling relationships, with distinct correlates.

Sibling-sibling influences

Thus far we have considered siblings as agents of social development by examining how the *quality* of sibling relationships influences interactions with others outside the home. However, siblings also influence each other's social behaviour more directly. Sibling similarities may occur through social learning processes where children observe and imitate their sibling's behaviour (Bandura, 1977), but also because older siblings act as gatekeepers by providing access to resources or peer networks necessary for certain activities (e.g., alcohol or drug use; Rowe & Gulley, 1992; Windle, 2000). Older siblings may be salient role models for younger children, as they are familiar and similar to the child, and may provide direct reinforcement when the child performs the learned behaviour (Bandura, 1977). Sibling influences can also serve to create differences between children: for example, children may actively differentiate themselves from their siblings through their behaviour and interests, in order to establish a unique identity within the family (Schachter, Shore, Feldman-Rotman, Marquis, & Campbell, 1976). Sibling influences have most commonly been examined in relation to risk-taking and antisocial behaviours (e.g., Brook, Brook, & Whiteman, 1999; Brook, Whiteman, Brook, & Gordon, 1991; Conger & Rueter, 1996; Fagan & Najman, 2005; Kowal & Blinn-Pike, 2004; Low, Shortt, & Snyder, 2012; Rowe & Gulley, 1992; Slomkowski, Rende, Conger, Simons, & Conger, 2001); here, in keeping with the theme of the chapter we consider sibling influences on gender development and peer competence.

Many studies have examined sibling influences on gender development by comparing the gender-typed qualities of children with sisters versus brothers. For example, using data from the Avon Longitudinal Study of Parents and Children study, Rust and colleagues (2000) showed that boys with older brothers, and girls with older sisters showed more gender-typed behaviour than children with opposite-sex siblings. Moreover, children who had an older brother showed more masculine and less feminine behaviour than other children, while boys with an older sister showed more feminine behaviour, and girls with an older sister showed less masculine behaviour. While these findings are consistent with a social learning approach, a significant limitation of this approach to examining sibling influences on gender is that the gender-typed behaviours of siblings were not measured (such that, for example, siblings of brothers were assumed to be exposed to more masculine role models), and parental influences on gender-typed behaviour were not considered.

To overcome these limitations McHale, Updegraff, Helms-Erikson and Crouter (2001) examined siblings' and parents' gender role qualities over a two-year period beginning when the siblings were eight and 10 years old. The study findings indicated that older siblings' gender role attitudes, and gender-typed personality characteristics and leisure activities predicted younger siblings' scores on the same constructs, even when controlling for parental influences. Moreover, in keeping with the tenets of social learning theory indicating that higher status models are more likely to be imitated, sibling influences were more prominent for younger siblings' than for older siblings' gender role qualities. In fact, when sibling effects were present for older siblings, they more often followed a pattern suggesting sibling differentiation rather than social learning.

Sibling influences on gender role qualities may occur through variation in the time spent with individuals of the same versus the opposite gender. For example, McHale, Kim, Whiteman and Crouter (2004) reported some links between the time spent with brothers versus sisters and children's gendered attitudes and personalities. Specifically, for girls, time spent with sisters was correlated with higher endorsement of traditional attitudes towards gender while time spent with brothers was correlated with lower endorsement of gendered attitudes. Certainly, given the highly gender-segregated nature of children's peer relationships and friendships, opposite-sex siblings may provide a unique opportunity to socialise with individuals of the other sex, that as mentioned earlier may facilitate later successful romantic relationships, at least among heterosexual adolescents (Doughty, McHale, et al., 2015). However, qualitative research examining sibling relationships presents a more nuanced picture. Drawing on longitudinal case studies, Edwards and Weller (2014) argue that sibling influences on gender are not static, but that young people's gendered identities are constructed and negotiated in different ways at different points in time, as the nature and context of sibling relationships change.

Sibling influences are also apparent in children's social competence. For example, an early study showed that primary-school-aged sibling pairs showed greater similarity than matched pairs of peers in peer ratings of social preference, teacher ratings of likeability, adaptive social behaviour and popularity, and observed positive behaviour in the playground (Lewin, Hops, Davis, & Dishion, 1993). Note, however, that this similarity does not necessarily imply direct sibling influence, as sibling similarity may reflect shared genetic or environment influences (e.g., parental influences on social behaviour). To examine sibling influence more directly, Whiteman, McHale and Crouter, (2007) developed a measure of perceived sibling influence and assessed how younger siblings' social competence varied with perceived sibling influence and their older siblings' level of social competence. Their findings indicated that, after controlling for sibling relationship quality, there was a marginally significant effect of perceived sibling influence on younger siblings' social competence. However, this effect was qualified by an interaction between sibling influence and older siblings' social competence, such that younger siblings reported particularly high levels of social competence when they reported high levels of sibling influence and their older sibling showed high social competence. Moreover, Whiteman et al.'s (2007) findings demonstrated that sibling influence was greater in sibling relationships characterised by high levels of intimacy and frequent shared activities. Thus, sibling influences on social competence appear to depend not only on the quality of the relationship between siblings but also on the extent to which the younger child perceives their older sibling as a competent role model.

Taken together, the findings in this chapter demonstrate the contribution of siblings to children's social development. Findings linking sibling relationship quality with relationship quality with other children generally point to spillover rather than compensatory processes, where positive relationships with siblings are associated with positive peer and friend relationships and higher levels of social competence. Associations between sibling and friend or peer relationships are not always straightforward, however, and may be influenced by a number of factors including the specific aspect of relationship quality studied, the gender composition of the sibling dyad, family composition and the child's age. Interestingly, in contrast with studies showing links between children's sibling relationships and their early socio-cognitive skills (reviewed in Chapter 6), which focus predominantly on the preschool period, the findings reviewed here suggest that sibling relationship quality may play a particularly important role in children's social relationships and social competence in later childhood, as children become less reliant on parents. Finally, siblings influence social development directly through processes of social learning and sibling differentiation, which are prominent in children's development of gender and social competence.

Take-home messages

1. Understanding how sibling relationships contribute to children's social competence is important because social abilities in childhood predict competence at work, academic attainment and social success in adulthood. Links between sibling relationships and social competence can be understood in terms of the

spillover and compensation processes discussed in the context of family systems theory in Chapter 4.

2. When considering the concordance in quality between children's relationships with siblings, friends and peers it is important to consider the different contexts of these three relationships. Friendships are both close and voluntary, while peer and sibling relationships may be involuntary and vary more in their quality.

3. In early childhood, findings regarding associations between sibling and friend relationship quality have been mixed, perhaps reflecting studies' differing focus on specific behaviours and aspects of relationship quality.

4. In adolescence, however, several studies have shown a bidirectional relationship between the quality of children's relationships with siblings and friends.

5. Early studies suggested little overlap in the quality of sibling and peer relationships. However, more recent studies suggest a more nuanced picture in which links between sibling and peer relationships are evident, but vary with sibling gender composition and family factors.

6. Early prosocial behaviour towards siblings appears to predict later prosocial behaviour with peers more strongly than prosocial behaviour towards friends.

7. Studies from different stages of the lifespan suggest that the quality of sibling relationships is a consistently important predictor of children's social competence.

8. The few studies that have compared the contribution of both sibling and parent-child relationships to children's social competence suggest that each relationship predicts unique variance in social abilities.

9. Findings from the Cambridge Toddlers Up study suggest that in the preschool and early school years parent-child relationship quality is a stronger predictor of social competence than sibling relationship quality. However, in line with findings that peer influences on social development strengthen as children approach adolescence, in the late primary and early secondary school years sibling relationship quality became a stronger predictor of social competence than mother-child relationship quality.

10. Siblings exert direct influences on each other's behaviour through processes of social learning and sibling differentiation. Social learning processes appear to be particularly important in explaining predictive links between older and younger siblings' gender-typed attitudes and behaviour.

References

Abramovitch, R., Corter, C., Pepler, D., & Stanhope, L. (1986). Sibling and peer interaction: A final follow-up and a comparison. *Child Development, 57,* 217–229. doi: 10.2307/1130653

Aldercotte, A., White, N., & Hughes, C. (2016). Sibling and peer relationships in early childhood. In L. Balter and C. Tamis-LeMonda (Eds.), *Child psychology: A handbook of contemporary issues* (pp. 141–166). New York: Routledge.

Aristotle, Ross, W., & Brown, L. (2009). *The Nicomachean ethics.* Oxford: Oxford University Press.

Attili, G., Vermigli, P., & Roazzi, A. (2010). Children's social competence, peer status, and the quality of mother-child and father-child relationships. *European Psychologist, 15,* 23–33. doi: 10.1027/1016-9040/a000002.

Bandura, A. (1977). *Social learning theory.* Englewood Cliffs, NJ: Prentice Hall.

Bell, N. J., Avery, A. W., Jenkins, D., Feld, J., & Schoenrock, C. J. (1985). Family relationships and social competence during late adolescence. *Journal of Youth and Adolescence, 14,* 109–119. doi:10.1007/BF02098651.

Berndt, T., & Bulleit, T. (1985). Effects of sibling relationships on preschoolers' behavior at home and at school. *Developmental Psychology, 21,* 761–767. doi:10.1037/0012-1649. 21.5.761.

Bornstein, M., Hahn, C.-S., & Haynes, O. (2010). Social competence, externalizing, and internalizing behavioral adjustment from early childhood through early adolescence. *Development and Psychopathology, 22,* 717–735. doi:10.1017/S0954579410000416.

Bretherton, I. (1985). Attachment theory: Retrospect and prospect. In I. Bretherton & E. Waters (Eds.), *Growing points of attachment theory and research* (pp. 3–35): Monographs of the Society for Research in Child Development (No. 209).

Brody, G. H., Stoneman, Z., MacKinnon, C., & MacKinnon, R. (1985). Role relationships and behavior among preschool-aged and school-aged sibling pairs. *Developmental Psychology, 21,* 124–129. doi:10.1037/0012-1649.21.1.124.

Brook, J. S., Brook, D. W., & Whiteman, M. (1999). Older sibling correlates of younger sibling drug use in the context of parent-child relations. *Genetic, Social, and General Psychology Monographs, 125,* 451–468.

Brook, J. S., Whiteman, M., Brook, D. W., & Gordon, A. S. (1991). Sibling influences on adolescent drug use: Older brothers or younger brothers. *Journal of the American Academy of Child and Adolescent Psychiatry, 30,* 958–966. doi: 10.1097/00004583-199111000-00014

Brownell, C. A. (2016). Prosocial behavior in infancy: The role of socialization. *Child Development Perspectives, 10,* 222–227. doi:10.1111/cdep.12189.

Bryant, B. (1989). The child's perspective of sibling caretaking and its relevance to understanding social-emotional functioning and development. In P. Zukow (Ed.), *Sibling interaction across cultures: Theoretical and methodological issues* (pp. 143–164). New York: Springer-Verlag.

Buist, K. L., Deković, M., & Prinzie, P. (2013). Sibling relationship quality and psychopathology of children and adolescents: A meta-analysis. *Clinical Psychology Review, 33,* 97–106. doi:10.1016/j.cpr.2012.10.007.

Burbidge, J., & Minnes, P. (2014). Relationship quality in adult siblings with and without developmental disabilities. *Family Relations, 63,* 148–162. doi:10.1111/fare.12047.

Caspi, A., & Elder, G. (1988). Emergent family patterns: The intergenerational construction of problem behavior and relationships. In R. Hinde & J. Stevenson-Hinde (Eds.), *Relationships within families* (pp. 218–240). Oxford, UK: Oxford University Press.

Chen, X., Dong, Q., & Zhou, H. (1997). Authoritative and authoritarian parenting practices and social and school performance in Chinese children. *International Journal of Behavioral Development, 21,* 855–873. doi:10.1080/016502597384703.

Chow, H. P. H. (2010). Factors contributing to the subjective well-being of undergraduate students in a Canadian prairie city. *Prairie Forum, 35,* 103–117.

Conger, R., & Rueter, M. (1996). Siblings, parents and peers: A longitudinal study of social influences in adolescent risk for alcohol use and abuse. In G. H. Brody (Ed.), *Sibling relationships: Their causes and consequences* (pp. 1–30). Norwood, NJ: Ablex.

Conger, R. D., Cui, M., Bryant, C. M., & Elder, G. H. (2000). Competence in early adult romantic relationships: A developmental perspective on family influences. *Journal of Personality and Social Psychology, 79,* 224–237. doi:10.1037//0022-3514.79.2.224.

Costin, S. E., & Jones, D. C. (1992). Friendship as a facilitator of emotional responsiveness and prosocial interventions among young children. *Developmental Psychology, 28*, 941–947. doi:10.1037/0012-1649.28.5.941.

Crick, N., & Dodge, K. (1994). A review and reformulation of social information processing mechanisms in children's social adjustment. *Psychological Bulletin, 115*, 74–101. doi: 10.1037/0033-2909.115.1.74.

Doughty, S. E., Lam, C. B., Stanik, C. E., & McHale, S. M. (2015). Links between sibling experiences and romantic competence from adolescence through young adulthood. *Journal of Youth and Adolescence, 44*, 2054–2066. doi:10.1007/s10964-014-0177-9.

Doughty, S. E., McHale, S. M., & Feinberg, M. E. (2015). Sibling experiences as predictors of romantic relationship qualities in adolescence. *Journal of Family Issues, 36*, 589–608. doi:1 0.1177/0192513X13495397.

Dunn, J. (1983). Sibling relationships in early childhood. *Child Development, 54*, 787–811.

Dunn, J., & McGuire, S. (1992). Sibling and peer relationships in childhood. *Journal of Child Psychology and Psychiatry, 33*, 67–105.

Dunn, J., Slomkowski, C., Donelan, N., & Herrera, C. (1995). Conflict, understanding, and relationships: Developments and differences in the preschool years. Special Issue: Conflict resolution in early social development. *Early Education and Development, 6*, 303–316. doi:10.1207/s15566935eed0604_2.

Edwards, R., & Weller, S. (2014). Sibling relationships and the construction of young people's gendered identities over time and in different spaces. *Families, Relationships and Societies, 3*, 185–199. doi: 10.1332/204674314X13951457865780.

Fagan, A. A., & Najman, J. M. (2005). The relative contributions of parental and sibling substance use to adolescent tobacco, alcohol, and other drug use. *Journal of Drug Issues, 35*, 869–884. doi:10.1177/002204260503500410.

Furman, W., & Buhrmester, D. (1992). Age and sex differences in perceptions of networks of personal relationships. *Child Development, 63*, 103–115. doi:10.1111/j.1467-8624.1992. tb03599.x.

Garcia, M. M., Shaw, D. S., Winslow, E. B., & Yaggi, K. E. (2000). Destructive sibling conflict and the development of conduct problems in young boys. *Developmental Psychology, 36*, 44–53. doi:10.1037/0012-1649.36.1.44.

Gest, S., Sesma, A., Masten, A., & Tellegen, A. (2006). Childhood peer reputation as a predictor of competence and symptoms 10 years later. *Journal of Abnormal Child Psychology, 34*, 509–526. doi:10.1007/s10802-006-9029-8.

Hakvoort, E. M., Bos, H. M. W., Van Balen, F., & Hermanns, J. M. A. (2010). Family relationships and the psychosocial adjustment of school-aged children in intact families. *Journal of Genetic Psychology, 171*, 182–201. doi:10.1080/00221321003657445.

Harrist, A. W., Achacoso, J. A., John, A., Pettit, G. S., Bates, J. E., & Dodge, K. A. (2014). Reciprocal and complementary sibling interactions: Relations with socialization outcomes in the kindergarten classroom. *Early Education and Development, 25*, 202–222. doi:10.1080/10409289.2014.848500.

Healy, K., Sanders, M., & Iyer, A. (2013). Parenting practices, children's peer relationships and being bullied at school. *Journal of Child and Family Studies. 24*, 127–140. doi:10.1007/ s10826-013-9820-4.

Healy, K. L., Sanders, M. R., & Iyer, A. (2015). Facilitative parenting and children's social, emotional and behavioral adjustment. *Journal of Child and Family Studies, 24*, 1762–1779. doi:10.1007/s10826-014-9980-x.

Howe, N., Ross, H. S., & Recchia, H. (2011). Sibling relations in early and middle childhood. In P. K. Smith & C. H. Hart (Eds.), *The Wiley-Blackwell handbook of childhood social development* (2nd ed., pp. 356–372). New York: Wiley.

Hughes, C., & Dunn, J. (1997). "Pretend you didn't know": Preschoolers' talk about mental states in pretend play. *Cognitive Development, 12,* 477–499. doi: 10.1016/ S0885-2014(97)90019-8.

Hughes, C., & Dunn, J. (2007). Children's early relationships with other children. In C. Brownell & C. Kopp (Eds.), *Transitions in early socioemotional development: The toddler years* (pp. 177–200). New York: Guilford Press.

Ingoldsby, E. M., Shaw, D. S., & Garcia, M. M. (2001). Intrafamily conflict in relation to boys' adjustment at school. *Development and Psychopathology, 13,* 35–52. doi: 10.1017/ S0954579401001031.

Jack, A. (2005). *Shaggy dogs and black sheep: The origins of even more phrases we use every day.* London: Penguin Books.

Kim, J. E., Hetherington, E. M., & Reiss, D. (1999). Associations among family relationships, antisocial peers, and adolescents' externalizing behaviors: Gender and family type differences. *Child Development, 70,* 1209–1230. doi: 10.1111/1467-8624.00088.

Kowal, A. K., & Blinn-Pike, L. (2004). Sibling influences on adolescents' attitudes toward safe sex practices. *Family Relations, 53,* 377–384. doi: 10.1111/j.0197-6664.2004.00044.x.

Kramer, L., & Gottman, J. (1992). Becoming a sibling: "With a little help from my friends". *Developmental Psychology, 28,* 685–699. doi:10.1037/0012-1649.28.4.685.

Kramer, L., & Kowal, A. (2005). Sibling relationship quality from birth to adolescence: The enduring contributions of friends. *Journal of Family Psychology, 19,* 503–511. doi:10.1037/0893-3200.19.4.503.

Lamb, M. E. (1978). The development of sibling relationships in infancy: A short-term longitudinal study. *Child Development, 49,* 1189–1196. doi:10.2307/1128759.

Lamborn, S., Mounts, N., Steinberg, L., & Dornbusch, S. (1991). Patterns of competence and adjustment among adolescents from authoritative, authoritarian, indulgent, and neglectful families. *Child Development, 62,* 1049–1065. doi:10.1111/j.1467-8624.1991.tb01588.x.

Lewin, L. M., Hops, H., Davis, B., & Dishion, T. J. (1993). Multimethod comparison of similarity in school adjustment of siblings and unrelated children. *Developmental Psychology, 29,* 963–969. doi:10.1037/0012-1649.29.6.963.

Lindsey, E. W., Cremeens, P., & Caldera, Y. (2010). Mother-child and father-child mutuality in two contexts: Consequences for young children's peer relationships. *Infant and Child Development, 19,* 142–160. doi: 10.1002/icd.645.

Lippman, L. H., Moore, K. A., & McIntosh, H. (2011). Positive indicators of child well-being: A conceptual framework, measures, and methodological issues. *Applied Research in Quality of Life, 6,* 425–449. doi:10.1007/s11482-011-9138-6.

Low, S., Shortt, J. W., & Snyder, J. (2012). Sibling influences on adolescent substance use: The role of modeling, collusion, and conflict. *Development and Psychopathology, 24,* 287–300. doi:10.1017/S0954579411000836.

McElwain, N. L., & Volling, B. L. (2005). Preschool children's interactions with friends and older siblings: Relationship specificity and joint contributions to problem behavior. *Journal of Family Psychology, 19,* 486–496. doi: 10.1037/0893-3200.19.4.486.

McHale, S. M., & Crouter, A. C. (1996). The family contexts of children's sibling relation-ships. In G. H. Brody (Ed.), *Sibling relationships: Their causes and consequences* (pp. 173–195). Norwood, NJ: Ablex.

McHale, S. M., Kim, J. Y., Whiteman, S., & Crouter, A. C. (2004). Links between sex-typed time use in middle childhood and gender development in early adolescence. *Developmental Psychology, 40,* 868–881. doi:10.1037/0012-1649.40.5.868

McHale, S. M., Updegraff, K. A., Helms-Erikson, H., & Crouter, A. C. (2001). Sibling influ-ences on gender development in middle childhood and early adolescence: a longitudinal study. *Developmental Psychology, 37,* 115–125. doi:10.1037/0012-1649.37.1.115.

Marks, A. (2010). *Children's interactions with siblings from ages 3 to 6: Developmental trajectories and links with children's peer experiences.* (Unpublished doctoral dissertation). University of Cambridge. Cambridge, UK.

Masten, A., Desjardins, C., McCormick, C., Kuo, S., & Long, J. (2010). The significance of childhood competence and problems for adult success in work: A developmental cascade analysis. *Development and Psychopathology, 22,* 679–694. doi:10.1017/S0954 579410000362.

Mendelson, M., Aboud, F., & Lanthier, R. (1994). Kindergartners' relationships with siblings, peers and friends. *Merrill Palmer Quarterly, 40,* 416–427.

Milevsky, A. (2005). Compensatory patterns of sibling support in emerging adulthood: Variations in loneliness, self-esteem, depression and life satisfaction. *Journal of Social and Personal Relationships, 22,* 743–755. doi:10.1177/0265407505056447.

Morgan, J. K., Shaw, D. S., & Olino, T. M. (2012). Differential susceptibility effects: The interaction of negative emotionality and sibling relationship quality on childhood internalizing problems and social skills. *Journal of Abnormal Child Psychology, 40,* 885–899. doi:10.1007/s10802-012-9618-7.

Parke, R., MacDonald, K., Beitel, A., & Bhavnagri, N. (1988). The role of the family in the development of peer relationships. In R. McMahon & R. Peters (Eds.), *Social learning and systems approaches to marriage and the family* (pp. 17–44). Philadelphia, PA: Brunner/Mazel.

Parker, J., & Asher, S. (1987). Peer relations and later personal adjustment: Are low-accepted children at risk? *Psychological Bulletin, 192,* 357–389. doi:10.1037/0033-2909.102.3.357.

Patterson, G. (1986). The contribution of siblings to training for fighting: A microsocial analysis. In D. Olweus, J. Block & M. Radke-Yarrow (Eds.), *Development of antisocial and prosocial behavior* (pp. 235–261). New York: Academic Press.

Paulus, M. (2014). The emergence of prosocial behavior: Why do infants and toddlers help, comfort, and share? *Child Development Perspectives, 8,* 77–81. doi:10.1111/cdep.12066.

Pike, A., Coldwell, J., & Dunn, J. (2005). Sibling relationships in early/middle childhood: Links with individual adjustment. *Journal of Family Psychology, 19,* 523–532. doi:10. 1037/0893-3200.19.4.523.

Ponzetti, J., & James, C. M. (1997). Loneliness and sibling relationships. *Journal of Social Behavior and Personality, 12,* 103–112.

Rowe, D. C., & Gulley, B. L. (1992). Sibling effects on substance use and delinquency. *Criminology, 30,* 217–234. doi:10.1111/j.1745-9125.1992.tb01103.x.

Rust, J., Golombok, S., Hines, M., Johnston, K., & Golding, J. (2000). The role of brothers and sisters in the gender development of preschool children. *Journal of Experimental Child Psychology, 77,* 292–303. doi:10.1006/jecp.2000.2596.

Ryff, C. D., & Keyes, C. L. M. (1995). The structure of psychological well-being revisited. *Journal of Personality and Social Psychology, 69,* 719–727. doi:10.1037/0022-3514. 69.4.719.

Schachter, F. F., Shore, E., Feldman-Rotman, S., Marquis, R. E., & Campbell, S. (1976). Sibling deidentification. *Developmental Psychology, 12,* 418–427. doi:10.1037/0012-1649.12.5.418.

Sherman, A. M., Lansford, J. E., & Volling, B. L. (2006). Sibling relationships and best friendships in young adulthood: Warmth, conflict, and well-being. *Personal Relationships, 13,* 151–165. doi:10.1111/j.1475-6811.2006.00110.x.

Slomkowski, C., Rende, R., Conger, K., Simons, R., & Conger, R. (2001). Sisters, brothers, and delinquency: Evaluating social influence during early and middle adolescence. *Child Development, 72,* 271–283. doi:10.1111/1467-8624.00278.

Stocker, C. (1994). Children's perceptions of their relationships with siblings, friends and mothers: Compensatory processes and links with adjustment. *Journal of Child Psychology and Psychiatry, 35,* 1447–1459. doi: 10.1111/j.1469-7610.1994.tb01286.x.

Stocker, C., & Dunn, J. (1990). Sibling relationships in childhood: Links with friendships and peer relationships. *British Journal of Developmental Psychology*, *8*, 227–244. doi:10.1111/j.2044-835X.1990.tb00838.x.

Stormshak, E. A., Bellanti, C. J., Bierman, K. L., Coie, J. D., Dodge, K. A., Greenberg, M. T., & McMahon, R. J. (1996). The quality of sibling relationships and the development of social competence and behavioral control in aggressive children. *Developmental Psychology*, *32*, 79–89. doi:10.1037/0012-1649.32.1.79.

Sturgess, W., Dunn, J., & Davies, L. (2001). Young children's perceptions of their relationships with family members: Links with family setting, friendships, and adjustment. *International Journal of Behavioral Development*, *25*, 521–529. doi: 10.1080/01650250042000500.

Trumbull, H. C. (1893). *The blood covenant: A primitive rite and its bearings on scripture.* Philadelphia: John D. Wattles.

White, N. (2014). *Sibling relationships from preschool to pre-adolescence: Change, correlates, and consequences.* (Unpublished doctoral dissertation). University of Cambridge. Cambridge, UK.

White, N., Ensor, R., Marks, A., Jacobs, L., & Hughes, C. (2014). "It's mine!" Does sharing with siblings at age 3 predict sharing with siblings, friends, and unfamiliar peers at age 6? *Early Education and Development*, *25*, 185–201. doi:10.1080/10409289.2013.825189.

Whiteman, S. D., McHale, S. M., & Crouter, A. C. (2007). Explaining sibling similarities: Perceptions of sibling influences. *Journal of Youth and Adolescence*, *36*, 963–972. doi:10.1007/s10964-006-9135-5.

Windle, M. (2000). Parental, sibling, and peer influences on adolescent substance use and alcohol problems. *Applied Developmental Science*, *4*, 98–110. doi:10.1207/S1532480XADS0402_5.

Yeh, H. C., & Lempers, J. D. (2004). Perceived sibling relationships and adolescent development. *Journal of Youth and Adolescence*, *33*, 133–147. doi:10.1023/B:JOYO.0000013425.86424.0f.

6

SIBLINGS, SOCIAL UNDERSTANDING AND SUCCESS AT SCHOOL

In a particularly charming documentary about the natural world, David Attenborough describes the dastardly way in which some Adélie penguins pilfer stones that others have carefully collected to form a nest, while keeping a vigilant eye to avoid being robbed by other "criminal penguins". In the frozen Antarctic, rivalry for scarce resources is rife and individuals who develop devious means of outwitting others are likely to be rewarded with reproductive success. Families are another context in which rivalry can play a prominent part: siblings routinely compete for parental attention or use their knowledge of each other to evoke a response that is likely to elicit parental disapproval. The first half of this chapter is devoted to the question of how sibling rivalry and other salient features of sibling interactions (including conflict, pretend play, mental state talk and attunement) might stimulate children's understanding of others' minds. In the second half of this chapter we turn to the question of how sibling relationships can influence children's academic performance.

Do sibling rivalry and conflict stimulate children's socio-cognitive development?

In a wonderfully honest book, written in the last few months of a life cut short by cancer, Kate Gross (2014) describes the rocky first few decades in her relationship with her younger sister. In this account, she recalls how she would tyrannise her little sister and assign her to subservient roles in their games of pretend play. Lacking the physical power to retaliate, Kate's younger sister Jo found ways of drawing their mother into their arguments, using means (such as surreptitious pinching) that may hoodwink the mother into a mistaken belief about who started the dispute. In other words, the drive to outwit or outmanoeuvre a sibling provides children with a powerful motivation for refining their understanding of others' thoughts and feelings. Indeed, naturalistic observational studies have shown that children's earliest efforts at deception often take the form of attempts to shift the blame for a misdeed onto a sibling (Wilson, Smith, & Ross, 2003).

Sibling rivalry is therefore reason enough to predict that the presence of siblings accelerates children's social understanding. In support of this proposal, an early study by Perner, Ruffman and Leekam (1994) showed that having a sibling was associated with an advantage equivalent to approximately six months in age in children's understanding of false belief (widely viewed as the litmus test for crediting children with a "theory of mind"). Several subsequent studies have replicated this finding, although typically with smaller effects, qualified by factors such as birth order, age gap or family socioeconomic status (McAlister & Peterson, 2006; Ruffman, Perner, Naito, Parkin, & Clements, 1998; Tompkins, Farrar, & Guo, 2013). In an effort to make sense of the mixed findings in this field, Devine and Hughes (2016) conducted a meta-analysis of data from 45 separate studies, involving a total of 4,996 children aged three to seven years and found a small but significant positive association between the number of siblings a child has and success on tests of false belief understanding: $r = .15, p < .01$.

Although this effect is weak, it is worth noting that it runs counter to the findings from numerous large-scale investigations showing a negative relationship between family size and child outcomes (e.g., Downey, 2001; Lawson & Mace, 2009, see Chapter 1). A cognitive advantage associated with being in a larger family is therefore unusual and suggests that interactions with other children (rather than with adults) provide a particularly valuable context for children's developing understanding of others' minds.

Consistent with this view, moderation analyses within Devine and Hughes's (2016) meta-analysis showed that the association between number of siblings and false belief understanding was significantly stronger in studies that focused on child-aged siblings. In other words, it is not having a sibling per se that contributes to children's understanding of others' minds, but rather having a sibling who is the right age to be a playmate and rival. Indeed, as the above example of squabbling sisters illustrates, sibling conflict may be as useful as sibling harmony in promoting children's growing awareness of others' minds. Piaget (1955, p. 83) noted that "it may well be through quarrelling that children first come to feel the need for making themselves understood" (cited in Randell & Peterson, 2009). Consistent with this view, Foote and Holmes-Lonergan (2003) have found, in a small-scale observational study of 22 children, that engagement in "other-oriented" reasoning (e.g., compromise, negotiation) within sibling conflict predicted false belief understanding, above and beyond effects of age and language ability. Similarly, Slomkowski and Dunn (1992) reported an association between children's use of other-oriented and self-oriented argument within sibling conflict and their ability to understand others' emotions seven months later.

In contrast, in a mother-report study, Randell and Peterson (2009) found that children's understanding of mind was unrelated to the frequency, topic or mode of resolution of disputes. However, it showed a specific association with the affective elements of sibling disputes. That is, preschoolers who performed well on false belief tasks were rated by mothers as showing less negative affect during sibling disputes and less post-conflict distress (e.g., tears, anger, sulking); this association remained even when effects of age and verbal ability were controlled. As Randell and Peterson (2009) noted, this association is likely to be bidirectional: while reasoned arguments with siblings can stimulate children's growing awareness of other minds, children with a good understanding of others' thoughts and feelings are probably more predisposed to listen, to use persuasion or to suggest compromises to resolve disagreements with siblings.

Somewhat more complex findings have emerged from a study of slightly older sibling dyads (aged, on average, 6.0 and 8.4 years old). Recchia and Howe (2009) found that the likelihood of compromise was related to younger siblings' interpretative understanding of conflict (i.e., how well they could understand the reasons for two characters' conflicting perspectives in a vignette), but only for dyads rated as low in relationship quality. For high relationship quality dyads, compromise was equally frequent regardless of whether the younger sibling had a good or poor interpretative understanding of conflict. That is, as a result of the striking variation in sibling relationship quality, there may be distinct processes underpinning the link between sibling conflict and social understanding in different families.

Does pretend play and talk about feelings with siblings provide a fertile context for learning about minds?

The example from Kate Gross's account of her relationship with her younger sister (given at the start of this chapter) also highlights another dimension of individual differences in children's sibling relationships that has been shown to be salient for children's understanding of mind, namely the frequency of pretend play. Early theoretical work by Leslie (1987) highlighted the "structural isomorphism" between pretense and belief. That is, both involve a decoupling from reality: for example, one can pretend (or think) that a cup is full of tea, even if this is not true (or indeed, even if the cup does not actually exist). In a seminal study of young siblings' interactions, Dunn and Dale (1984) found that 25–33% of preschool siblings showed frequent and sustained joint pretend play. Two separate later studies (Hughes & Dunn, 1997; Hughes, Fujisawa, Ensor, Lecce, & Marfleet, 2006) showed that children are much more likely to discuss their own and others' thoughts and feelings during pretend play with siblings and friends than when engaged in other forms of play, even when age, verbal ability and overall rates of talk were controlled. Indeed, this may be one reason why, by the age of four, children have been found, on average, to refer to their own and others' feelings three times as often during conversations with siblings than during conversations with mothers (Brown & Dunn, 1992). Moreover, studies of young children's interactions with friends and peers have demonstrated a specific association between frequency of shared pretend play and success on false belief tasks (Dunn & Cutting, 1999). It therefore seems likely that siblings facilitate children's acquisition of a theory of mind not only through rivalry and conflict but also by providing rich opportunities for sustained collaborative fantasy play.

Mental state conversations such as those occurring in sibling pretend play may be particularly fertile contexts for the development of theory of mind abilities because, unlike parent-child conversations, which typically focus on the child's mental states, such child-child talk tends to include references to both participants' mental states (Brown & Dunn, 1992). References to others' mental states appear to be particularly strongly linked to children's developing socio-cognitive abilities (Hughes, Lecce, & Wilson, 2007), and several studies have documented concurrent associations between sibling mental state talk and theory of mind abilities (Brown, Donelan-McCall, & Dunn, 1996; Hughes et al., 2007). Currently the longitudinal data are lacking to give any indication of the causal direction of this link, but Hughes and Dunn (1998) showed an equivalent association for talk between friends. Specifically, mental state talk between young friends was associated with enhanced false belief understanding 13 months later. Given the similarities between conversations with siblings and friends (e.g., talk about both individuals' feelings) this finding is highly suggestive of important longitudinal links between sibling mental state talk and theory of mind development.

Opportunities for exposure to mental state talk include not only encounters that demand direct engagement in a discussion of one's own and others' thoughts and feelings, but also the chance to eavesdrop on siblings' conversations with parents. In Chapter 2, for example, we noted that the birth of a second child is accompanied by an increase in the frequency with which mothers talk about mental states – for example, in discussions of what the new baby might want or like (Dunn & Kendrick, 1982). Similarly, Hughes (2011) compared the rate at which mothers referred to cognitive states (thoughts, beliefs, memories) at two different time points in the Cambridge Toddlers Up study, when the target children were aged two and six years old, and found an 18-fold increase in the average frequency of mothers' cognitive state talk. Clearly then, children with older siblings are likely to be immersed in a much richer linguistic environment – which may go some way to off-setting any "dilution of resources" that results from siblings' competing demands for parental attention.

Direct evidence in support of this proposal comes from a detailed study in which 37 children were each observed at home for a total of nine hours: four-year-old children with older siblings were indeed exposed to much more frequent talk about cognitive states and engaged in such talk more often than did four-year-olds without older siblings (Jenkins, Turrell, Kogushi, Lollis, & Ross, 2003). Moreover, in a recent training study, Gola (2012) presented preschoolers with videos including 128 mental state utterances in either an interactive or an overheard interaction style. Children who overheard talk about others' mental states showed significant improvements in false belief understanding after four sessions, whereas children who had been presented equivalent information in an interactive format did not show a similar improvement.

Does attunement between siblings matter for children's theory of mind?

Given that sibling relationships (perhaps more than any other close relationship) show striking variation in quality (e.g., Howe, Ross, & Recchia, 2011), it seems likely that the benefit of having a sibling for children's growing understanding of mind will depend on the frequency, content and quality of sibling interactions. One particularly salient dimension for individual differences in relationship quality may be the extent to which siblings are "in tune" or "on the same wavelength". While some siblings nearly always seem to know exactly what the other one is thinking, others show much less evidence of mutual understanding. Take, for example, two quotes from a pair of siblings interviewed in one of Dunn's Cambridge studies:

Nancy (age 10): Well, he's nice to me. And he sneaks into my bed at night time from Mummy. I think I'd be very lonely without Carl. I play with him a lot, and he thinks up ideas and it's very exciting. He comes to meet me at the gate after school and I think that's very friendly [...] He's very kind [...] Don't really know what I'd do without a brother.

Carl (age 6): She's pretty disgusting and we don't talk to each other much. I don't really know much about her. [*Interviewer:* What is it you particularly like about her?] Nothing. Sometimes when I done something wrong she tells me off quite cruelly. (Dunn & McGuire, 1994, pp. 119–120)

This amusing contrast in the two siblings' views of each other is reminiscent of the different viewpoints within marital relationships reported by Bernard (1972), but also suggests that variation in attunement within the sibling relationship is likely to be important for children's understanding of each other's minds. Indeed, in the very first empirical study to highlight the association between sibling interactions and children's understanding of mind, Dunn, Brown, Slomkowski, Tesla and Youngblade (1991) reported that the frequency with which 33-month-old children engaged in cooperative interactions with an older sibling (which, one might assume, depend upon being in tune with the other child's goals) predicted the likelihood of succeeding on a test of false belief understanding administered seven months later. Moreover, our work with the Cambridge Toddlers Up sample revealed a positive longitudinal association between children's false belief understanding and their connectedness of communication (defined as the proportion of utterances that are directly related to the semantic content of the previous utterance) within mother-child conversations recorded at an earlier time-point (Ensor & Hughes, 2008). While researchers have yet to look specifically at connectedness in sibling conversations these results suggest that, while not in itself sufficient to promote children's understanding of mind, having a child-age sibling is likely to increase opportunities for connected conversations that provide a window into others' thoughts and feelings.

We hope that the findings presented here will, collectively at least, convince the reader that children with siblings are immersed in an enriched social world that has at least the potential for stimulating an accelerated understanding of mind. The positive impact of siblings on this cognitive domain are particularly striking given that, in general, the effects of family size on children's cognitive development have been characterised in terms of the negative impact of "resource dilution" (Downey, 2001). The next section of this chapter provides a critique of this model and considers ways in which siblings can help as well as hinder children's academic achievement.

Siblings and children's learning and academic achievement

At the outset, it is worth noting that academic achievement and theory of mind are two important outcomes that, while distinct, do share some overlap. In particular, as discussed in an earlier book (Hughes, 2011), having a theory of mind can help children succeed at school via a number of distinct paths, including both direct paths (e.g., better comprehension of story narratives, enabling more rapid progress towards literacy) and indirect paths, involving positive relationships with peers (see Slaughter, Imuta, Peterson, & Henry, 2015 for a meta-analytic review) and increased ability to respond adaptively to teacher feedback (Lecce, Caputi, & Pagnin, 2014). Moreover, there is growing evidence from several sources, including neuroscientific studies of animals, that playful exchanges (that we have seen are valuable for children's understanding of mind) are important vehicles for learning (see Whitebread, Basilio, Kuvalja, & Verma, 2012 for a review). It is for this reason that we decided to consider the evidence for siblings' influence on theory of mind and on school success within the same chapter, with pretend play serving as a neat illustration of this overlap. In a paper entitled "*I've got some swords and you're dead!*", Dunn and Hughes (2001) describe the way in which children's games of shared pretend play can provide a window into their preoccupations, interests and concerns.

For many children, fantasy play often reflects everyday life. As a result, once older siblings start at school, such play frequently involves a re-enactment of school rituals, such as taking the register – with the older sibling playing the teacher (of course) and the younger sibling (and perhaps an array of soft toys) representing docile pupils. This is interesting, because (as we shall see shortly) older siblings also often provide genuine teaching to their younger siblings, explaining how a toy works or coaching them in a new game. Indeed, as noted by Recchia, Howe and Alexander (2009), sibling interactions provide a perfect example of what both Piagetian and Vygotskian theoretical perspectives identify as ideal for learning: namely interactions that involve an asymmetry in knowledge but not in authority. Moreover, Howe and Recchia (2005; 2009) have argued that good playmates also make good teachers, supporting this claim with evidence for a weak but significant cross-sectional and longitudinal association between the quality of sibling interactions in settings that elicit reciprocal (play) and complementary (teaching) interactions.

Investigating siblings' teaching styles in more detail, Howe, Brody and Recchia (2006) gave two sets of block design tasks (one easy, one hard) to 28 middle-class sibling dyads and found that: (1) the older siblings were able to adjust their teaching strategies according to both the younger siblings' age and the level of task difficulty; (2) the younger siblings were not passive recipients of learning but instead often asked questions or even refused offers of help. Overall, their findings emphasise the value of such sibling interactions both as a means of enhancing children's skill learning and as a context for strengthening sibling bonds.

Further insights into sibling interactions as a vehicle for learning come from a recent study in which, in order to investigate naturally occurring episodes of sibling teaching, Howe, Della Porta, Recchia, Funamoto and Ross (2015) filmed 39 sibling dyads (mean ages six and four years) for a total of nine hours of unstructured activity at home and identified over a thousand teaching episodes that were independent of parental involvement and that ranged in length from two to 114 conversational turns. Expressed as an hourly rate per sibling dyad, the average number of teaching episodes was 2.3 (range = 0.3–9) with most (80%) of these episodes initiated by the older sibling.

In other words, as argued by Strauss and Ziv (2012), teaching appears to be a natural human cognitive activity, even for very young children. Interestingly, much of the teaching in Howe and colleagues' study was conceptual rather than procedural. Commonly used teaching strategies included direct instruction, demonstration and correction of errors; less frequent strategies included explanation, positive feedback, planning and clarification. Echoing Howe et al.'s (2006) finding that children adjust their teaching strategies according to task difficulty, the children in this study varied their teaching strategies according to both the type of knowledge being taught (conceptual/procedural) and the context (e.g., who initiated the episode).

As we have seen earlier, however, interactions between siblings show remarkable variation in quality. Within these teaching/learning interactions, older siblings show marked contrasts in their cognitive sensitivity (i.e., in their use of praise, encouragement and other forms of positive control), with significant consequences for younger siblings' learning. For example, in a large and detailed study of 385 preschool sibling dyads filmed during a cooperative building task, Prime et al. (2014; 2016) coded the older siblings' interactional style in order to categorise them as

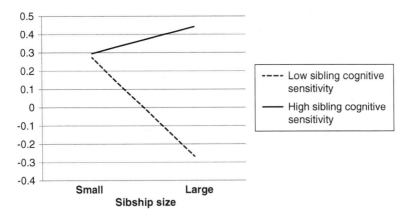

FIGURE 6.1 Older siblings' cognitive sensitivity influences the strength of the relationship between sibship size and children's theory of mind.

Source: Prime, Plamondon, Pauker, Perlman and Jenkins (2016, p. 99); with kind permission from Elsevier.

high or low in cognitive sensitivity. As shown in the figure, for the two cognitive outcomes assessed in the younger siblings (receptive vocabulary and false belief understanding), families with older siblings rated as low in cognitive sensitivity showed the decline in performance with sibship size predicted by the resource dilution model. In contrast, for families with older siblings rated as high in cognitive sensitivity, performance was maintained as sibship size increased.

Overall, the findings from the studies described above provide compelling evidence that young siblings are actively engaged in sharing their knowledge of the world with each other and so should not be overlooked in models of children's cognitive development. All of the studies considered thus far in this chapter have involved sibling dyads in which both siblings, or at least the younger siblings, were preschoolers. However, researchers investigating learning trajectories across the transition to adolescence have also begun to recognise that, alongside the influence of parents and peers, siblings also act as powerful role models.

For example, in a US study of 451 families, Melby and colleagues (2008) have shown that support from both parents and siblings in adolescence was associated with educational attainment 13 years later, through a link between family support and educational engagement. Interestingly, both the initial level and change in sibling support in adolescence were associated with academic engagement. Indeed, studies based in the United States indicate that older siblings' academic support contributes to younger siblings' motivation and achievement at school in several ethnic minority groups (Alfaro & Umaña-Taylor, 2010; Bankston, 1998).

Other researchers suggest that links between sibling relationships and academic adjustment may be more complicated. Bouchey, Shoulberg, Jodl and Eccles (2010) analysed data from the Maryland Adolescent Development in Context study, focusing on 251 families with siblings aged 12 and 15, with 161 families successfully tracked for two years. The first finding to emerge from this study was that younger siblings' academic adjustment (measured by three factors: perceived importance of school, academic self-concept and GPA) increased over time if their older siblings reported high academic engagement and success. Importantly, this association was independent of parental support and background demographic factors. Interestingly, however, younger siblings' perception of their older sibling's academic engagement was not related to changes in academic adjustment, except for a link to increases in GPA for same-sex dyads only. These findings highlight the importance of taking into account both siblings' views of the relationships when considering the implications of sibling relationships for children's adjustment.

Bouchey and colleagues also examined the role of sibling support in predicting changes in academic adjustment. Their analyses showed that support from an older sibling was associated with decreases in academic adjustment over time, and this was true regardless of whether the younger or older sibling provided information about sibling support. The authors attributed this link to deidentification processes (e.g., Schachter, Shore, Feldman-Rotman, & Marquis, 1976), whereby children who have academically successful siblings may pursue different interests (e.g., sport, music) in order to create their own unique identity, or reduce competition for parental attention. Likewise, in a study of 16-year-old twins, dyads who reported higher levels of co-dependence were more likely to go into vocational education rather than to stay at high school than were twins who reported less co-dependence (Penninkilampi-Kerola, Moilanen, & Kaprio, 2005).

At this point, it is worth noting that most studies of family influence on children's academic achievement have focused on parents rather than on siblings. For example, parents' support for and engagement in their child's learning, and the quality of the parent-child relationship have both been shown to predict children's success at school (Fan & Chen, 2001; Melby & Conger, 1996). With the exception of Melby and colleagues' (2008) study of adolescents, however, few studies have examined the interplay of parent and sibling influences on academic achievement. Using data from the Cambridge Toddlers Up study, we sought to examine how the quality of relationships with parents and older siblings contribute to children's academic achievement over the transition to secondary school (White, 2014). We reasoned that older siblings might be particularly important sources of information and support at a new school. Accordingly, we expected supportive sibling relationships to be more strongly related to academic achievement relative to parent-child relationships after the transition to secondary school than when children were in primary school.

Our findings were initially surprising. There were few links between positivity in sibling and mother-child relationships and children's academic achievement either before (age ten) or after (age 12) the transition to secondary school, except for an interaction effect at age 12 whereby children's academic achievement was higher when they experienced positive relationships with both their mother and older sibling. In contrast, concurrent sibling conflict was linked to children's academic achievement at both time points, but in different ways. At age ten, sibling conflict was linked to poorer academic achievement, while at age 12 sibling conflict predicted higher academic achievement. Mother-child conflict also predicted lower academic achievement at age 12.

Negative associations between family conflict and academic competence may be explained in several ways: for example, conflict may distract children from academic activities, and children who experience family conflict may be more likely to exhibit behaviour problems (e.g., Garcia, Shaw, Winslow, & Yaggi, 2000; Kim, Hetherington, & Reiss, 1999) that hinder their academic progress. The positive link between sibling conflict and academic achievement between siblings at age 12 is less intuitive but may be explained by sibling rivalry, such that children try to outperform their sibling at school. Study children were more likely to be at the same school as their older sibling following the move to secondary school, and so academic rivalry may have been more pronounced than at the previous time point. Alternatively, by age 12, conflict between siblings may be an indicator of more involved sibling relationships that facilitate success at school.

This finding of a positive link between sibling conflict and academic achievement resonates with the opening tenet of this chapter, that conflict between siblings can facilitate children's early understanding of others' minds. While the negative effects of sibling conflict are discussed in the next chapter, we hope we have demonstrated that there is a cognitive silver lining to this irritating facet of family life, which may provide some comfort to exasperated parents. The studies presented in this chapter highlight the myriad and often complex ways in which siblings can contribute to children's cognitive development. What is less clear is how sibling influences interact with other sources (e.g., parents and peers) to predict cognitive outcomes, and future research should take a family systems perspective to understanding children's cognitive and academic development.

Take-home messages

1. Contrary to the predictions from theories that emphasise resource dilution, there is a small but significant positive association between success on tests of false belief understanding and the number of siblings in a family. This association is stronger for child-aged siblings.
2. Conflict may be an important context for children to learn about others' thoughts and feelings, although the findings from empirical explorations of the links between sibling conflict and social understanding are complex.
3. Between a quarter and a third of young preschool siblings show frequent and sustained joint pretend play, which in turn appears to be a fertile context for conversational reference to mental states. Together, these findings suggest that pretend play may be a valuable context for children's growing understanding of others' minds.
4. There are a number of prerequisites for shared pretend play, of which perhaps the most important is that children are "on the same wave-length". This quality of attunement is known to be pivotal in accounts of how parent-child conversations contribute to theory of mind, but has yet to be examined in studies of siblings.
5. Siblings also provide an opportunity for children to overhear complex conversations. Young children with older siblings are exposed to more frequent talk about cognitive states and engage in such talk more often than children without older siblings.
6. Sibling interactions involve an asymmetry in knowledge but not authority, and this juxtaposition makes them ideal contexts for learning.
7. Teaching occurs naturally in sibling interactions. Older siblings are effective teachers and modify their teaching strategies according to their sibling's age and task difficulty, while younger siblings are active participants in the learning process.
8. Older siblings' cognitive sensitivity toward their younger sibling can buffer against "resource dilution" effects on children's vocabulary.
9. Research with adolescents suggests that older siblings may be important sources of academic support, and that this support is linked to increased academic motivation and success among younger siblings.

10. A new study with the Cambridge Toddlers Up sample suggests that links between sibling conflict and academic achievement change over the transition to secondary school. While at age ten sibling conflict predicted lower academic achievement, this association had reversed by age 12, perhaps due to increased academic rivalry.

References

Alfaro, E. C., & Umaña-Taylor, A. J. (2010). Latino adolescents' academic motivation: The role of siblings. *Hispanic Journal of Behavioral Sciences, 32*, 549–570. doi: 10.1177/0739986310383165.

Bankston, C. L. (1998). Sibling cooperation and scholastic performance among Vietnamese-American secondary school students: An ethnic social relations theory. *Sociological Perspectives, 41*, 167–184. doi:10.2307/1389358.

Bernard, J. (1972). *The future of marriage*. New Haven: Yale University Press.

Bouchey, H. A., Shoulberg, E. K., Jodl, K. M., & Eccles, J. S. (2010). Longitudinal links between older sibling features and younger siblings' academic adjustment during early adolescence. *Journal of Educational Psychology, 102*, 197–211. doi: 10.1037/a0017487.

Brown, J., Donelan-McCall, N., & Dunn, J. (1996). Why talk about mental states? The significance of children's conversations with friends, siblings, and mothers. *Child Development, 67*, 836–849. doi: 10.1111/j.1467-8624.1996.tb01767.x.

Brown, J., & Dunn, J. (1992). Talk with your mother or your sibling? Developmental changes in early family conversations about feelings. *Child Development, 63*, 336–349. doi:10.1111/j.1467-8624.1992.tb01631.x.

Devine, R. T., & Hughes, C. (2016). Family correlates of false belief understanding in early childhood: A meta-analysis. *Child Development*. Advance online publication. doi:10.1111/cdev.12682.

Downey, D. B. (2001). Number of siblings and intellectual development: The resource dilution explanation. *American Psychologist, 56*, 497–504. doi:10.1037/0003-066X.56.6-7.497.

Dunn, J., Brown, J., Slomkowski, C., Tesla, C., & Youngblade, L. (1991). Young children's understanding of other people's feelings and beliefs: Individual differences and their antecedents. *Child Development, 62*, 1352–1366. doi: 10.1111/j.1467-8624.1991.tb01610.x.

Dunn, J., & Cutting, A. (1999). Understanding others, and individual differences in friendship interactions in young children. *Social Development, 8*, 201–219. doi:10.1111/1467-9507.00091.

Dunn, J., & Dale, N. (1984). I a Daddy: 2-year-olds' collaboration in joint pretend with sibling and with mother. In I. Bretherton (Ed.), *Symbolic play: The development of social understanding* (pp. 131–158). San Diego, CA: Academic Press.

Dunn, J., & Hughes, C. (2001). "I got some swords and you're dead!": Fantasy and friendship in young "hard to manage" children. *Child Development, 72*, 491–505. doi: 10.1111/1467-8624.00292.

Dunn, J., & Kendrick, C. (1982). *Siblings: Love, envy, & understanding*. London: Grant McIntyre Ltd.

Dunn, J., & McGuire, S. (1994). Young children's nonshared experiences: A summary of studies in Cambridge and Colorado. In E. M. Hetherington, D. Reiss & R. Plomin (Eds.), *Separate social worlds of siblings: The impact of nonshared environment on development* (pp. 111–128). Hillsdale, NJ: Lawrence Erlbaum Associates.

Ensor, R., & Hughes, C. (2008). Content or connectedness? Early family talk and theory of mind in the toddler and preschool years. *Child Development, 79,* 201–216. doi:10.1111/j.1467-8624.2007.01120.x.

Fan, X., & Chen, M. (2001). Parental involvement and students' academic achievement: A meta-analysis. *Educational Psychology Review, 13,* 1–22. doi: 10.1023/A:1009048817385.

Foote, R., & Holmes-Lonergan, H. (2003). Sibling conflict and theory of mind. *British Journal of Developmental Psychology, 21,* 45–58. doi:10.1348/026151003321164618.

Garcia, M. M., Shaw, D. S., Winslow, E. B., & Yaggi, K. E. (2000). Destructive sibling conflict and the development of conduct problems in young boys. *Developmental Psychology, 36,* 44–53. doi:10.1037/0012-1649.36.1.44.

Gola, A. (2012). Mental verb input for promoting children's theory of mind: A training study. *Cognitive Development, 27,* 64–76. doi: 10.1016/j.cogdev.2011.10.003.

Gross, K. (2014). *Late fragments: Everything I want to tell you (about this magnificent life).* London: William Collins.

Howe, N., Brody, M. H., & Recchia, H. (2006). Effects of task difficulty on sibling teaching in middle childhood. *Infant and Child Development, 15,* 455–470. doi:10.1002/icd.470.

Howe, N., Della Porta, S., Recchia, H., Funamoto, A., & Ross, H. (2015). "This bird can't do it 'cause this bird doesn't swim in water": Sibling teaching during naturalistic home observations in early childhood. *Journal of Cognition and Development, 16,* 314–332. doi: 10.1080/15248372.2013.848869.

Howe, N., & Recchia, H. (2005). Playmates and teachers: Reciprocal and complementary interactions between siblings. *Journal of Family Psychology, 19,* 497–502. doi:10.1037/0893-3200.19.4.497.

Howe, N., & Recchia, H. (2009). Individual differences in sibling teaching in early and middle childhood. *Early Education and Development, 20,* 174–197. doi:10.1080/10409280802206627.

Howe, N., Ross, H. S., & Recchia, H. (2011). Sibling relations in early and middle childhood. In P. K. Smith & C. H. Hart (Eds.), *The Wiley-Blackwell handbook of childhood social development* (2nd ed., pp. 356–372). New York: Wiley.

Hughes, C. (2011). *Social understanding and social lives: From toddlerhood through to the transition to school.* London: Psychology Press.

Hughes, C., & Dunn, J. (1997). "Pretend you didn't know": Preschoolers' talk about mental states in pretend play. *Cognitive Development, 12,* 477–499. doi: 10.1016/S0885-2014(97)90019-8.

Hughes, C., & Dunn, J. (1998). Understanding mind and emotion: Longitudinal associations with mental-state talk between young friends. *Developmental Psychology, 34,* 1026–1037. doi:10.1037/0012-1649.34.5.1026.

Hughes, C., Fujisawa, K., Ensor, R., Lecce, S., & Marfleet, R. (2006). Cooperation and conversations about the mind: A study of individual differences in two-year-olds and their siblings. *British Journal of Developmental Psychology, 24,* 53–72. doi:10.1348/026151005X82893.

Hughes, C., Lecce, S., & Wilson, C. (2007). "Do you know what I want?" Preschoolers' talk about desires, thoughts and feelings in their conversations with sibs and friends. *Cognition and Emotion, 21,* 330–350. doi: 10.1080/02699930600551691.

Jenkins, J., Turrell, S., Kogushi, Y., Lollis, S., & Ross, H. (2003). A longitudinal investigation of the dynamics of mental state talk in families. *Child Development, 74,* 905–920. doi:10.1111/1467-8624.00575.

Kim, J. E., Hetherington, E. M., & Reiss, D. (1999). Associations among family relationships, antisocial peers, and adolescents' externalizing behaviors: Gender and family type differences. *Child Development, 70,* 1209–1230. doi: 10.1111/1467-8624.00088.

Lawson, D. W., & Mace, R. (2009). Trade-offs in modern parenting: A longitudinal study of sibling competition for parental care. *Evolution and Human Behavior, 30,* 170–183. doi:10.1016/j.evolhumbehav.2008.12.001.

Lecce, S., Caputi, M., & Pagnin, A. (2014). Long-term effect of theory of mind on school achievement: The role of sensitivity to criticism. *European Journal of Developmental Psychology, 11,* 305–318. doi:10.1080/17405629.2013.821944.

Leslie, A. (1987). Pretense and representation: The origins of "theory of mind". *Psychological Review, 94,* 412–426. doi:10.1037/0033-295X.94.4.412.

McAlister, A., & Peterson, C. C. (2006). Mental playmates: Siblings, executive functioning and theory of mind. *British Journal of Developmental Psychology, 24,* 733–751. doi:10.1348/026151005X70094.

Melby, J. N., & Conger, R. (1996). Parental behaviors and adolescent academic performance: A longitudinal analysis. *Journal of Research on Adolescence, 1,* 113–137.

Melby, J. N., Conger, R. D., Fang, S. A., Wickrama, K. A. S., & Conger, K. J. (2008). Adolescent family experiences and educational attainment during early adulthood. *Developmental Psychology, 44,* 1519–1536. doi:10.1037/a0013352.

Penninkilampi-Kerola, V., Moilanen, I., & Kaprio, J. (2005). Co-twin dependence, social interactions, and academic achievement: A population-based study. *Journal of Social and Personal Relationships, 22,* 519–541. doi:10.1177/0265407505054521.

Perner, J., Ruffman, T., & Leekam, S. (1994). Theory of mind is contagious: You catch it from your sibs. *Child Development, 65,* 1228–1238. doi:10.1111/j.1467-8624.1994.tb00814.x.

Prime, H., Pauker, S., Plamondon, A., Perlman, M., & Jenkins, J. (2014). Sibship size, sibling cognitive sensitivity, and children's receptive vocabulary. *Pediatrics, 133,* 394–401. doi:10.1542/peds.2012-2874.

Prime, H., Plamondon, A., Pauker, S., Perlman, M., & Jenkins, J. M. (2016). Sibling cognitive sensitivity as a moderator of the relationship between sibship size and children's theory of mind: A longitudinal analysis. *Cognitive Development, 39,* 93–102. doi:10.1016/j.cogdev.2016.03.005.

Randell, A., & Peterson, C. (2009). Affective qualities of sibling disputes, mothers' conflict attitudes, and children's theory of mind development. *Social Development, 18,* 857–874. doi:10.1111/j.1467-9507.2008.00513.x.

Recchia, H., & Howe, N. (2009). Associations between social understanding, sibling relationship quality, and siblings' conflict strategies and outcomes. *Child Development, 80,* 1564–1578. doi:10.1111/j.1467-8624.2009.01351.x.

Recchia, H. E., Howe, N., & Alexander, S. (2009). You didn't teach me, you showed me: Variations in sibling teaching strategies in early and middle childhood. *Merrill-Palmer Quarterly, 55,* 55–78. doi:10.1353/mpq.0.0016.

Ruffman, T., Perner, J., Naito, M., Parkin, L., & Clements, W. (1998). Older (but not younger) siblings facilitate false belief understanding. *Developmental Psychology, 34,* 161–174. doi:10.1037/0012-1649.34.1.161.

Schachter, F. F., Shore, E., Feldman-Rotman, S., Marquis, R. E., & Campbell, S. (1976). Sibling deidentification. *Developmental Psychology, 12,* 418–427. doi:10.1037/0012-1649.12.5.418.

Slaughter, V., Imuta, K., Peterson, C. C., & Henry, J. D. (2015). Meta-analysis of theory of mind and peer popularity in the preschool and early school years. *Child Development, 86,* 1159–1174. doi:10.1111/cdev.12372.

Slomkowski, C., & Dunn, J. (1992). Arguments and relationships within the family: Differences in young children's disputes with mother and sibling. *Developmental Psychology, 28,* 919–924. doi:10.1037/0012-1649.28.5.919.

Strauss, S., & Ziv, M. (2012). Teaching is a natural cognitive ability for humans. *Mind, Brain, and Education, 6,* 186–196. doi:10.1111/j.1751-228X.2012.01156.x.

Tompkins, V., Farrar, M. J., & Guo, Y. (2013). Siblings, language, and false belief in low-income children. *Journal of Genetic Psychology, 174*, 457–463. doi:10.1080/00221325.2012.694918.

White, N. (2014). *Sibling relationships from preschool to pre-adolescence: Change, correlates, and consequences.* (Unpublished doctoral dissertation). University of Cambridge. Cambridge, UK.

Whitebread, D., Basilio, M., Kuvalja, M., & Verma, M. (2012). The importance of play: a report on the value of children's play with a series of policy recommendations. Brussels, Belgium: Toys Industries for Europe.

Wilson, A., Smith, M., & Ross, H. (2003). The nature and effects of young children's lies. *Social Development, 12*, 21–45. doi: 10.1111/1467-9507.00220.

7

SIBLING RELATIONSHIPS AND PSYCHOLOGICAL WELL-BEING

On their website (www.youngminds.org.uk), the children and adolescent mental health charity Young Minds notes that recent societal changes and technological advances have made the world an increasingly difficult place for young people to grow up into healthy adults (see Chapter 10 for a discussion of the impact of these changes on family relationships). In our digital age, media pressure to have the perfect body and lifestyle is inescapable, and the rise of social media has provided avenues for bullying online as well as offline. Moreover, with a challenging job market, young people are under increasing pressure to pass exams at school to gain university entrance, a process that has become considerably more competitive and expensive in recent years.

In this context, it is perhaps unsurprising that approximately one in ten five- to 16-year-olds in the United Kingdom, or roughly three children in every classroom, have a diagnosable mental disorder (Green, McGinnity, Meltzer, Ford, & Goodman, 2005). This estimate likely underestimates the scale of behavioural and psychological difficulties among young people, as it does not include children who are experiencing significant difficulties but do not meet the specific diagnostic criteria for a mental disorder. We also know that half of all mental disorders are manifest before 14 years of age, even though individuals may not receive a formal diagnosis or treatment until later in life (Patel, Flisher, Hetrick, & McGorry, 2007; World Health Organization, 2014). Furthermore, childhood mental health problems can have far-reaching and long-term consequences. For example, children with conduct disorder are at increased risk for a range of negative outcomes, including poorer educational achievement (Fergusson, Horwood, & Lynskey, 1993), unemployment (Colman et al., 2009) and substance abuse (Hopfer et al., 2013). Identifying and providing support for children and adolescents at risk for poor psychological adjustment is therefore a key priority for governments and health providers.

The role of parents in children's mental health is well established, in terms of both direct influences on well-being through the quality of parent-child interactions or parenting styles (e.g., Parkes, Sweeting, & Wight, 2016), and indirect influences through the home environment (e.g., Evans, Gonnella, Marcynyszyn, Gentile, & Salpekar, 2005), social disadvantage (e.g., Flouri & Midouhas, 2016), or parental depression (e.g., Wachs, Black, & Engle, 2009). Moreover, clinical interventions for children often directly involve parents: parent-child interactions may be the target of the intervention (as, for example, in parent-child interaction therapy, Eyberg, 1988) or parents may implement behavioural management programmes for their child. Less is known about the role of sibling relationships in psychological well-being and siblings are not typically involved in clinical interventions (although see the Siblings are Special intervention program for a notable exception; Feinberg, Sakuma, Hostetler, & McHale, 2013; Feinberg, Solmeyer, et al., 2013; Updegraff et al., 2016).

There are a number of reasons why sibling interactions may contribute to children's adjustment. Sibling interactions are often involuntary, frequent and begin early, and thus may provide a model for future behaviour and relationships. Moreover, the unique "no-holds-barred" nature of sibling relationships provides an important early context for children to develop key socio-emotional skills. In adolescence, older siblings are often role models and so may provide their younger siblings with an entry point into risky behaviours. In this chapter we review the evidence for links between individual differences in sibling relationship quality and psychological adjustment, focusing particularly on externalising (e.g., conduct disorder, antisocial behaviour) and internalising (e.g., anxiety, depression) problems. We begin by discussing theoretical perspectives and meta-analytic evidence examining sibling relationships and adjustment. Next we consider the factors that may influence the strength of associations between sibling relationship quality and adjustment, including whether links with adjustment persist into young adulthood and beyond. We end the chapter by considering how culture may influence links between sibling relationships and psychological well-being.

Theoretical perspectives on siblings and adjustment

Several theoretical perspectives can be used to explain links between sibling relationship quality and psychological adjustment. For example, from an attachment perspective, insecure attachment to a caregiver may cause individuals to develop negative views of the self as unworthy of love (potentially leading to anxiety and depression) or of the world as untrustworthy (potentially leading to aggression and antisocial behaviour; Bowlby, 1973; Bretherton, 1985). By analogy, lack of warmth in the sibling relationship (i.e., insecure attachment to a sibling) might be expected to predict both internalising and externalising problems (e.g., Ainsworth, 1989; Fraley & Tancredy, 2012). High levels of sibling conflict may also disrupt attachment bonds and lead to internalising problems, because feelings of hopelessness or guilt about sibling conflict contribute to a negative attribution style (e.g., Buist, Deković, & Prinzie, 2013).

Interestingly, however, some researchers have demonstrated *positive* links between sibling warmth and externalising behaviours, particularly in at-risk or clinical samples, and among brothers (Fagan & Najman, 2003; Rende, Slomkowski, Lloyd-Richardson, & Niaura, 2005; Slomkowski, Rende, Conger, Simons, & Conger, 2001). Such findings provide support for a "partners in crime" model (Slomkowski et al., 2001) whereby siblings engage in antisocial behaviour together, echoing research showing that association with deviant peers may maintain children's antisocial behaviour (e.g., Patterson, DeBaryshe, & Ramsey, 1989). Another perspective on associations between sibling conflict and externalising behaviours is that of social learning theory (Bandura, 1977), whereby behaviour experienced in sibling interactions is generalised to different contexts (e.g., Parke, MacDonald, Beitel, & Bhavnagri, 1988). According to the "siblings as key pathogens" theory (e.g., Patterson, 1984; Slomkowski et al., 2001), siblings' influence on antisocial behaviour is both direct and indirect: children observe conflict between siblings and parents, and then practise negative behaviours in sibling interactions.

Empirical evidence for siblings' impact on adjustment

Buist, Deković and Prinzie (2013) have recently conducted a set of meta-analyses, based on 34 studies with a total of 12,257 children aged four to 18 years old, to investigate sibling warmth and conflict and parental differential treatment in relation to children's internalising and externalising problems. These meta-analyses showed that low levels of sibling warmth, high levels of sibling conflict and high levels of differential treatment were each associated with both internalising and externalising problems. This relationship was stronger for sibling conflict than for either sibling warmth or differential treatment, but for each aspect of sibling relationship quality effect sizes were similar for internalising and externalising problems.

Buist and her colleagues also examined whether the links between sibling relationship quality and children's adjustment were stronger for particular groups of children or in particular contexts. Possible moderators examined in these analyses included factors relating to the samples (e.g., child's gender, sibling gender constellation, age difference, developmental period and SES) and factors concerning the study methods or publication quality (e.g., study design, informant for relationship quality/child behaviour problems, journal impact factor, publication year). For all six meta-analyses, only four variables influenced the strength of the association with adjustment. First, the association between sibling conflict and internalising problems was stronger for children with small age gap between siblings. This finding may suggest that sibling conflict is more distressing to children with close-in-age siblings perhaps because they are expected to spend more time together than siblings who are more different in age. In addition, the strength of the link between parental differential treatment and internalising difficulties varied with sibling gender composition, developmental period and study publication year. These effects showed that the association was particularly strong in studies (1) with a high proportion of pairs of brothers, (2) with child compared to adolescent siblings and

(3) that were published less recently. These findings suggest that brothers may be more sensitive to differences in parental treatment than other sibling dyads, and that as children get older they become more able to justify the legitimate reasons what parents might treat them and their siblings differently.

This set of meta-analyses provides compelling evidence of a link between sibling relationship quality and children's internalising and externalising problems. However, given that we know from family systems theory that the quality of relationships clusters in families, this link could reflect the general family climate rather than the quality of the sibling relationship per se. To address this possibility several researchers have examined whether sibling relationships predict unique variance in children's adjustment above and beyond that explained by the quality of other family relationships. For example, in a study of siblings aged from four to eight years, Pike, Coldwell and Dunn (2005) compared links between both parent-child and sibling relationship quality and children's problem behaviours and found that sibling positivity predicted additional variance in parental reports of children's behaviour problems, over and above the variance explained by parent-child positivity and negativity.

Similar findings have emerged from the early adolescent time points of the Cambridge Toddlers Up study. Here, self-reported relationship positivity with a sibling at age 12 predicted unique variance in children's behavioural problems both concurrently and one year later, even after controlling for gender, parent-child relationship quality, exposure to social adversity and previous levels of behaviour problems (White, Cassels, Foley, Gee, & Hughes, 2017). Moreover, in a recent US longitudinal study Harper, Padilla-Walker and Jensen (2014) showed that sibling hostility in mid-to-late adolescence predicted depressive symptoms two years later even after taking into account adolescents' relationships with their mother, father and best friend. Interestingly, in this study sibling hostility also predicted externalising behaviours but only among boys. Taken together, these findings show that, independently of parent-child relationships, the quality of sibling relationships plays a unique role in children's behavioural adjustment in childhood and adolescence.

Links between sibling relationship quality and children's adjustment are typically interpreted to indicate that the quality of sibling relationships influences children's later behaviour. As a result, many longitudinal studies that examine sibling relationship quality as a predictor of children's adjustment fail to consider the reverse association. However, as discussed in Chapter 5, there is evidence that early behaviour with friends (which is likely to be related to child adjustment) predicts the quality of sibling relationships (Kramer & Kowal, 2005), suggesting that this is a significant omission. To address this gap, Pike and Oliver (2016) have recently analysed data from 2,573 families in the Avon Longitudinal Study of Parents and Children to test the direction of links between sibling relationship quality and children's behaviour. In this study, maternal ratings at two time points (when the younger child was four and seven years old) revealed bidirectional relationships between sibling relationship and both children's conduct problems and prosocial behaviour.

Specifically, for both children, sibling positivity predicted later prosocial behaviour, while sibling negativity predicted later conduct problems. In addition, (1) initial levels of older siblings' prosocial behaviour predicted both sibling positivity and younger siblings' prosocial behaviour at the second time point; (2) initial levels of both older and younger siblings' conduct problems predicted later difficulties in the sibling relationship; and (3) initial levels of older siblings' conduct problems predicted the younger siblings' conduct problems at the later time point. Together, these findings highlight the interactive relationship between sibling interactions and children's behaviour. Children who enjoy warm and supportive sibling relationships show high levels of positive social behaviour with others; equally children's prosocial or antisocial behaviour with peers leads to warmth or conflict (respectively) in the sibling relationship. It is also interesting to note that the older sibling's prosocial or antisocial behaviour was a stronger predictor of later sibling relationship quality and behaviour than the younger sibling's behaviour. This finding suggests older children may be more dominant in the sibling relationship such that their behavioural tendencies have a stronger influence on later relationship quality and the other sibling's behaviour.

Individual variation in the strength of links with adjustment

With the development of sophisticated statistical modelling techniques, researchers have become able to examine more complex links between sibling interactions and behaviour problems. While most research has examined how sibling relationship quality measured at one time point predicts concurrent or later behaviour problems, Ensor, Marks, Jacobs and Hughes (2010) used latent growth modelling of longitudinal data to investigate how individual trajectories of sibling behaviour were associated with children's behavioural outcomes. Using the Cambridge Toddlers Up sample these authors examined how individual trajectories of negative behaviour with siblings at age three and age six predicted harming and bullying unfamiliar peers at age six. Their analyses showed that children who showed sustained high or increasing trajectories of antisocial behaviour with a sibling from age three to six showed higher rates of antisocial behaviour with a peer at age six. This finding highlights the value of viewing the sibling relationship as a dynamic process and echoes research into the effects of stress indicating that chronic exposure to stress may be more strongly linked to depression than acute stress (e.g., McGonagle & Kessler, 1990).

The influence of sibling relationship quality on psychological adjustment may also be particularly important for children facing adversity. The evidence from several studies suggests that a supportive sibling relationship can protect children from developing internalising problems following stressful life events or peer difficulties (East & Rook, 1992; Gass, Jenkins, & Dunn, 2007; Sapouna & Wolke, 2013). Similarly, a recent study showed that warm, harmonious sibling relationships could prevent intergenerational transmission of parental psychopathology (Keeton, Teetsel, Dull, & Ginsburg, 2015). Conversely, in a study of five-year-old boys, Garcia, Shaw, Winslow and Yaggi (2000) showed that destructive sibling conflict predicted unique variance in teachers' ratings of aggression but only in the context of rejecting parenting. Taken together, these studies suggest that sibling relationships have a larger impact, which can be positive or negative, when children are facing additional difficulties in their family or social life.

While the above studies have focused on sibling relationships in the context of one particular risk factor (e.g., rejecting parenting, social isolation, parental psycho-pathology), the rich data available about the Cambridge Toddlers Up families, enabled us to use a multi-informant, global measure of adversity to test the hypothesis that sibling relationships would be more strongly associated with children's adjustment in the context of risk (White et al., 2017). Models of risk and resilience indicate that exposure to risk acts in a cumulative fashion, suggesting the utility of measuring gradients of risk exposure rather than the presence or absence of specific risk factors (e.g., Evans, Li, & Whipple, 2013). To measure risk we created an aggregate measure of adversity using information from three sources: (1) mothers' reports of negative family events, their education, the amount of time spent as a single parent and their depressive symptoms; (2) children's reports of family affluence (using the Family Affluence Scale; Boyce, Torsheim, Currie, & Zambon, 2006); and (3) researchers' rating of the home environment and (very rare) cases of parental neglect. We used regression analyses to examine (1) how children's reports of positivity in their sibling relationship at age 12 predicted mothers' reports of behavioural problems both concurrently and one year later, and (2) whether there was an interaction effect of sibling positivity and adversity. The cross-sectional analyses showed a main effect of sibling positivity on behavioural problems but no interaction. However, in the analyses predicting adjustment a year later, a significant interaction effect revealed that sibling positivity was more strongly related to psychological adjustment among children facing high levels of adversity. These findings suggest that long-term effects of variation in sibling relationship quality are greater when children are facing adversity. They also have clear policy implications, for example, in the placement of siblings in foster care (see Chapter 10). In particular, these reasonably consistent protective effects of supportive sibling relationships suggest that interventions for at-risk children may be more effective if they include siblings.

Adjustment throughout the lifespan

Most of the existing research examining the contribution of sibling relationships to psychological well-being has focused on childhood and adolescence, but how does the quality of sibling relationships contribute to well-being in adulthood when siblings no longer live together and have more separate lives? A small body of research with college students suggests that sibling support continues to play an important role in psychological well-being in young adulthood. Milevsky (2005) found that university students who reported high levels of support from their siblings also reported higher self-esteem and life satisfaction, and lower levels of depression and loneliness than students who felt less supported by their siblings. Importantly, there was some evidence that high levels of support from siblings buffered against the negative effects (e.g., depression, poor life satisfaction, loneliness) associated with low support from parents and friends. Similarly, Ponzetti and James (1997) showed that the closeness of sibling relationships predicted unique variance in undergraduate students' self-reported loneliness, such that students with closer sibling relationships felt less lonely.

Other researchers have suggested that it may be sibling conflict rather than closeness that is linked to psychological adjustment in adulthood. Stocker, Lanthier and Furman (1997) showed that sibling conflict but not warmth or rivalry was associated with self-reported symptoms of mental health difficulties in a sample of college students. Similarly, using cluster analysis to classify sibling relationship types, Sherman, Lansford and Volling (2006) reported that young adults with a harmonious (high warmth/low conflict) sibling relationship reported higher self-esteem and lower levels of loneliness than young adults with an affect-intense (high warmth/high conflict) relationship.

In later adulthood, too, close sibling relationships seem to be linked with fewer symptoms of depression and lower levels of loneliness, although the strength of these associations varies with gender and relationship status. In an early study of 83 older adults (aged 61–91 years), Cicirelli (1989) showed that adults who felt closer to their sister reported fewer symptoms of depression. In addition, women who reported high levels of conflict or indifference in their relationships with a sister showed more symptoms of depression. Cicirelli explained these findings in terms of gender differences in family roles. He argued that siblings, and in particular sisters, are important sources of help and support in later life, such that a distant or conflictual relationship with a sister may be associated with the loss of an important source of support.

A more recent study of middle-aged to older adults highlighted the potential importance of relationship status in determining links between sibling relationship quality and well-being. Pinquart (2003) examined how contact with adult children, siblings, friends and neighbours predicted 53- to 79-year-olds' self-reported loneliness. In this study, the quality of contact with a sibling predicted lower levels of loneliness among never-married adults, but higher levels of loneliness among married adults. While this finding suggests that sibling relationships may be of particular importance for adults who have not married, the result for married adults is more difficult to interpret. It may be that married adults turn to siblings in times of difficulty, for example as a way to compensate for difficulties in their couple relationship, or when they are experiencing loneliness or depression. Alternatively, married adults may find close relationships with their sibling intrusive.

These studies of the consequences of sibling relationships in adulthood begin to suggest that individual differences in sibling relationship quality continue to matter for well-being in adulthood. However, at least two key limitations of these studies deserve note. First, the studies rely on self-reports of both the sibling relationship and psychological well-being and thus some of the association between relationships and well-being maybe due to shared measurement variance. Second, these studies are all cross-sectional, and so we cannot make any conclusions about the direction of effect. Support from siblings may help individuals combat depression and loneliness (and sibling conflict may add to this burden) but equally individuals experiencing depression may withdraw from family relationships, or their behaviour may provoke conflict within the sibling relationship. Further research using data from sources outside the individual in question (e.g., psychologists' assessments of well-being, the other siblings' view of the relationship), and employing a longitudinal design, is needed to fully understand the links between sibling relationships and psychological adjustment in adulthood.

Two final points are worth noting. First, in the adult literature researchers have used internalising problems (e.g., depression, loneliness) as a measure of psychological adjustment. It is not clear, therefore, whether sibling relationships continue to contribute to aggression and antisocial tendencies in adulthood. Second, researchers interested in adult sibling relationships have typically focused on university students and older adults, and (as noted in Chapter 3) sibling relationships in middle adulthood have been overlooked. This oversight may reflect that middle adulthood is a time when individuals are traditionally focused on creating and raising their own family, and thus sibling relationships may be somewhat on the periphery. That said, the fact that siblings may have recently gone through similar life events (e.g., getting married, having children) may make brother and sisters important sources of advice and support in this period, as in other stages of life. Indeed, the fact that many people name one of their siblings as a legal guardian for their children in the event of their own death suggests that siblings are often trusted and valued members of the family.

Cultural differences in links with adjustment

An important limitation of current research on sibling relationships and children's adjustment is a focus on White Western ethnic majority groups. Siblings' roles within the family vary dramatically with culture such that there are mean-level differences in relationship quality between ethnic groups (a topic that will be discussed in more depth in Chapter 9). However, it is not yet clear what these group differences in sibling relationship quality mean for children's adjustment. According to an *ethnic equivalence* model (Lamborn & Felbab, 2003), family influences may transcend cultural values such that individual differences in sibling relationship quality predict children's behavioural outcomes in the same way in different cultures. For example, this view would suggest that children who engage in more frequent sibling conflict should show poorer behavioural adjustment regardless of their cultural background. The alternative view is a *cultural values* model whereby similar family experiences have different implications for children's adjustment because of the different cultural meanings attached to these experiences (Lamborn & Felbab, 2003). For example, in Western families a moderate amount of sibling conflict may not predict negative outcomes for a child because this conflict is viewed as a normal part of sibling relationships and as an important context to develop understanding of others. In contrast, in some non-Western cultures sibling conflict may be more detrimental for children's development because it is at odds with cultural norms of social harmony.

Several research groups have begun to explore family relationships in US ethnic minority groups, and this one-culture research suggests that the quality of children's sibling relationships also plays an important role in children's social and behavioural adjustment among ethnic minority families. For example, in a study of 63 Mexican-American families with preschoolers, Modry-Mandle, Gamble and Taylor (2007) showed that sibling warmth predicted unique variance in children's teacher-rated social competence and mother-rated behavioural adjustment, even when controlling for a variety of aspects of the wider family environment. Studies with African-American families have also highlighted the way in which sibling influence varies with the quality of the relationship between the two children. For example, Brody and Murry (2001) showed that similarity between siblings in terms of social and academic competence was reduced in the context of high levels of sibling conflict, while in a study by Whiteman, Bernard and McHale (2010) younger siblings reported higher rates of social learning from their older sibling in the context of high sibling warmth and low sibling negativity.

Exploring the ethnic equivalence and cultural values models more directly, a recent study used latent growth curve modelling to compare links between sibling relationship quality and adjustment among Dutch and Moroccan adolescents living in the Netherlands. Buist et al. (2013) found mean-level differences in sibling relationship quality across ethnic groups, such that Moroccan adolescents reported more support from, and less conflict with their siblings than their Dutch counterparts. Despite these group differences, individual variation in the quality of sibling relationships predicted externalising problems, depression and anxiety in a similar way within each ethnic group. Specifically, sibling conflict was associated with higher levels of all three problem behaviours, whereas sibling support was associated with lower levels of depression and anxiety. Buist and her colleagues frame these findings as evidence of an ethnic equivalence model of links between family experience and adjustment (Lamborn & Felbab, 2003), where family influences transcend differences in cultural values and practices to predict children's behaviour.

Future research is needed with families from different cultural groups to explore whether this model of ethnic equivalence in the links between sibling relationship quality and adjustment generalises to other cultural groups and to other countries. Indeed, one study with American young adults from different ethnic backgrounds suggests that there may be important cultural differences in links between family interactions and well-being. Using data from a sample of 220 European, Filipino, East Asian (predominantly Chinese) and Latino young adults living in the United States, Fuligni and Masten (2010) reported that overall the amount of leisure time participants spent with family was associated with greater well-being, while conflict with family members was linked to distress and guilt. However, there were some cultural contrasts between European and Filipino families such that links between family leisure time and happiness were stronger for Filipino families, and conflict between family members was associated with feelings of guilt only among Filipino young adults. These studies represent only the beginning of our attempts to understand how cultural values may affect links between family relationship quality and psychological well-being. As our world increasingly seeks solutions to the global problem of poor child mental health, policymakers must be aware of cultural differences in factors that contribute to psychological adjustment.

Take-home messages

1. Mental health, and in particular children's mental health, needs to be a key priority for governments and health providers.
2. Links between sibling relationships and psychological adjustment are most commonly explained using an attachment or social learning theory perspective.
3. Meta-analyses indicate robust associations between sibling conflict or parental differential treatment and both internalising and externalising problems. A lack of warmth within the sibling relationship also seems to be associated with behavioural difficulties, but the association with internalising problems may not be robust.
4. Research controlling for the quality of children's other close relationships suggests that associations between sibling relationship quality and psychological adjustment reflect something unique about the sibling relationship and not just an effect of family emotional climate.
5. Poor quality sibling interactions may be particularly harmful to children's mental health when experienced over an extended period, or when relationships deteriorate over a period of time.
6. Children facing difficulties at home or at school may be particularly susceptible to the effects of individual variation in sibling relationship quality.
7. Despite no longer living together, sibling support and conflict remain significant predictors of depression, loneliness and self-esteem among university students.
8. In later adulthood, close sibling relationships are also associated with psychological well-being, but these links seem to be influenced by gender and relationship status.
9. Further longitudinal research is needed to establish causal links between sibling relationship quality and well-being in adulthood, and to investigate how siblings might contribute to psychological adjustment in middle adulthood.
10. Mean-level differences in the quality of sibling relationships between different cultural groups do not necessary entail differences in the association between sibling relationships and psychological adjustment. Recent research in the Netherlands provides support for such an *ethnic equivalence* model.

References

Ainsworth, M. (1989). Attachments beyond infancy. *American Psychologist, 44,* 709–716. doi:10.1037/0003-066X.44.4.709.

Bandura, A. (1977). *Social learning theory.* Englewood Cliffs, NJ: Prentice Hall.

Bowlby, J. (1973). *Attachment and loss: Vol. 2. Separation.* New York: Basic Books.

Boyce, W., Torsheim, T., Currie, C., & Zambon, A. (2006). The Family Affluence Scale as a measure of national wealth: Validation of an adolescent self-report measure. *Social Indicators Research, 78,* 473–487. doi:10.1007/s11205-005-1607-6.

Bretherton, I. (1985). Attachment theory: Retrospect and prospect. In I. Bretherton & E. Waters (Eds.), *Monographs of the society for research in child development* (Vol. 50 Serial No. 209 (1–2), pp. 3–35). Chicago: University of Chicago Press.

Brody, G. H., & Murry, V. M. (2001). Sibling socialization of competence in rural, single-parent African American families. *Journal of Marriage and Family, 63*, 996–1008. doi:10.1111/j.1741-3737.2001.00996.x.

Buist, K. L., Deković, M., & Prinzie, P. (2013). Sibling relationship quality and psychopathology of children and adolescents: A meta-analysis. *Clinical Psychology Review, 33*, 97–106. doi:10.1016/j.cpr.2012.10.007.

Buist, K. L., Paalman, C. H., Branje, S. J. T., Deković, M., Reitz, E., Verhoeven, M., Meeus, W. H., Koot, H. M., & Hale, W. W. (2013). Longitudinal effects of sibling relationship quality on adolescent problem behavior: A cross-ethnic comparison. *Cultural Diversity and Ethnic Minority Psychology, 20*, 266–275. doi:10.1037/a0033675.

Cicirelli, V. (1989). Feelings of attachment to siblings and well-being in later life. *Psychology and Aging, 4*, 211–216. doi:10.1037/0882-7974.4.2.211.

Colman, I., Murray, J., Abbott, R. A., Maughan, B., Kuh, D., Croudace, T. J., & Jones, P. B. (2009). Outcomes of conduct problems in adolescence: 40 year follow-up of national cohort. *BMJ (Online), 338*, 208–211. doi:10.1136/bmj.a2981.

East, P. L., & Rook, K. S. (1992). Compensatory patterns of support among children's peer relationships: A test using school friends, nonschool friends, and siblings. *Developmental Psychology, 28*, 163–172. doi: 10.1037/0012-1649.28.1.163.

Ensor, R., Marks, A., Jacobs, L., & Hughes, C. (2010). Trajectories of antisocial behaviour towards siblings predict antisocial behaviour towards peers. *Journal of Child Psychology and Psychiatry, 51*, 1208–1216. doi:10.1111/j.1469-7610.2010.02276.x.

Evans, G. W., Gonnella, C., Marcynyszyn, L. A., Gentile, L., & Salpekar, N. (2005). The role of chaos in poverty and children's socioemotional adjustment. *Psychological Science, 16*, 560–565. doi: 10.1111/j.0956-7976.2005.01575.x.

Evans, G. W., Li, D., & Whipple, S. S. (2013). Cumulative risk and child development. *Psychological Bulletin, 139*, 1342–1396. doi:10.1037/a0031808.

Eyberg, S. (1988). Parent-child interaction therapy: Integration of traditional and behavioral concerns. *Child and Family Behavior Therapy, 10*, 33–46. doi:10.1300/J019v10n01_04.

Fagan, A. A., & Najman, J. M. (2003). Sibling influences on adolescent delinquent behaviour: An Australian longitudinal study. *Journal of Adolescence, 26*, 547–559. doi:10.1016/S0140-1971(03)00055-1.

Feinberg, M. E., Sakuma, K. L., Hostetler, M., & McHale, S. M. (2013). Enhancing sibling relationships to prevent adolescent problem behaviors: Theory, design and feasibility of Siblings Are Special. *Evaluation and Program Planning, 36*, 97–106. doi:10.1016/j.evalprogplan.2012.08.003.

Feinberg, M. E., Solmeyer, A. R., Hostetler, M. L., Sakuma, K. L., Jones, D., & McHale, S. M. (2013). Siblings Are Special: Initial test of a new approach for preventing youth behavior problems. *Journal of Adolescent Health, 53*, 166–173. doi:10.1016/j.jadohealth.2012.10.004.

Fergusson, D. M., Horwood, L. J., & Lynskey, M. T. (1993). The effects of conduct disorder and attention deficit in middle childhood on offending and scholastic ability at age 13. *Journal of Child Psychology and Psychiatry and Allied Disciplines, 34*, 899–916. doi:10.1111/j.1469-7610.1993.tb01097.x.

Flouri, E., & Midouhas, E. (2016). School composition, family poverty and child behaviour. *Social Psychiatry and Psychiatric Epidemiology, 51*, 817–826. doi:10.1007/s00127-016-1206-7.

Fraley, R. C., & Tancredy, C. M. (2012). Twin and sibling attachment in a nationally representative sample. *Personality and Social Psychology Bulletin, 38*, 308–316. doi:10.1177/0146167211432936.

Fuligni, A., & Masten, C. L. (2010). Daily family interactions among young adults in the United States from Latin American, Filipino, East Asian, and European backgrounds. *International Journal of Behavioral Development, 34*, 491–499. doi:10.1177/0165025409360303.

Garcia, M. M., Shaw, D. S., Winslow, E. B., & Yaggi, K. E. (2000). Destructive sibling conflict and the development of conduct problems in young boys. *Developmental Psychology, 36*, 44–53. doi:10.1037/0012-1649.36.1.44.

Gass, K., Jenkins, J., & Dunn, J. (2007). Are sibling relationships protective? A longitudinal study. *Journal of Child Psychology and Psychiatry and Allied Disciplines, 48*, 167–175. doi:10.1111/j.1469-7610.2006.01699.x.

Green, H., McGinnity, A., Meltzer, H., Ford, T., & Goodman, R. (2005). *Mental health of children and young people in Great Britain, 2004.* London: Palgrave.

Harper, J. M., Padilla-Walker, L. M., & Jensen, A. C. (2014). Do siblings matter independent of both parents and friends? Sympathy as a mediator between sibling relationship quality and adolescent outcomes. *Journal of Research on Adolescence, 26*, 101–114. doi:10.1111/jora.12174.

Hopfer, C., Salomonsen-Sautel, S., Mikulich-Gilbertson, S., Min, S. J., McQueen, M., Crowley, T., Young, S., Corley, R., Sakai, J., Thurstone, C., Hoffenburg, A., Hartman, C., & Hewitt, J. (2013). Conduct disorder and initiation of substance use: A prospective longitudinal study. *Journal of the American Academy of Child and Adolescent Psychiatry, 52*, e511–518. doi:10.1016/j.jaac.2013.02.014.

Keeton, C. P., Teetsel, R. N., Dull, N. M. S., & Ginsburg, G. S. (2015). Parent psychopathology and children's psychological health: Moderation by sibling relationship dimensions. *Journal of Abnormal Child Psychology, 43*, pp. 1333–1342. doi:10.1007/s10802-015-0013-z.

Kramer, L., & Kowal, A. (2005). Sibling relationship quality from birth to adolescence: The enduring contributions of friends. *Journal of Family Psychology, 19*, 503–511. doi:10.1037/0893-3200.19.4.503.

Lamborn, S. D., & Felbab, A. J. (2003). Applying ethnic equivalence and cultural values models to African-American teens' perceptions of parents. *Journal of Adolescence, 26*, 605–622. doi: 10.1016/S0140-1971(03)00059-9.

McGonagle, K. A., & Kessler, R. C. (1990). Chronic stress, acute stress, and depressive symptoms. *American Journal of Community Psychology, 18*, 681–706. doi:10.1007/BF00931237.

Milevsky, A. (2005). Compensatory patterns of sibling support in emerging adulthood: Variations in loneliness, self-esteem, depression and life satisfaction. *Journal of Social and Personal Relationships, 22*, 743–755. doi:10.1177/0265407505056447.

Modry-Mandell, K. L., Gamble, W. C., & Taylor, A. R. (2007). Family emotional climate and sibling relationship quality: Influences on behavioral problems and adaptation in preschool-aged children. *Journal of Child and Family Studies, 16*, 59–71. doi:10.1007/s10826-006-9068-3.

Parke, R., MacDonald, K., Beitel, A., & Bhavnagri, N. (1988). The role of the family in the development of peer relationships. In R. McMahon & R. Peters (Eds.), *Social learning and systems approaches to marriage and the family* (pp. 17–44). Philadelphia, PA: Brunner/Mazel.

Parkes, A., Sweeting, H., & Wight, D. (2016). What shapes 7-year-olds' subjective well-being? Prospective analysis of early childhood and parenting using the Growing Up in Scotland study. *Social Psychiatry and Psychiatric Epidemiology, 51*, 1417–1428. doi:10.1007/s00127-016-1246-z.

Patel, V., Flisher, A. J., Hetrick, S., & McGorry, P. (2007). Mental health of young people: A global public-health challenge. *Lancet, 369*, 1302–1313. doi:10.1016/S0140-6736(07)60368-7.

Patterson, G. (1984). Siblings: Fellow travelers in coercive family process. In R. Blanchard & D. Blanchard (Eds.), *Advances in the study of aggression* (Vol. 1, pp. 173–215). Orlando, FL: Academic Press.

Patterson, G. R., DeBaryshe, B. D., & Ramsey, E. (1989). A developmental perspective on antisocial behaviour. *American Psychologist, 44,* 329–335. 10.1037/0003-066X.44.2.329

Pike, A., Coldwell, J., & Dunn, J. (2005). Sibling relationships in early/middle childhood: links with individual adjustment. *Journal of Family Psychology, 31,* 250–255. doi:10.1037/0893-3200.19.4.523.

Pike, A., & Oliver, B. R. (2016). Child behavior and sibling relationship quality: A cross-lagged analysis. *Journal of Family Psychology.* doi:10.1037/fam0000248.

Pinquart, M. (2003). Loneliness in married, widowed, divorced, and never-married older adults. *Journal of Social and Personal Relationships, 20,* 31–53. doi:10.1177/02654075030201002.

Ponzetti, J., & James, C. M. (1997). Loneliness and sibling relationships. *Journal of Social Behavior and Personality, 12,* 103–112.

Rende, R., Slomkowski, C., Lloyd-Richardson, E., & Niaura, R. (2005). Sibling effects on substance use in adolescence: Social contagion and genetic relatedness. *Journal of Family Psychology, 19,* 611–618. doi:10.1037/0893-3200.19.4.611.

Sapouna, M., & Wolke, D. (2013). Resilience to bullying victimization: The role of individual, family and peer characteristics. *Child Abuse and Neglect, 37,* 997–1006. doi:10.1016/j.chiabu.2013.05.009.

Sherman, A. M., Lansford, J. E., & Volling, B. L. (2006). Sibling relationships and best friendships in young adulthood: Warmth, conflict, and well-being. *Personal Relationships, 13,* 151–165. doi:10.1111/j.1475-6811.2006.00110.x.

Slomkowski, C., Rende, R., Conger, K., Simons, R., & Conger, R. (2001). Sisters, brothers, and delinquency: Evaluating social influence during early and middle adolescence. *Child Development, 72,* 271–283. doi:10.1111/1467-8624.00278.

Stocker, C., Lanthier, R. P., & Furman, W. (1997). Sibling relationships in early adulthood. *Journal of Family Psychology, 11,* 210–221. doi:10.1037/0893-3200.11.2.210.

Updegraff, K. A., Umaña-Taylor, A. J., Rodríguez de Jesús, S.A., McHale, S. M., Feinberg, M. F., & Kuo, S. I. C. (2016). Family-focused prevention with Latinos: What about sisters and brothers? *Journal of Family Psychology.* Advance online publication. doi:10.1037/fam0000200.

Wachs, T. D., Black, M. M., & Engle, P. L. (2009). Maternal depression: A global threat to children's health, development, and behavior and to human rights. *Child Development Perspectives, 3,* 51–59. doi: 10.1111/j.1750-8606.2008.00077.x.

White, N., Cassels, M., Foley, S., Gee, N., & Hughes, C. (2017). *Sibling and pet relationships in pre-adolescence: Links with adversity and adjustment.* Manuscript in preparation.

Whiteman, S. D., Bernard, J. M. B., & McHale, S. M. (2010). The nature and correlates of sibling influence in two-parent African American families. *Journal of Marriage and Family, 72,* 267–281. doi:10.1111/j.1741-3737.2010.00698.x.

World Health Organization. (2014). *Health for the world's adolescents – a second chance in the second decade.* Geneva, Switzerland: World Health Organization.

8

SIBLING RELATIONSHIPS IN THE CONTEXT OF DISABILITY OR CHRONIC ILLNESS

"Unhappy (and happy) in their own way." By modifying the famous opening lines of Tolstoy's *Anna Karenina* to create a title for their review of research on families raising a child with Autism Spectrum Conditions (ASC), Gardiner and Iarocci (2012) highlight a new direction for research with families where one child has a disability. That is, the long-held narrow "deficit" model of family experiences in the context of disability or illness is yielding to the recognition that families can, with appropriate support, display remarkable resilience in adjusting to the life changes associated with caring for a child with special developmental or health needs.

Also worth noting is that any elevated incidence of problems among siblings will, at least in part, reflect shared genetic risk rather than a causal impact of the disability upon siblings' well-being. Of course, this point will apply more to some conditions than others, and contrasts in the level of shared genetic risk are likely to explain why siblings of children with ASC consistently display more difficulties than siblings of children with Down Syndrome (DS) (Heller & Arnold, 2010). Indeed, empirical reviews of the literature on siblings of children with DS (Cuskelly & Gunn, 2006) or children with physical disabilities (Dew, Balandin, & Llewellyn, 2008) indicate that, overall, these groups show good adjustment and are not deprived of normal childhood experiences. In contrast, the outcomes for siblings of individuals with ASC are more varied. In their meta-analytic review of this field, Yirmiya, Shaked and Erel, (2001) proposed a diathesis-stress model, which highlighted the interplay between genetic vulnerability to autistic traits (diathesis) and environmental stress. In a first test of this model, Orsmond and Seltzer (2009) focused on adolescence as a time of multiple transitions and stressors. Gathering ratings of depressive and anxiety symptoms from adolescent siblings of individuals with ASC they found that, as predicted from the diathesis-stress model, these ratings were only elevated for siblings who showed both sub-threshold autism characteristics (diathesis) and a high number of stressful life events.

With the caveat that adjustment problems in siblings may reflect shared genetic risk rather than adverse effects of disability on siblings, we turn now to consider the literature on adjustment and relationship quality for siblings in families raising a child with a disability or chronic illness. At the outset, it is worth noting that this literature shows a geographical fault-line in that researchers in the United Kingdom and the United States have typically adopted different methods and focused on different questions. Specifically, while US studies have focused on siblings' self-concepts, emotional reactions, academic outcomes and peer relations, British research is rooted in sociology and so has emphasised the importance of family, school and cultural contexts. Detailed coverage of research on siblings of children with disabilities would therefore require a whole volume (e.g., Burke, 2004). The more modest aim of this chapter is to contextualise the literature on siblings of children with disabilities and illnesses. We will do this in two ways. First, after discussing how the term "disability" is best defined and noting the importance of definitions for establishing reliable prevalence estimates, we review the research on sibling adjustment and relationship quality in families raising a child with a disability alongside the parallel (but much smaller) literatures on chronic or mental illness. For many years, this comparison was limited by both differences and weaknesses in research methods but recent years have seen the emergence of population-based studies that provide a much firmer base for comparing the impact of disability and mental illness upon sibling relationships. Next, we consider demographic findings related to the prevalence of childhood disability and its association with financial disadvantage; this provides a context for discussing the various psychosocial challenges facing siblings of children with disabilities.

Definition and prevalence of disability in childhood

Medical students receive very little training about children with disabilities and so may struggle as physicians to provide accurate information when asked by expectant parents how disability affects sibling relationships. One problem is that early studies lacked a clear and consistent definition of disability. In contrast with the medical definition of disability as "long-term physical, mental, intellectual or sensory impairments" adopted by the United Nations (Convention on the Rights of Persons with Disabilities, 2006, para. 1) with its implicit portrayal of the individual with a disability as in need of help to be 'put right', advocacy groups typically define disability in terms of the limitations experienced by individuals in society. This social model highlights the interplay between impairment and experience: being confined to a wheelchair is, for example, only a disability when no ramps or lifts are available. The social model of disability has been explicitly recognised in legislation: in the United Kingdom the 1995 Disability Discrimination Act (DDA, reiterated in the 2010 Equality Act) defines a disabled person as someone who has "a physical or mental impairment which has a substantial and long-term adverse effect on his ability to carry out normal day-to-day activities" (Disability Discrimination Act, 1995, p.1). Thus the DDA recognises that society has a responsibility to ensure that people with disabilities are given the same rights as others. Achieving this is likely to require a variety of forms of social education to promote acceptance and to identify the changes needed to break down the barriers that exclude people with disabilities from participating in society.

The DDA definition of disability is also useful from a research perspective, in that it enables surveys to adopt standardised questions, leading to more consistent prevalence estimates. Findings from the age-seven wave of the Millennium Cohort Study (MCS), which involves more than 19,000 children in the United Kingdom born in 2000–2001 and has adopted three alternative measures of disability (long-term limiting illness, special educational needs and developmental delay) illustrate how prevalence estimates vary with definition of disability. Specifically, 31% of participants showed one or more aspect of disability, but only 1% showed all three (Institute of Education, 2013). Adopting the DDA definition of disability in a 2004/5 survey of more than 16,000 British children (aged 0–18 years), Blackburn, Spencer and Read (2010) reported an overall prevalence of 7.3%. This prevalence of disability is higher in boys than in girls, both overall and for difficulties with physical coordination, communication, memory, concentration and learning (Blackburn et al., 2010). Importantly it is estimated that 80% of children with a disability have non-disabled siblings (Atkinson & Crawford, 1995).

Challenges for siblings of children with disabilities

According to Burke and Montgomery (2001), nearly half of children with disabilities receive a diagnosis before the age of 12 months, with a further third receiving a diagnosis between the ages of one and five years. In other words, the diagnosis of a disability often comes at a time when older children in the family may still be adjusting to the life changes that accompany the arrival of a new baby. Recent findings from research on adoptive families and families with children conceived by gamete donation highlight the advantages of beginning discussions with these children at a very early age (e.g., Ilioi & Golombok, 2015); by extrapolation, families with a new baby who has a disability may welcome guidance in explaining the disability to the baby's siblings very early in life. This is an important point, as diagnostic information is often conveyed to parents in a coded manner, reducing the likelihood that siblings will understand what the diagnosis actually means (Burke, 2004). For example, phrases such as "developmental delay" can lead to confusion as to whether or not the child is expected to "catch up" eventually.

Given the need for reassuring information, the scarcity of prominent characters with disabilities in the media is striking. Disability is virtually non-existent within commercial children's television, although BBC programmes for children have included characters such as Penny Pocket in *Balamory*, Hannah Sparks in *Fireman Sam* and Rachel Burns in *Grange Hill*, played by the very talented comedian with cerebral palsy, Francesca Martinez. Overall, however, the general absence of positive portrayals of people with disabilities in the media requires urgent attention, as ignorance about the disability can lead to feelings of self-blame or guilt, or a misunderstanding of challenging behaviour as directed at them personally (Sibs, 2016). Understanding the diagnosis is also vital in enabling siblings to challenge prejudice and negative attitudes. These appear widespread: according to the UK charity Scope (2014), for example, two out of three people in the United Kingdom feel uncomfortable talking to people with disabilities.

Perhaps the most important challenge faced by siblings of children with disabilities is, however, lack of parental attention. This may go beyond the direct impact of caregiving for the child with a disability to include other demands upon parents' time, including involvement in disability causes (Sibs, 2016). The effects of reduced parental attention can also be compounded by experiences of isolation. For example, in their examination of the factors that contribute to school-aged children's well-being, Layard and Dunn (2009) noted the importance of being able to bring friends home; yet this kind of social activity is particularly difficult for families of children with a disability. Experiences of differential parenting are also particularly common among children with disabled siblings (McHale & Pawletko, 1992) and have complex outcomes. For example, differential treatment can evoke feelings of jealousy, anxiety and guilt, even if recognised as legitimate. Children with typically developing versus disabled siblings also appear to display contrasting consequences of differential treatment. Specifically, more favourable parental treatment predicts more positive self-concepts but more negative relationships among typically developing siblings, but is associated with more anxiety and guilt among children with disabled siblings (McHale & Pawletko, 1992). These contrasts in the impact of differential parenting across specific outcomes and across different groups of children highlight the complex and potentially contradictory ways in which children evaluate differential parenting.

Sibling adjustment, age and type of disability/disorder

Rossiter and Sharpe (2001) conducted the first meta-analytic review of research on siblings of children with developmental delays; this review included data from 25 studies published between 1972 and 1999 and revealed an increased prevalence of behavioural problems and depression relative to siblings of typically developing children. This group difference was, however, small in magnitude and did not include any control for shared genetic risk. For each of these reasons then, mental health professionals should avoid interpreting behavioural problems among typically developing siblings as reflecting the challenges of having a sibling with a disability (Goeke & Ritchey, 2011). The group difference was also only evident among child-aged siblings, a finding that can be interpreted in at least three ways. First, the reduction in parental attention to siblings may become less marked over time, as the child grows up and the parents acquire confidence or social support. Second, developmental increases in siblings' autonomy may lessen the *need* for parental attention. Third, as children get older, their peers may become more understanding, reducing the stressors associated with having a disabled sibling.

A further caveat regarding the group difference in adjustment reported by Rossiter and Sharpe (2001) is that this effect may be specific rather than general. For example, siblings of individuals with ASC appear more likely than siblings of individuals with DS to describe difficult experiences, such as their sibling's embarrassing or destructive behaviour or social isolation, or to voice concerns about their brother or sister's future (for a review, see Orsmond and Seltzer, 2007b).

Effects of disability on sibling relationship quality

Among adult siblings, Orsmond and Seltzer (2007a) have reported less contact, less warmth and more worry among siblings of adults with ASC, as compared with siblings of adults with DS, with variability in sibling relationship quality related to the similarity in cognitive functioning between affected and unaffected siblings. That is, when the adult with ASC was relatively high functioning, or when the sibling had lower levels of education the outcomes appeared more positive. Thus, efforts to promote reciprocity between siblings may be valuable in increasing relationship satisfaction for siblings of adults with ASC.

Heller and Arnold (2010) conducted a systematic review of all studies (between 1970 and 2008) of siblings of adults with developmental disabilities, addressing three topics: psychosocial adjustment, sibling relationship quality and planning for future care. While this systematic review revealed variation in sibling adjustment that was linked to type of disability, sex and age of either sibling, severity of disability and geographical proximity, it also provided an encouraging picture of positive sibling relationships, echoing the findings from an early study by Gamble and McHale (1989). Also of note is that the type of disability was significant not only with respect to adjustment but also with regard to sibling relationship quality. For example, in a national (US) online survey, Hodapp and Urbano (2007) found that adult siblings of individuals with DS reported more positive sibling relationships than did siblings of adults with ASC. Overall, women were more involved than men in caring for their disabled siblings, but effects of birth order and severity of disability were not consistent across studies. With regards to geographical proximity, a study of older adults with intellectual disabilities showed that almost half of siblings became primary carers after their parents' death, at least temporarily (Bigby, 1997). In discussing their findings, Heller and Arnold (2010) note that individuals with disabilities now enjoy longer lives and are less likely to be living in institutions, highlighting the need for more research that includes adults with disabilities' own perspectives on their sibling relationships. Taking up this challenge, Burbidge and Minnes (2014) have emphasised the bidirectional nature of sibling support: for example, many of the adults with disabilities interviewed in their study reported helping their siblings with housework. These adults with disabilities also expressed a desire for more contact with siblings, a finding that led Burbidge and Minnes (2014) to call for more training to enable adults with disabilities to use technology to stay in close contact with siblings.

Sibling roles in the context of childhood disability

In a seminal early study, McHale and Gamble (1989) found that siblings of children with intellectual disabilities (especially sisters) reported more caregiving than did siblings of typically developing children. Interestingly, brothers of children with intellectual disabilities engaged in as much caregiving as did sisters of typically developing children, suggesting that gender roles are loosened within families who have a disabled child. This impact of disability on sibling roles may depend on birth order. For example, when it is the younger sibling who has a disability, there is likely to be a sustained asymmetry in sibling roles. In contrast, when it is the older sibling who has a disability there is likely to be a period of cognitive crossover, during which sibling roles may shift dramatically. As will be discussed in Chapter 9, caregiving is, in many parts of the world, a common feature of sibling relationships and so judgements as to whether caregiving responsibilities should be viewed as a "burden" on siblings should be made with care. Indeed, findings reviewed by Stoneman (2005) indicate that many siblings embrace opportunities to teach and care for their sibling with a disability.

Insider and outsider views of the impact of disability

Another conclusion that emerges from research in this field is that views within and outside families regarding the impact of disability or illness often show strik-ing contrasts. For example, a prenatal diagnosis of DS will lead to a termination of pregnancy in 85–95% of cases (e.g., Caruso, Westgate, & Holmes,1998). One factor that contributes to this decision is the belief that the child's disability will adversely affect family relationships. For example, in a Dutch survey of 71 women who terminated a pregnancy after a DS diagnosis, Korenromp et al. (2007) found that 73% decided that the "burden" of DS would be too heavy for their other chil-dren (as compared with 64% who considered the burden too heavy for themselves). However, a US survey of 822 brothers and sisters of individuals with DS (divided into two age groups: above and below the age of 12) conducted by Skotko, Levine and Goldstein, (2011) indicated that children were generally positive about their family life. Specifically, the vast majority of this large sample of siblings described feelings of love and pride towards their sibling coupled with a willingness to assume increased responsibilities and to remain involved in their sibling's life as they both age. Moreover, just 19% of the younger group and 12% of the older group reported that their parents gave their DS sibling too much time or attention, while 89–90% (across age groups) reported that their friends were comfortable being around their brother or sister with DS and just 5% of the older group felt that their social life suffered because of their DS sibling. Of course, any survey study raises questions about how non-respondents might have answered, but these positive findings are backed by conclusions from at least two reviews of studies adopting a variety of research methods (e.g., direct observations and both sibling and parental report; Roper, Allred, Mandleco, Freeborn, & Dyches, 2014; Stoneman, 2005). Similar informant effects have been reported in studies of siblings of children with physical disabilities (Dew et al., 2008) and children with autism (Rivers & Stoneman, 2003), and in a meta-analysis of studies of sibling relationships in the context of chronic illness (Rossiter & Sharpe, 2001). The encouraging conclusion from this literature is that, across a wide variety of disabilities and conditions, siblings appear generally positive in their views about the impact on family life.

Understanding why the impact of disability differs across families

Although the early study conducted by Gamble and McHale (1989) showed no difference in self-reported stressors for siblings of children with intellectual disabilities and siblings of typically developing children, more recent studies employing objective rather than subjective measures suggest a rather different picture. In particular, children with disabilities are more likely than other children to live in a single-parent household or in a family facing deprivation, debt and poor housing, or to have at least one parent who also has a disability (Blackburn et al., 2010). Moreover, raising a child with disabilities is approximately three times more expensive than raising a typically developing child (Dobson & Middleton, 1998), which obviously magnifies the impact of the association between disability and low family income. Furthermore, family cohesion, a key predictor of positive sibling relationships in the context of disability, is related to both socioeconomic status and knowledge about the disability or illness (e.g., Williams et al., 2002). This context of environmental disadvantage is therefore worth considering when assessing the impact of disability upon sibling relationships.

Ideas about the impact of disability on families have shifted from a focus on adverse effects to a recognition that outcomes can be quite diverse and that this variation is often closely related to contextual factors (such as disadvantage) that might accentuate the impact, as well as to protective factors (such as family support) that might serve as a buffer. For example, in a study of 172 families raising typically developing children or a child with a disability, Roper et al. (2014) applied a structural equation modelling approach to examine the interplay between type of disability, caregiver burden and sibling relationship quality. Their results indicated that: (1) sibling relationship quality was *less* positive for typically developing sibling dyads than for sibling dyads that included a child with either DS or multiple disabilities; (2) caregiving was more burdensome for parents of children with ASC or multiple disabilities; and (3) the increased caregiving burden associated with ASC accounted for the association between ASC and sibling relationship difficulties.

Likewise, echoing the family systems perspective discussed in Chapter 4, an observational study of 50 families with a child with ASC has shown that compromised sibling relationships are associated with both stress in the marital relationship and siblings' dissatisfaction with differential parenting (Rivers & Stoneman, 2003, 2008). Rivers and Stoneman's (2008) study also highlighted temperamental persistence as a buffer that maintains the quality of family relationships. Specifically, low levels of persistence in the typically developing child (and, to a lesser extent, in the child with ASC) were associated with increased negativity in the sibling relationship and with higher rates of differential parenting. As noted by Rivers and Stoneman (2008), temperamental persistence may enhance typically developing siblings' ability to ignore distracting verbalisations or other disturbing behaviour from the sibling with ASC, to make repeated efforts to begin or restore social interactions, and to sustain a solitary activity while parents focus their attention on the child with ASC. More generally, these findings indicate that rather than simply focusing, as previous studies have done, on the characteristics of the child with a disability, it is important to attend to the attributes of both children in the sibling relationship.

Sibling adjustment in the context of chronic illness

Hot on the heels of their meta-analysis of studies of siblings of children with disabilities (Rossiter & Sharpe, 2001), Sharpe and Rossiter (2002) conducted a meta-analysis of 51 published studies of siblings of children with a chronic illness. While this study showed a much more substantial effect on siblings' adjustment, the effect was significantly weaker in more recent studies, suggesting that changing attitudes to illness and disability are beginning to bear fruit. Moreover, variation in the impact on the healthy sibling was linked to contrasts in daily treatment regimes rather than the specific nature of the illness.

In discussing their findings, Sharpe and Rossiter (2002) noted that adjustment problems in siblings appear comparable in nature and magnitude with those reported for the children with chronic illness (Lavigne & Faier-Routman, 1992). As interventions focused on children with chronic illness appear effective in reducing emotional and behavioural problems (Kibby, Tyc, & Mulhern, 1998), there is obvious merit in extending similar interventions to siblings. Sharpe and Rossiter (2002) also noted that these adjustment problems do not typically affect the sibling relationship, which they argue may be resilient and perhaps even enhanced in the context of illness.

One particularly large group of children with chronic illnesses are those affected by paediatric cancers: in the United Kingdom approximately 1,800 children are diagnosed with cancer every year (Cancer Research UK, 2016), with five-year survival rates of just over 80% (Office for National Statistics, 2016). In a systematic review of 65 quantitative and qualitative studies of siblings of children with cancer published between 1997 and 2008, Alderfer et al. (2010) noted both negative and positive outcomes. A significant subset of siblings experienced post-traumatic stress symptoms, negative emotional reactions (e.g., fear, worry, anger or guilt), as well as low quality of life in emotional, family and social domains. These symptoms, often related to loss of parental attention, were typically most striking in the immediate aftermath of the cancer diagnosis and were particularly common among adolescent siblings. At the same time, compared with other children of their age, siblings of children with cancer appeared to display increased maturity and empathy. These findings lend support to two distinct theoretical models. The first of these is the post-traumatic stress framework in which distress is seen as a normative reaction to a life-threatening illness that can actually lead to positive outcomes, such as increased maturity or empathy. The second model is the developmental social ecology model, which highlights the way in which both within-person characteristics (e.g., gender, biological predispositions) and specific life events and social contexts shape child development.

Support for these findings comes from a recent qualitative study of siblings of children with cancer (D'Urso, Mastroyannopoulou, & Kirby, 2016), adopting a post-traumatic stress/growth framework. Three key themes emerged from interviews with 12- to 18-year-old siblings of children who had been treated for either leukaemia or a brain tumour. First, children reported experiencing a number of difficult emotions, including shock, fear and uncertainty when their sibling was diagnosed, and guilt, anger, helplessness, sadness and jealousy during their sibling's treatment. However, children also reported the strengthening of relationships both within the family, particularly with fathers, and outside the family with peers and professionals. Finally, children emphasised opportunities for personal development, reporting that were now more confident, mature and empathic, and had a different outlook on life. However, these personal changes were not necessarily completely positive: some children reported concern at having to take on more adult roles within the family, as well as worry about the future. These findings echo the opening statement of this chapter, and also highlight the importance of social and emotional support from relationships within and outside the family in aiding children to cope with their sibling's illness.

Siblings in the context of mental illness

In a recent epidemiological study that stands apart from previous studies in its methodological rigour, Wolfe, Song, Greenberg and Mailick (2014) used 50 years of population-level data drawn from the Wisconsin Longitudinal Study (rather than volunteer siblings, as typified by previous research) to compare siblings of individuals with developmental delay or mental illness. Importantly, this study ($N = 7,265$ at the last wave) enabled Wolfe et al., (2014) to control for family factors that preceded the birth of the siblings (e.g. parental divorce, death or low socioeconomic status) as well as subsequent risk factors that may have jeopardised outcomes (e.g., parental divorce, binge-drinking, ill health). In addition, genetic data were available for just over half of the final sample, enabling the authors to perform robustness tests to assess the likelihood that genetic factors underpinned any emergent contrasts.

With all of the above checks in place, Wolfe et al. (2014) found that in families where a brother or sister had schizophrenia, bipolar disorder or major depression, the well siblings completed fewer years of education and were more likely to be unemployed in the early years of midlife. For families where a brother or sister had a developmental delay, group contrasts in education and employment were less pronounced but the well siblings showed lower rates of marriage and elevated rates of marital disruption. These results highlight the value of a developmental perspective in understanding effects of disability on family life. For example, DS and other forms of developmental delay are (as noted earlier) typically diagnosed in the first few years of life and have a relatively constant impact on children's behaviour, such that the siblings can adjust to construct stable positive relationships. In contrast, mental illness typically first emerges in adolescence or early adulthood and has an unpredictable impact on behaviour.

Mental illness is also much more likely to disrupt family relationships and evoke distress in siblings. For example, siblings of individuals with severe mental illness are more likely to experience depressive episodes than are siblings of individuals with intellectual disabilities or siblings in families described as normative (e.g., Taylor, Greenberg, Seltzer, & Floyd, 2008). In a review aimed at health professionals, Lukens and Thorning (2011) noted several protective factors that illustrate the value of adopting a family systems perspective (see Chapter 4). For example, outcomes for both the well and the affected sibling were more positive in the context of reciprocity and mutuality in the sibling relationship, general family cohesion and siblings' empathy and appreciation of demands on parents. These findings indicate that the effectiveness of existing practice could be enhanced by: (1) further research to achieve a fuller understanding of siblings' involvement in caregiving, which can extend over many decades; (2) developing and extending psycho-educational support for siblings to increase quality of life for all family members; and (3) paying more attention to the voices of affected individuals to enable them to engage in more reciprocal and satisfying interactions with their siblings.

Future directions

A common theme within the reviews cited in this chapter is the need for greater methodological rigour to increase the clarity and reliability of study findings. Alongside this general methodological point (e.g., use of population rather than volunteer samples that are sufficiently sized to examine moderating effects of developmental stage, family circumstances and child characteristics; greater consistency in methods of measurement), several conceptual areas remain very under-researched. These gaps include: longitudinal research to examine changes in sibling relationships in the early months and years following a diagnosis; the exploration of how disability might affect relationships *between* typically developing siblings (i.e., in families that have one child with a disability and two or more typically developing children), and the use of multi-informant approaches that, where possible, include the perspective of the child with disability alongside that of siblings and parents. Much more research is also needed to ensure that the findings from basic science have a positive impact, for example in developing clinical services to support siblings of children and adults with disabilities, disorders and chronic mental or physical illness.

Take-home messages

1. Over the past few decades there has been a valuable shift in how disability is defined, from early medical "deficit" models to more contemporary definitions, such as that adopted in the Disability Discrimination Act, that emphasise the importance of breaking down barriers to participating in society.

2. Related to the change in definitions, there have been historical shifts in the experiences of families caring for children with disability. These reflect other changes, such as increased longevity, reduced institutionalisation and technology as a medium for communication.

3. The impact of disability on siblings varies markedly with aetiology: siblings of individuals with DS show better adjustment and more positive sibling relationships than siblings of individuals with ASC or mental illness.

4. The impact of disability on siblings also varies markedly with context, highlighting the importance of family processes discussed earlier in this volume (e.g., spillover and compensation effects; see Chapter 4).

5. The impact of disability on siblings also varies markedly by informant: when sibling views are gathered directly, they are generally more positive than those gathered from parental reports.

6. A developmental perspective can help elucidate the varying impact of disability or illness on sibling relationships. For example, one reason mental illness has a stronger impact on siblings than developmental delay is the acute nature of its onset, often in adolescence, a time that is often already characterised by changes and stress. A developmental perspective is also needed to understand the way in which disability can affect adult sibling relationships, which often involve transitions into caregiver roles.

7. The presumption of burden is generally not supported by evidence: sibling relationships when one child has a disability or illness can be as positive as (or even more positive than) relationships between typically developing siblings. Moreover, caregiving is often embraced, more in line with sibling relationships in non-Western cultures (see Chapter 9).

8. As in sibling relationships in families without a child with a disability or illness, characteristics of the typically developing sibling (e.g., temperamental persistence) may help to explain variation in relationship quality.

9. Financial disadvantage often compounds the challenges faced by families in which one child has a disability or long-term illness. Caring for children with disabilities is both expensive and time-consuming, such that urgent changes are needed to maximise the potential of all children.

10. Important gaps in the research field include (1) exploring how disability affects other sibling relationships in families that have a child with a disability and two or more typically developing children and (2) using multi-informant approaches that, where possible, include the perspective of the child with a disability.

References

Alderfer, M. A., Long, K. A., Lown, E. A., Marsland, A. L., Ostrowski, N. L., Hock, J. M., & Ewing, L. J. (2010). Psychosocial adjustment of siblings of children with cancer: A systematic review. *Psycho-Oncology, 19,* 789–805. doi:10.1002/pon.1638.

Atkinson, N., & Crawford, M. (1995). *All in the family: Siblings and disability.* London: NCH Action for Children.

Bigby, C. (1997). Parental substitutes? The role of siblings in the lives of older people with intellectual disability. *Journal of Gerontological Social Work, 29*, 3–21. doi:10.1300/J083v29n01_02.

Blackburn, C. M., Spencer, N. J., & Read, J. M. (2010). Prevalence of childhood disability and the characteristics and circumstances of disabled children in the UK: Secondary analysis of the Family Resources Survey. *BMC Pediatrics, 10*(21). doi:10.1186/1471-2431-10-21.

Burbidge, J., & Minnes, P. (2014). Relationship quality in adult siblings with and without developmental disabilities. *Family Relations, 63*, 148–162. doi:10.1111/fare.12047.

Burke, P. (2004). *Brothers and sisters of disabled children*. London: Jessica Kingsley Publishers.

Burke, P., & Montgomery, S. (2001). Brothers and sisters: Supporting the siblings of children with disabilities. *Practice: Social Work in Action, 13*, 27–28. doi:10.1080/09503150108415469.

Cancer Research UK. (2016). Children's cancer statistics. Retrieved from http://www.cancerresearchuk.org/health-professional/cancer-statistics/childrens-cancers - heading-Zero.

Caruso, T. M., Westgate, M. N., & Holmes, L. B. (1998). Impact of prenatal screening on the birth status of fetuses with Down syndrome at an urban hospital, 1972-1994. *Genetics in Medicine, 1*, 22–28. doi:10.1097/00125817-199811000-00006.

Convention on the Rights of Persons with Disabilities. (2006). Retrieved from http://www.disabilityaction.org/centre-on-human-rights/human-rights-and-disability/united-nations-convention-on-the-rights-of-persons-with-disabilities/.

Cuskelly, M., & Gunn, P. (2006). Adjustment of children who have a sibling with Down syndrome: Perspectives of mothers, fathers and children. *Journal of Intellectual Disability Research, 50*, 917–925. doi:10.1111/j.1365-2788.2006.00922.x.

D'Urso, A., Mastroyannopoulou, K., & Kirby, A. (2016). Experiences of posttraumatic growth in siblings of children with cancer. *Clinical Child Psychology and Psychiatry, 22*, 301–317. doi:10.1177/1359104516660749.

Dew, A., Balandin, S., & Llewellyn, G. (2008). The psychosocial impact on siblings of people with lifelong physical disability: A review of the literature. *Journal of Developmental and Physical Disabilities, 20*, 485–507. doi:10.1007/s10882-008-9109-5.

Disability Discrimination Act. (1995). Retrieved from http://www.legislation.gov.uk/ukpga/1995/50/section/1.

Dobson, B., & Middleton, S. (1998). *Paying to care: The cost of childhood disability*. York: Joseph Rowntree Foundation. Retrieved from https://www.jrf.org.uk/report/paying-care-cost-childhood-disability.

Gamble, W. C., & McHale, S. M. (1989). Coping with stress in sibling relationships: A comparison of children with disabled and nondisabled siblings. *Journal of Applied Developmental Psychology, 10*, 353–373. doi:10.1016/0193-3973(89)90035-X.

Gardiner, E., & Iarocci, G. (2012). Unhappy (and happy) in their own way: A developmental psychopathology perspective on quality of life for families living with developmental disability with and without autism. *Research in Developmental Disabilities, 33*, 2177–2192. doi:10.1016/j.ridd.2012.06.014.

Goeke, J., & Ritchey, K. (2011). Siblings of individuals with disabilities. In J. Caspi (Ed.), *Sibling development: Implications for mental health practitioners* (pp. 167–193). New York: Springer.

Heller, T., & Arnold, C. K. (2010). Siblings of adults with developmental disabilities: Psychosocial outcomes, relationships, and future planning. *Journal of Policy and Practice in Intellectual Disabilities, 7*, 16–25. doi:10.1111/j.1741-1130.2010.00243.x.

Hodapp, R. M., & Urbano, R. C. (2007). Adult siblings of individuals with Down syndrome versus with autism: Findings from a large-scale US survey. *Journal of Intellectual Disability Research, 51*, 1018–1029. doi:10.1111/j.1365-2788.2007.00994.x.

Ilioi, E. C., & Golombok, S. (2015). Psychological adjustment in adolescents conceived by assisted reproduction techniques: A systematic review. *Human Reproduction Update, 21*, 84–96. doi:10.1093/humupd/dmu051.

Institute of Education. (2013). *What is the prevalence of child disability?* London: Institute of Education. Retrieved from http://www.closer.ac.uk/wp-content/uploads/Briefing-1-Prevalence-of-child-disability-Nov-20131.pdf.

Kibby, M. Y., Tyc, V. L., & Mulhern, R. K. (1998). Effectiveness of psychological intervention for children and adolescents with chronic medical illness: A meta-analysis. *Clinical Psychology Review, 18*, 105–117. doi:10.1016/S0272-7358(97)00049-4.

Korenromp, M. J., Page-Christiaens, G. C. M. L., van den Bout, J., Mulder, E. J. H., & Visser, G. H. A. (2007). Maternal decision to terminate pregnancy in case of Down syndrome. *American Journal of Obstetrics and Gynecology, 196*, 149e.1–149e.11. doi:10.1016/j.ajog.2006.09.013.

Lavigne, J. V., & Faier-routman, J. (1992). Psychological adjustment to pediatric physical disorders: A meta-analytic review. *Journal of Pediatric Psychology, 17*, 133–157. doi:10.1093/jpepsy/17.2.133.

Layard, R., & Dunn, J. (2009). *A good childhood: Searching for values in a competitive age.* London: Penguin.

Lukens, E., & Thorning, H. (2011). Siblings in families with mental illness. In J. Caspi (Ed.), *Sibling development: Implications for mental health practitioners* (pp. 195–219). New York: Springer.

McHale, S. M., & Gamble, W. C. (1989). Sibling relationships of children with disabled and nondisabled brothers and sisters. *Developmental Psychology, 25*, 421–429. doi:10.1037/0012-1649.25.3.421.

McHale, S. M., & Pawletko, T. M. (1992). Differential treatment of siblings in two family contexts. *Child Development, 63*, 68–81. doi:10.1111/j.1467-8624.1992.tb03596.x.

Office for National Statistics. (2016). *Childhood cancer survival in England: Children diagnosed from 1990 to 2009 and followed up to 2014 (experimental statistics).* London: Office for National Statistics. Retrieved from https://www.ons.gov.uk/peoplepopulationandcommunity/healthandsocialcare/conditionsanddiseases/bulletins/childhoodcancersurvivalinengland/childrendiagnosedfrom1990to2009andfollowedupto2014experimentalstatistics5-year-survival-for-children-diagnosed-between-1990-and-2009.

Orsmond, G. I., & Seltzer, M. M. (2007a). Siblings of individuals with autism or Down syndrome: Effects on adult lives. *Journal of Intellectual Disability Research, 51*, 682–696. doi:10.1111/j.1365-2788.2007.00954.x.

Orsmond, G. I., & Seltzer, M. M. (2007b). Siblings of individuals with autism spectrum disorders across the life course. *Mental Retardation and Developmental Disabilities Research Reviews, 13*, 313–320. doi:10.1002/mrdd.20171.

Orsmond, G. I., & Seltzer, M. M. (2009). Adolescent siblings of individuals with an autism spectrum disorder: Testing a diathesis-stress model of sibling well-being. *Journal of Autism and Developmental Disorders, 39*, 1053–1065. doi:10.1007/s10803-009-0722-7.

Rivers, J. W., & Stoneman, Z. (2003). Sibling relationships when a child has autism: Marital stress and support coping. *Journal of Autism and Developmental Disorders, 33*, 383–394. doi:10.1023/A:1025006727395.

Rivers, J. W., & Stoneman, Z. (2008). Child temperaments, differential parenting, and the sibling relationships of children with autism spectrum disorder. *Journal of Autism and Developmental Disorders, 38*, 1740–1750. doi:10.1007/s10803-008-0560-z.

Roper, S. O., Allred, D. W., Mandleco, B., Freeborn, D., & Dyches, T. (2014). Caregiver burden and sibling relationships in families raising children with disabilities and typically developing children. *Families, Systems and Health, 32*, 241–246. doi:10.1037/fsh0000047.

Rossiter, L., & Sharpe, D. (2001). The siblings of individuals with mental retardation: A quantitative integration of the literature. *Journal of Child and Family Studies, 10*, 65–84. doi:10.1023/A:1016629500708.

Scope. (2014). *Current attitudes towards disabled people*. Retrieved from http://www.scope.org.uk/Scope/media/Images/PublicationDirectory/Current-attitudes-towards-disabled-people.pdf?ext=.pdf.

Sharpe, D., & Rossiter, L. (2002). Siblings of children with a chronic illness: A meta-analysis. *Journal of Pediatric Psychology, 27*, 699–710. doi:10.1093/jpepsy/27.8.699.

Sibs. (2016). The needs of young children. Retrieved from https://www.sibs.org.uk/supporting-young-siblings/professionals/needs-of-young-siblings/.

Skotko, B. G., Levine, S. P., & Goldstein, R. (2011). Having a brother or sister with Down syndrome: Perspectives from siblings. *American Journal of Medical Genetics, Part A, 155*, 2348–2359. doi:10.1002/ajmg.a.34228.

Stoneman, Z. (2005). Siblings of children with disabilities: Research themes. *Mental Retardation, 43*, 339–350. doi:10.1352/0047-6765(2005)43[339: SOCWDR]2.0.CO;2.

Taylor, J. L., Greenberg, J. S., Seltzer, M. M., & Floyd, F. J. (2008). Siblings of adults with mild intellectual deficits or mental illness: Differential life course outcomes. *Journal of Family Psychology, 22*, 905–914. doi:10.1037/a0012603.

Williams, P. D., Williams, A. R., Graff, J. C., Hanson, S., Stanton, A., Hafeman, C., Liebergen, A., Leuenberg, K., Setter, R. K., Ridder, L., Curry, H., Barnard, M., & Sanders, S. (2002). Interrelationships among variables affecting well siblings and mothers in families of children with a chronic illness or disability. *Journal of Behavioral Medicine, 25*, 411–424. doi:10.1023/A:1020401122858.

Wolfe, B., Song, J., Greenberg, J. S., & Mailick, M. R. (2014). Ripple effects of developmental disabilities and mental illness on nondisabled adult siblings. *Social Science and Medicine, 108*, 1–9. doi:10.1016/j.socscimed.2014.01.021.

Yirmiya, N., Shaked, M., & Erel, O. (2001). Comparison of siblings of individuals with autism and siblings of individuals with other diagnoses: An empirical summary. In N. Schopler, N. Yirmiya, C. Shulman & L. Marcus (Eds.), *The research basis for autism intervention* (pp. 59–73). New York: Kluwer/Plenum.

9

SIBLING RELATIONSHIPS IN CULTURAL CONTEXT

In 1979 the Republic of China implemented a "one-child policy" in a bid to control the country's rapidly increasing population. This policy encouraged couples to marry late and provided both education about birth control and financial incentives for families with only one child. Amid worries about the enforcement of the policy and the increased burden on individuals to care for their aging parents and grandparents, researchers and policy-makers voiced their disquiet about the social consequences of raising a whole nation of only children (e.g., Jiao, Ji, & Jing, 1986). Specifically, there was concern that, compared with children with siblings, these only children, often referred to as "little emperors", would show poorer social skills and be more selfish and less family-oriented.

Responding to these concerns, numerous studies have compared the adjustment of only children and children with siblings in China. Contrary to initial fears, the evidence from these studies suggests that, compared with Chinese children with siblings, Chinese singletons hold similar attitudes about family support, and show similar if not enhanced social, behavioural and academic outcomes (e.g., Lee, 2012; Liu, Lin, & Chen, 2010). These findings suggest that the advantages and disadvantages of having a sibling for children's development are not universal but vary with prevailing cultural values. In a country such as China where having one child is the norm, and financial and social sanctions are levied against those who do not comply with the norm, having a sibling may be detrimental to children's well-being. In contrast, in the West where the majority of children grow up with a sibling, having a sibling may procure a small early social advantage. One study in China neatly demonstrates how the shift in cultural attitudes affected the relative adjustment of only children and children with siblings. Yang, Ollendick, Dong, Xia and Lin (1995) compared these two groups in three cohorts of children born before, during and after the implementation of the policy. Alongside higher rates of anxiety for children with siblings in all three cohorts, they found elevated levels of depression among children that were restricted to the cohorts born during or after implementation of the one-child policy. In other words, changes in public opinion and cultural values about family size lead to changes in the impact of having a sibling. In line with this conclusion, in a recent quantitative synthesis of Chinese data from 22 studies of psychopathology in late adolescence, Falbo and Hooper (2015) found small but consistent and significant advantages for only children compared to their peers with siblings.

We return to a discussion of the impact of being an only child in Western cultures in Chapter 10; however, the example of China's one-child policy clearly demonstrates how cultural values can influence the impact of family size on adjustment. The current chapter continues with the theme of individual differences to examine whether cultural values also affect the *quality* of sibling relationships. In line with the field, the other chapters in this book have focused on psychological research on sibling relationships in White ethnic majority families living in the United States, United Kingdom or other Western countries; the goal of this chapter is to expand this narrow ethnic focus by reviewing research from several disciplines. The first cultural perspectives on siblings came from anthropologists' observational studies of families in traditional communities in Asia, Oceania and Africa. More recently, psychologists have also begun to examine sibling processes among ethnic minority groups (primarily in the United States) and a few studies have directly compared the quality of sibling relationships in two or more cultural groups. In this chapter we discuss each strand of research in turn, before concluding with a discussion of cultural differences in factors that influence sibling relationship quality.

Definitions of siblings

In an early review of cross-cultural research on siblings, Cicirelli (1994) noted that one difficulty with comparing family relationships in traditional cultures with those in Western cultures is that the word "sibling" has different meanings in different cultures. In the West, siblings are defined as sharing at least one biological, adoptive or step parent but in other cultures definitions are more varied. Some non-Western cultures include just biological siblings (Kirkpatrick, 1983), while other cultures include cousins (Hecht, 1983; Watson-Gegeo & Gegeo, 1989), relatives of the same gender (Rubinstein, 1983) or all children in a community (Wenger, 1989). Differences in cultural values regarding the family are also reflected in the vocabulary available to describe sibling relationships. For example, Kolenda (1993) notes that in Southern Indian languages there are no words for "sister" and "brother"; instead, one must refer to one's "older" or "younger" sibling, reflecting the strong age-based hierarchy among siblings. Many Polynesian languages (including Māori) also have separate words for older and younger siblings, although typically only for siblings of the same gender, suggesting that in these cultures hierarchies are based on gender as well as age (Firth, 1970).

Sibling roles in childhood

Despite these differences in definition, Cicirelli (1994) highlights clear cultural contrasts in siblings' roles within the family. In Western contemporary societies there are few set cultural roles governing sibling relationships. Childhood siblings are playmates (and sparring partners), but are generally not expected to play a major role in their younger siblings' care or learning. Sibling caretaking may occur occasionally, but this typically takes the form of short-term babysitting (Bryant, 1989). For example, an older sibling may be asked to look after their younger sibling so the parent can go to the shops, but in this case the older sibling's job is simply to entertain the younger child and ensure he or she does not come to any harm. Similarly, as discussed in Chapter 6, informal teaching occurs relatively frequently in sibling interactions (Howe, Della Porta, Recchia, Funamoto, & Ross, 2015), but older siblings are not considered in anyway responsible for younger children's educational attainment. In the West when siblings leave home, sibling relationships become largely voluntary. Adult siblings may help each other in times of need, but such help is usually dictated by the ability and inclination of one sibling to aid the other rather than a sense of family obligation. Note, however, that historically children in the West may have played a larger role in care for their siblings: in her book exploring Victorian sibling relationships, Davidoff (2012) provides many examples of siblings, and especially sisters, taking a prominent caregiving role within the family.

In contrast, siblings have a much more established role in family life in non-Western cultures. In traditional South Asian cultures, for example, the sibling relationship rather than the parent-child relationship is considered the primary family bond and siblings play important roles in each other's lives throughout the lifespan (Nuckolls, 1993). In non-Western cultures siblings also typically play a formalised role in caregiving. In many traditional African communities, for example, older siblings may be the main day-to-day caregivers for younger children while parents are busy with other chores, while in Oceanic cultures older sisters may help their mother with the care of younger children (e.g., Watson-Gegeo & Gegeo, 1989; Whittemore & Beverly, 1989). Similarly, in Eastern Indian cultures siblings may care for younger children as part of a socialisation process that is shared between all members of the extended family (Seymour, 1993).

Importantly, in non-Western cultures the role of sibling caregiving is not simply to entertain the younger child; instead, older siblings are expected to play an active role in socialising and teaching their younger sibling so that the younger child can contribute to the community as an adult. Accordingly, parents train older children to look after younger siblings, and teach younger children to be obedient to older children (Cicirelli, 1994). This formalised caregiving may promote sibling interdependence and reduce rivalry, and several researchers have noted lower levels of rivalry among young siblings in Southern Asia (Beals & Esson, 1993; Seymour, 1993). For example, in contrast to the fuss made over a new baby in Western cultures, Seymour (1993) reported that in an Eastern Indian community a new sibling was not given any special attention but was immediately incorporated into a process of family caregiving and expected to learn to cooperate with the other members of the family. Sibling involvement in care may also provide important opportunities for engagement in observational learning. In an observational study where target children were given a distractor toy to play with while their sibling was shown how to make a novel toy, Correa-Chávez and Rogoff (2009) observed cultural differences in children's attention towards the sibling, and the subsequent help they required to make the novel toy, among Guatemalan Mayan and European-American families. Specifically, Guatemalan children from traditional Mayan families (where mothers had little involvement in Western schooling) paid more attention to their siblings than did European-American children or Mayan children whose mothers had more involvement in Western schooling.

Cultural expectations of adult siblings

Sibling caregiving may also establish hierarchies among siblings and expectations of mutual support that endure through the lifespan. In many traditional South Asian cultures, brothers are expected to provide material support, including a dowry, for their adult sisters, while sisters are expected to provide hospitality and affection to their brother. This strong bond between brothers and sisters is epitomised in the Hindu festival of Raksha Bandhan in which sisters give their brothers a decorative thread to wear around their wrist and pray for their well-being, while brothers pledge to protect and provide for their sister (de Munck, 1993). The anthropological studies in Cicirelli's (1994) review paint a compelling picture of large differences in the role of siblings in Western urbanised families, as compared with families in rural agricultural communities in a variety of non-industrialised countries. These contrasts reflect extreme cultural differences as these traditional communities differ from Westernised societies in terms of the physical environment and daily life styles.

Psychological approaches to exploring cultural variation in sibling relationships

In contrast with the anthropological focus on prototypical patterns of interaction within a culture, psychological research into cross-cultural variation in sibling relationships has typically sought to explain individual differences in sibling interactions. This research has tended to involve ethnic minority groups living in Westernised cultures or modern urban non-Western samples, rather than rural communities. In exploring how culture affects family life, psychologists have typically either examined variation in sibling relationship quality within one ethnic group or compared individual differences in sibling relationships across two or more cultural groups. These two approaches provide different perspectives on the role of culture in sibling relationships. The former allows us to understand the factors (such as gender, ethnic identity, endorsement of family values) that contribute to individual variation within a culture, while comparing two cultural groups provides a broader view of how cultural values impact on sibling behaviours and roles.

Mono-cultural research. Mono-cultural research on siblings has typically focused on either Latino-American or African-American families, which represent the largest ethnic minority groups in the United States (Humes, Jones, & Ramirez, 2011). Research with these ethnic groups has shown that some (but not all) of the predictors of variation in sibling relationship are similar to those found in White ethnic majority groups; additional factors that appear to have particular relevance for ethnic minority families include cultural values regarding the family and ethnic identity. For example, echoing studies of White ethnic majority children (see Chapter 4), Gamble and Yu (2014) showed that high quality sibling relationships (i.e., those high in warmth and low and conflict) among preschoolers were associated with supportive parenting and emotional expressivity. In addition, mothers' cultural values relating to harmony within relationships (*simpatía*) and fathers' endorsement of values of family support and solidarity (*familism*) were each associated with sibling warmth. These findings align with work with Mexican-American adolescents conducted by Updegraff and her colleagues. For example, Updegraff, McHale, Whiteman, Thayer and Delgado (2005) reported that Mexican-American siblings spend large amounts of time in shared activities and that adolescents' own endorsement of familism predicted the intimacy of sibling relationships, particularly among girls. Similarly, Killoren, Thayer and Updegraff (2008) reported that adolescents' cultural orientation (i.e., the extent to which they identified with Mexican versus Western cultural values) was associated with the types of strategies they used in conflict with a sibling, which then predicted relationship quality.

Among African-American families too, the quality of children's sibling relationships shows similar links with the child's wider environment. In a study of 172 African-American families, McHale, Whiteman, Kim and Crouter (2007) used cluster analysis to divide sibling relationships into three types: positive, negative and distant. Positive sibling relationships were associated with higher levels of ethnic identity and parents' religiosity, and lower levels of parental education. Conversely, negative sibling relationships were associated with children's poor well-being, mothers' experiences of discrimination and older siblings' risk-taking behaviour. These findings resonate with an earlier study by Brody, Stoneman, Smith and Gibson (1999), which reported links between family relationships and sibling relationships among school-aged African-American siblings living in a rural setting. Interestingly, this study also showed that children's self-regulation and parents' psychological functioning predicted more positive sibling relationships. These studies of the correlates of sibling relationship quality among ethnic minority groups in the United States echo Bronfenbrenner's (1979) ecological perspective that children's behaviour and relationships are a product of interactions with individual characteristics and features of the wider environment.

Mono-cultural studies have given us valuable insight into individual differences in family relationships among ethnic minority families. However, several limitations are worth noting. First, this research has had a very narrow focus in terms of the cultures studied. In their review of sibling relationships in a range of family contexts, McGuire and Shanahan (2010) note that families from Asian cultures have been particularly overlooked in sibling research, despite making up approximately 5% of the US population (Humes et al., 2011). In addition, research outside of the United States would aid our understanding of acculturation processes in different Western contexts, and family processes in modern non-Western cultures. Second, as well as a narrow cultural focus, this research has focused on a narrow time frame from middle childhood to adolescence. Further research taking a lifespan perspective to sibling relationships in ethnic minority cultures is therefore needed to enhance our understanding of cultural variation in sibling relationships across development.

Cross-cultural studies. Cross-cultural studies are scarce but generally point to differences in the quality of sibling relationships across ethnic groups. In a study of adolescents' connectedness to members of their social network, Karcher and Sass (2010) showed that, compared with their Caucasian counterparts, African-American and Latino adolescents in the United States reported feeling more connected to their siblings. A large-scale study of over 13,000 adult American siblings found generally similar results (Riedmann & White, 1996). Specifically, Hispanic and African-American adults had more frequent contact with their sibling, and perceived their sibling as more supportive than European-American adults. In contrast, European-American siblings reported higher levels of exchange of support than other cultures. In addition, in a rare study of Asian families, French, Rianasari, Pidada, Nelwan and Buhrmester (2001) showed that school-aged children and adolescents living in Indonesia reported more companionship, intimacy and satisfaction and less conflict with a sibling than children of a similar age living in the United States.

Outside of the United States, a recent Dutch study by Buist and her colleagues (Buist et al., 2013) expanded previous cross-cultural work by using multiple-groups modelling to compare mean-level differences in sibling relationship quality. Using data from 159 Dutch and 159 Moroccan adolescents living in the Netherlands, the authors showed that Moroccan adolescents reported, on average, more positivity and less conflict with their sibling than their Dutch counterparts. Similar cross-cultural contrasts were observed in a large-scale study of adult siblings from five ethnic groups in the Netherlands: adults from most ethnic minority groups reported more contact and emotional support from siblings than adults in the Dutch group (Voorpostel & Schans, 2011). However, in this study Turkish and Antillean adults also reported more conflict with their sibling than their Dutch counterparts.

An important methodological limitation of these studies is that, with the exception of Karcher and Sass (2010), the researchers did not check for measurement invariance in sibling relationship measures before comparing across groups. Measurement invariance analyses assess whether the factor structure, factor loadings and item intercepts of a questionnaire or test are equivalent across groups (Brown, 2006). Such analyses, therefore, determine whether a questionnaire measures the same underlying constructs (i.e., has the same latent factors) in two or more groups, and whether answers to individual items are related to the underlying constructs to a similar extent in the groups. Simulation studies suggest that establishing measurement invariance is a crucial initial step to ensure that group differences are robust. In a paper entitled *What happens if we compare chopsticks with forks?* Chen (2008) showed that if measurement invariance is lacking, cross-cultural comparisons yield artificial group differences. Thus, it is difficult to infer from the extant literature whether there are real cultural differences in sibling relationship quality or whether observed group differences are methodological artefacts. To overcome these methodological difficulties, we conducted a study using multiple-groups modelling to assess measurement invariance and then examine cultural differences in sibling relationship quality among children of Asian and European descent living in the United Kingdom and New Zealand (White, Darshane, & Hughes, 2017).

Our findings showed that ratings of sibling relationship quality on an abbreviated version of the Network of Relationships Inventory (NRI; Furman & Buhrmester, 1985) showed measurement invariance across the United Kingdom and New Zealand and across children of Asian and European descent. This means that children in both countries and from both cultures answered the individual questions about their siblings in a similar way and these item scores were related to overall factor scores (Conflict, Companionship, Intimate Disclosure and Warmth) to a similar extent. Importantly, measurement invariance allows us to be confident that subsequent comparisons of mean NRI scores across countries or cultures are reliable, and provides preliminary support for the NRI as a non-culturally-biased research tool.

Having established measure invariance, we compared ratings of sibling relationship quality both across cultures (Asian and European) and across countries (New Zealand and the United Kingdom). As noted earlier, Asian families have been neglected in sibling research despite clear anthropological evidence of the prominence of sibling relationships in many Asian cultures. Similarly, the generalisability of sibling findings across Western countries has typically been assumed, despite many differences in immigration and settlement between nations. For example, in New Zealand, European settlement occurred relatively recently, and indigenous Māori culture places a strong emphasis on *whānau*, or extended family, with a rare observational study suggesting that Māori mothers spent more time playing interactively with and teaching their children than New Zealand European mothers (Podmore & St. George, 1986). Thus, to the extent that Māori cultural values about family influence the general social climate in New Zealand, we might expect children living in New Zealand to report more positive sibling relationships than children living in the United Kingdom.

In contrast to our hypotheses, ratings of sibling relationship quality were not significantly different between British and New Zealand children, perhaps suggesting that cultural values about the family among majority ethnic groups are relatively uninfluenced by indigenous culture or the values of other ethnic groups. This finding, however, provides some initial support for the application of sibling findings across European samples, by suggesting that children's perceptions of their sibling relationships are relatively similar across two Western countries.

In contrast to these cross-country similarities, Asian and European children's reports of the quality of their sibling relationships differed substantially. Asian children's reports of conflict with a sibling were approximately half a standard deviation (a difference equivalent to a medium effect size) lower than those from European children, and Asian children's reports of companionship, intimate disclosure and warmth with a sibling were approximately half a standard deviation higher than those for European children. These results extend previous anthropological studies of traditional South Asian cultures (Kolenda, 1993), and more recent cross-cultural work comparing children living in the United States and Indonesia (French et al., 2001), by demonstrating differences between children of Asian and European descent even when both groups live in a Western nation.

The clear differences between these two cultural groups in both countries are, in some ways, surprising, as the Asian children in the United Kingdom and New Zealand came from quite different ethnic backgrounds. The British Asian children were primarily of South Asian heritage, while the New Zealand Asian sample was more diverse, encompassing 13 different cultural groups. The cultural contrasts observed may, therefore, reflect general differences in roles and values surrounding family relationships associated with collectivism versus individualism rather than characteristics of a specific ethnic group. For example, Markus and Kitayama (1991) have proposed that individuals from collectivist cultures hold an interdependent construal of the self as part of a larger social system, thus valuing harmony and cohesion in social relationships, while individuals from individualistic cultures view the self as independent from others, and therefore as stable across social relationships and contexts. This is, of course, not to say that sibling relationships are necessarily homogenous within different collectivist cultures, however, and more fine-grained research is needed to explore differences in sibling relationships within specific cultural groups.

Cultural differences in the correlates of sibling relationship quality

Chapter 3 explored how characteristics of children and the dyad, such as age, gender, age gap and temperament, influence the quality of sibling relationships, but are these influences universal? As discussed earlier, mono-cultural research has suggested that in Latin American and African American families predictors of sibling relationship quality are broadly similar to those in European families, although additional factors such as the endorsement of cultural values about the family and ethnic identity may also be important. However, mono-cultural research does not allow for the comparison of the relative strength of these influences between cultures. In French et al.'s (2001) study of Indonesian and American children, effects of age and gender were similar for children from both cultures, except that among Indonesian but not American children reports of sibling conflict were higher for secondary- than for primary-school children. Similarly, in Voorpostel and Schans' (2011) research with adults from different ethnic groups within the Netherlands few cultural differences in the effects of gender on sibling relationships emerged, but sibling relationship quality varied with the relative age of the sibling (i.e., whether the sibling was older or younger than the respondent) in different ways between ethnic groups.

In our own study (White et al., 2017) children from both countries and cultures reported less intimate disclosure and more conflict with a younger sibling than with an older sibling, but gender differences varied with culture. Specifically, for European (but not Asian) children, girls reported higher levels of sibling warmth than boys. The cultural specificity of this gender difference in sibling warmth may suggest that the emphasis on cohesive and amicable family relationships in Asian cultures overrides gender differences in social relationships such that Asian boys' sibling relationships are as positive as girls' sibling relationships. Alternatively, differing cultural norms and values may mean that Asian boys feel more comfortable than European boys in *reporting* affection for their sibling. Clearly then there is a great need for further cross-cultural work to examine the correlates of sibling relationship quality in different groups, and the use of observations and interviews may be critical to fully understanding the *meaning* of cultural contrasts.

Conclusions

The sparse literature on cultural differences in sibling relationships discussed in this chapter present a convincing argument of the need to expand the study of siblings beyond a European Western context. A lifespan perspective will be particularly important in this endeavour, as cultural differences may be particularly evident at certain life stages. For example, Seymour's (1993) observation that new babies were incorporated into family life with very little special attention in an Eastern Indian community suggests that firstborns' experiences of the transition to siblinghood may vary widely in different cultural contexts. Another important step in understanding cultural differences in sibling relationships will be to use observations and interviews in addition to self-report measures. As well as ensuring that cross-cultural differences do not simply represent differential susceptibility to demand characteristics, observational methods and interviews may help us understand whether there are specific behaviours that foster positive sibling relationships within different cultures, and provide insight into the *meaning* of cross-cultural differences. In sum, while research into cross-cultural variation in sibling relationships is in its infancy, this topic provides many exciting avenues for future research, that with increased globalisation are likely to have increasing relevance for public policy.

Take-home messages

1. The definition of a sibling varies with culture.
2. In contemporary Western cultures there are few culturally prescribed expectations surrounding sibling relationships, and social obligations between siblings are minimal.
3. Anthropological studies suggest that in traditional non-Western cultures children play an active role in their siblings' lives. In particular, older children often play a large role in teaching and socialising younger siblings.

4. In traditional non-Western cultures, obligations between siblings often extend into adulthood. For example, brothers may be expected to provide a dowry for their sister and help choose a spouse.

5. Research within ethnic minority groups in the United States suggests that there are similar associations between the quality of sibling relationships and child and family characteristics as in White ethnic majority groups. Ethnic identity, cultural values surrounding the family and the family's experience of discrimination are also important for relationship quality in these groups.

6. Although scarce, cross-cultural studies indicate group differences in several aspects of children's sibling relationships, but studies have been limited to specific cultural groups.

7. However, the lack of studies establishing measurement invariance before comparing groups makes it difficult to gauge the robustness of cross-cultural findings.

8. One new study that included analyses to establish measurement invariance, found no differences in children's reports of sibling relationship quality between children living in the United Kingdom versus New Zealand, suggesting similarities between sibling relationships in different Westernised cultures.

9. In contrast, this study showed large cultural contrasts in sibling relationship quality. Specifically, Asian children reported more positive and less conflictual relationships with their sibling than European children in both the United Kingdom and New Zealand.

10. Cultural contrasts in the correlates of sibling relationships also deserve note. One study of school-aged children reported gender differences in sibling warmth among European children but not Asian children, while a study of adults from different ethnic groups in the Netherlands suggested cultural differences in the influence of birth order on sibling relationship quality. Further observational and qualitative research is required to understand the meaning of such contrasts.

References

Beals, A., & Esson, M. (1993). Siblings in North America and South Asia. In C. Nuckolls (Ed.), *Siblings in South Asia: Brothers and sisters in cultural context* (pp. 71–101). New York: Guilford Press.

Brody, G. H., Stoneman, Z., Smith, T., & Gibson, N. M. (1999). Sibling relationships in rural African American families. *Journal of Marriage and the Family, 61*, 1046–1056. doi:10.2307/354023.

Bronfenbrenner, U. (1979). *The ecology of human development: Experiments by nature and design.* Cambridge, MA: Harvard University Press.

Brown, T. (2006). *Confirmatory factor analysis for applied research.* New York: The Guilford Press.

Bryant, B. (1989). The child's perspective of sibling caretaking and its relevance to understanding social-emotional functioning and development. In P. Zukow (Ed.), *Sibling interaction across cultures: Theoretical and methodological issues* (pp. 143–164). New York: Springer-Verlag.

Buist, K. L., Paalman, C. H., Branje, S. J. T., Deković, M., Reitz, E., Verhoeven, M., Meeus, W. H., Koot, H. M., & Hale, W. W. (2013). Longitudinal effects of sibling relationship quality on adolescent problem behavior: A cross-ethnic comparison. *Cultural Diversity and Ethnic Minority Psychology, 20*, 266–275 doi:10.1037/a0033675.

Chen, F. (2008). What happens if we compare chopsticks with forks? The impact of making inappropriate comparisons in cross-cultural research. *Journal of Personality and Social Psychology, 95*, 1005–1018. doi:10.1037/a0013193.

Cicirelli, V. (1994). Sibling relationships in cross-cultural perspective. *Journal of Marriage and Family, 56*, 7–20. doi:10.2307/352697

Correa-Chávez, M., & Rogoff, B. (2009). Children's attention to interactions directed to others: Guatemalan Mayan and European American patterns. *Developmental Psychology, 45*, 630–641. doi: 10.1037/a0014144.

Davidoff, L. (2012). *Thicker than water: Siblings and their relations 1780–1920.* Oxford, UK: Oxford University Press.

de Munck, V. (1993). The dialectics and norms of self interest: Cross-siblings in a Sri Lankan Muslim community. In C. Nuckolls (Ed.), *Siblings in South Asia: Brothers and sisters in cultural context* (143–162). New York: Guilford Press.

Falbo, T., & Hooper, S. Y. (2015). China's only children and psychopathology: A quantitative synthesis. *American Journal of Orthopsychiatry, 85*, 259–274. doi: 10.1037/ort0000058.

Firth, R. (1970). Sibling terms in Polynesia. *The Journal of the Polynesian Society, 79*, 272–287.

French, D. C., Rianasari, M., Pidada, S., Nelwan, P., & Buhrmester, D. (2001). Social support of Indonesian and U.S. children and adolescents by family members and friends. *Merrill-Palmer Quarterly, 47*, 377–394. doi:10.1353/mpq.2001.0015.

Furman, W., & Buhrmester, D. (1985). Children's perceptions of the personal relationships in their social networks. *Developmental Psychology, 21,* 1016–1024. doi: 10.1037/0012-1649.21.6.1016.

Gamble, W. C., & Yu, J. J. (2014). Young children's sibling relationship interactional types: Associations with family characteristics, parenting, and child characteristics. *Early Education & Development, 25*, 223–239. doi: 10.1080/10409289.2013.788434.

Hecht, J. (1983). The cultural contexts of siblingship in Pukapuka. In M. Marshall (Ed.), *Siblingship in Oceania: Studies in the meaning of kin relations* (pp. 53–77). Lanham, MD: University Press of America.

Howe, N., Della Porta, S., Recchia, H., Funamoto, A., & Ross, H. (2015). "This bird can't do it 'cause this bird doesn't swim in water": Sibling teaching during naturalistic home observations in early childhood. *Journal of Cognition and Development, 16*, 314–332. doi: 10.1080/15248372.2013.848869.

Humes, K. R., Jones, N. A., & Ramirez, R. R. (2011). *Overview of race and Hispanic origin: 2010.* United States Census Bureau. Retrieved from http://www.census.gov/content/dam/Census/library/publications/2011/dec/c2010br-02.pdf.

Jiao, S., Ji, G., & Jing, Q. (1986). Comparative study of behavioral qualities of only children and sibling children. *Child Development, 57*, 357–361. doi:10.2307/1130591.

Karcher, M., & Sass, D. (2010). A multicultural assessment of adolescent connectedness: Testing measurement invariance across gender and ethnicity. *Journal of Counseling Psychology, 57*, 274–289. doi:10.1037/a0019357.

Killoren, S. E., Thayer, S. M., & Updegraff, K. A. (2008). Conflict resolution between Mexican origin adolescent siblings. *Journal of Marriage and Family, 70*, 1200–1212. doi:10.1111/j.1741-3737.2008.00560.x.

Kirkpatrick, J. (1983). Meanings of siblingship in Marquesan society. In M. Marshall (Ed.), *Siblingship in Oceania: Studies in the meaning of kin relations* (pp. 17–51). Lanham, MD: University Press of America.

Kolenda, P. (1993). Sibling relations and marriage practices: A comparison of North, Central, and South India. In C. Nuckolls (Ed.), *Siblings in South Asia: Brothers and sisters in cultural context* (pp. 103–141). New York: Guilford Press.

Lee, M.-H. (2012). The one-child policy and gender equality in education in China: Evidence from household data. *Journal of Family and Economic Issues, 33*, 41–52. doi:10.1007/s10834-011-9277-9.

Liu, R. X., Lin, W., & Chen, Z.Y. (2010). School performance, peer association, psychological and behavioral adjustments: A comparison between Chinese adolescents with and without siblings. *Journal of Adolescence, 33*, 411–417. doi: 0.1016/j.adolescence.2009.07.007.

McGuire, S., & Shanahan, L. (2010). Sibling experiences in diverse family contexts. *Child Development Perspectives, 4*, 72–79. doi:10.1111/j.1750-8606.2010.00121.x

McHale, S. M., Whiteman, S. D., Kim, J.-Y., & Crouter, A. C. (2007). Characteristics and correlates of sibling relationships in two-parent African American families. *Journal of Family Psychology, 21*, 227–235. doi:10.1037/0893-3200.21.2.227.

Markus, H., & Kitayama, S. (1991). Culture and the self: Implications for cognition, emotion, and motivation. *Psychological Review, 98*, 224–253. doi:10.1037/0033-295X.98.2.224.

Nuckolls, C. (1993). An introduction to the cross-cultural study of sibling relations. In C. Nuckolls (Ed.), *Siblings in South Asia: Brothers and sisters in cultural context* (pp. 19–41). New York: Guilford Press.

Podmore, V. N., & St. George, R. (1986). New Zealand Maori and European mothers and their 3-year-old children: Interactive behaviors in pre-school settings. *Journal of Applied Developmental Psychology, 7*, 373–382. doi:10.1016/0193-3973(86)90006-7.

Riedmann, A., & White, L. (1996). Adult sibling relationships: Racial and ethnic comparisons. In G. Brody (Ed.), *Sibling relationships: Their causes and consequences* (pp. 105–126). Norwood, NJ: Ablex.

Rubinstein, R. (1983). Siblings in Malo culture. In M. Marshall (Ed.), *Siblingship in Oceania: Studies in the meaning of kin relations* (pp. 307–344). Lanham, MD: University Press of America.

Seymour, S. (1993). Sociocultural contexts: Examining sibling roles in South Asia. In C. Nuckolls (Ed.), *Siblings in South Asia: Brothers and sisters in cultural context* (pp. 45–69). New York: Guilford Press.

Updegraff, K., McHale, S., Whiteman, S., Thayer, S., & Delgado, M. (2005). Adolescent sibling relationships in Mexican American families: Exploring the role of familism. *Journal of Family Psychology, 19*, 512–522. doi:10.1037/0893-3200.19.4.512.

Voorpostel, M., & Schans, D. (2011). Sibling relationships in Dutch and immigrant families. *Ethnic and Racial Studies, 34*, 2027–2047. doi:10.1080/01419870.2010.496490.

Watson-Gegeo, K., & Gegeo, D. (1989). The role of sibling interaction in child socialization. In P. Zukow (Ed.), *Sibling interaction across cultures: Theoretical and methodological issues* (pp. 54–76). New York: Springer-Verlag.

Wenger, M. (1989). Work, play, and social relationships among children in a Giriama community. In D. Belle (Ed.), *Children's social networks amd social supports* (pp. 91–115). New York: Wiley Interscience.

White, N., Darshane, N., & Hughes, C. (2017). *Pre-adolescents' perceptions of their sibling relationship: Comparisons of Asian and European children in two countries.* Manuscript in preparation.

Whittemore, R., & Beverly, E. (1989). Trust in the Mandinka way: The cultural context of sibling care. In P. Zukow (Ed.), *Sibling interaction across cultures: Theoretical and methodological issues* (pp. 26–53). New York: Springer-Verlag.

Yang, B., Ollendick, T., Dong, Q., Xia, Y., & Lin, L. (1995). Only children and children with siblings in the People's Republic of China: Levels of fear, anxiety, and depression. *Child Development, 66,* 1301–1311. doi: 10.1111/j.1467-8624.1995.tb00936.x.

10

SIBLING RELATIONSHIPS AND SOCIETAL CHANGES

Looking back and looking forward

The second chapter in this book noted the contrast between early views of the transition to siblinghood as a time of trauma and current views in which the emphasis is on young children's resilience. As we argued, one reason for this shift is that medical advances across the twentieth and twenty-first century and related shifts in parental attitudes have transformed children's experiences such that the positives of becoming a sibling often (and perhaps typically) outweigh the accompanying challenges. As a parallel to this argument, in the current chapter we consider whether family life and hence, by implication, sibling relationships have been transformed by societal and technological changes over the 40 years since Dunn's seminal observational work (e.g., Dunn & Kendrick, 1982). Note that Golombok's (2015) groundbreaking volume *Modern Families* provides a broader discussion of the nature and impact of new family forms on children's adjustment and experiences of parenting.

Studies of historical shifts in parent behaviour indicate that relatively short periods of time can produce observable changes in parent-child interactions. For example, in a comparison of German mothers and three-month-old infants in two cohorts separated by just six years, Keller, Borke, Yovsi, Lohaus and Jensen (2005) reported significant contrasts in both play with toys (which increased over time) and in physical contact (which decreased over time). The relative scarcity of studies of siblings makes it difficult to make analogous direct comparisons of historical changes in sibling interactions, but this report of shifts in the relative frequency of different types of parent-child interactions highlights the likelihood of parallel changes over time in how brothers and sisters interact with each other.

Perhaps the most obvious change in family life over the past few decades is the rising prominence of screens and digital devices. As stated in a national open letter published in *The Guardian* (https://www.theguardian.com/science/head-quarters/2017/jan/06/screen-time-guidelines-need-to-be-built-on-evidence-not-hype) and signed by an international group of scientists working in the field, children's increasing use of technology at home requires evidence-based policies. At present, very little is known about how exposure to screens might affect children's development, adjustment or relationships. In perhaps the only study to address this question in relation to sibling relationships, Coyne, Jensen, Smith and Erickson (2016) surveyed 508 adolescents about their sibling relationships and their separate and shared use of video games. Just over half of this sample reported playing video games with their sibling, at least occasionally. The overall time spent playing video games was associated with lower levels of sibling affection, but the causal direction of this cross-sectional association is unclear.

Shared video play, however, was associated with increased sibling affection, for both boys and girls. Interestingly, among brothers, shared video play was, overall, associated with increased conflict but shared play on violent video games was associated with decreased conflict. In seeking to explain this rather puzzling finding, the authors note that in some of these games siblings can work cooperatively to defeat a common enemy: cooperative play on violent video games has been reported to increase cooperative behaviour (Ewoldsen et al., 2012). Clearly, much more fine-grained work is needed to elucidate the ways in which technology affects sibling interactions. This is therefore an important area for future research.

Another clear change in family life over the past few decades is the rising numbers of single-parent families and stepfamilies. We therefore begin by considering whether sibling relationships differ across different family types. Other important changes in family life over the past 40 years can be traced back to the dramatic growth of women's involvement in the workforce and so this chapter also discusses the impact of delayed childbearing on sibling relationships, through its effect on fertility and family size. Also linked to the rapid rise in dual-earner families is a (smaller) increase in fathers' involvement in childcare and in household chores. In Chapter 2, we saw that fathers' involvement was a key predictor of firstborn children's ability to make a successful transition to becoming a sibling. In this chapter, we provide a brief discussion of how shifts in gender roles appear to affect sibling relationships. Finally, we identify new questions that emerge from the recognition of changes and increased diversity in the nature of family life and that deserve close attention in future research.

Does the quality of sibling relationships vary with family structure?

Numerous studies have examined how parental divorce, remarriage and interparental conflict affect parent-child relationships, but the impact of family change and family structure on sibling relationships has been much less studied. As shown in Chapter 7, siblings can be a source of stress, such that sibling conflict is a good predictor of later maladjustment (e.g., Buist, Deković, & Prinzie, 2013). Equally, siblings can serve as sources of support in difficult times, such as during parental divorce (e.g., Hetherington & Clingempeel, 1992; Jacobs & Sillars, 2012). That said, evidence from the Avon Brothers and Sisters Study (which is nested within the large-scale Avon Longitudinal Study of Parents and Children, ALSPAC) indicates that, relative to children in intact "biological" families, children in stepmother/

complex stepfamilies and single-parent families show elevated rates of behavioural and emotional problems (O'Connor, Dunn, Jenkins, Pickering, & Rasbash, 2001). Importantly, this contrast in adjustment was not evident for children in simple stepfather families and, within the more complex family forms, was accompanied by marked within-family variation. Together, these findings highlight individual differences in children's resilience in the face of (potentially) stressful changes in family living arrangements.

The focus of this section, however, is on a related but distinct question, namely whether (and how) sibling *relationships* are affected by different kinds of family structure. Two studies that have addressed this question directly deserve particular mention. Noller, Feeney, Sheehan, Darlington and Rogers (2009) found that adolescents in separated/divorced families reported more conflict in all family relationships (partner, parent-child, sibling) than did adolescents in married families, lending support for the process of spillover in family relationships discussed in Chapter 4. In contrast, analyses of data from the Avon Brothers and Sisters Study when the target children were five years old suggest no significant differences in sibling negativity or positivity across intact versus stepfamilies, but elevated levels of sibling conflict and aggression in children from single-mother families (Deater-Deckard, Dunn, & Lussier, 2002).

While it is of course possible that the contrast between the findings from the two studies above simply reflects developmental differences between the two samples, it is nevertheless worth considering what might underpin the elevated sibling conflict in single-mother families reported by Deater-Deckard and colleagues (2002). Echoing the findings from families raising a child with a disability (discussed in Chapter 8), one simple explanation is that the contrast in sibling conflict reflects the elevated stress and reduced resources in single-mother households. Another account hinges on the possibility that children in single-mother families are more likely to have recent experiences of acute parental conflict. Future studies should therefore adopt a longitudinal design in order to establish the stability (or otherwise) of elevated sibling conflict in single-mother families. Indeed, underscoring the need for caution in interpreting contrasts across different types of family structure, a recent study of mother-child relationships and child adjustment in "single mother by choice" families demonstrates that single motherhood does not in itself result in psychological problems for children (Golombok, Zadeh, Imrie, Smith, & Freeman, 2016).

Returning to the Avon Brothers and Sisters study, Deater-Deckard et al. (2002) also found that, in general, full siblings were more negative than half or stepsiblings. While this contrast might reflect a difference in levels of engagement in the sibling relationship there was not a corresponding group difference in sibling positivity. As Deater-Deckard et al. (2002) note, this asymmetry highlights the need for positivity and negativity in sibling relationships to be studied separately (rather than as opposite poles of a single dimension). The lack of group difference in relation to sibling positivity also suggests that temperament, personality, empathy and emotional understanding are stronger than family context as predictors of sibling positivity.

Finally, Deater-Deckard et al. (2002) also found that the link between sibling relationship quality and adjustment did not depend on the degree of genetic relatedness but did vary by family type (and was strongest in intact families). This conclusion echoes the results from the larger ALSPAC sample of 3,681 sibling pairs. Specifically, by tracking this large and representative community sample over four years, Dunn, Deater-Deckard, Pickering and Golding (1999) were able to show that while social adversity and parent-child negativity predicted sibling conflict in a similar way for non-step and stepfamilies, mother-partner hostility was only related to sibling relationship quality in non-step families (perhaps because siblings may have ambivalent feelings towards the stepparent, and thus be less distressed by parental conflict). Building on this theme of social adversity, in the next section we turn to the small but growing literature on the special case of siblings who are separated or kept together as they navigate their way through the system of state care (i.e., "looked after" children), focusing on the largest group of children who enter foster care or become adopted.

Sibling relationships in foster and adoptive families

Each year, 0.6% of children in the United Kingdom and the United States are looked after by the state: 90,000 from a total of 15 million children in the United Kingdom and 400,000 from a total of 70 million children in the United States (Herrick and Piccus, 2005; Jones, 2015). Approximately two thirds of these children have siblings who are also in state care, but nearly half of these looked-after children are separated from at least one of their siblings (Casey Family Programs National Center for Resource Family Support, 2003). Echoing earlier findings that siblings can provide a much-needed source of support and stability during times of stress (see Chapter 7), the evidence suggests that co-locating siblings results in more stable placements that will give better child outcomes (Hegar, 2005; Hegar & Rosenthal, 2011; Herrick & Piccus, 2005), especially for girls (Tarren-Sweeney & Hazell, 2005).

The buffering effects of co-location noted above justify concerns about the relatively high proportions of children who are separated from their siblings as well as from their biological parents and raise questions about the barriers to co-location of siblings in care. Sadly, one barrier is simply that many child welfare workers see preserving the sibling bond as a low priority (Herrick & Piccus, 2005). Even when social workers are committed to co-locating siblings, however, this can be difficult, especially for larger groups of siblings. In addition, individual siblings may come into the care system at different points in time, making it difficult to balance the twin aims of stability and co-location (Hegar & Rosenthal, 2009). In response to this challenge, recent decades have seen a rise in kinship foster care as an alternative to traditional fostering arrangements. However, although kinship care is often valued by children (Chapman et al., 2004), traditional foster care is typically associated with better outcomes in terms of adult-rated behavioural adjustment (e.g., Hegar & Rosenthal, 2009), perhaps because families are carefully selected as likely to offer sensitive and consistent parenting.

Co-locating siblings within traditional foster care arrangements may therefore provide the best of both worlds, in maximising both contact with kin and the prospect of developing secure attachment relationships. In partial support of this hypothesis, Hegar and Rosenthal (2009) examined data from 1,415 children in the National Study of Child and Adolescent Well-Being in the United States and found that children placed with a sibling took significantly less time to feel settled and happy with their new family living arrangements.

As discussed later in the chapter, there are marked individual differences in how children define "sibling". As a result, more work is needed to incorporate less traditional definitions of siblings in order to gain a fuller understanding of the experiences of children in foster care. With this goal in mind, Lery, Shaw and Magruder (2005) have compared four different methods of identifying siblings (via the children, their mothers, their fathers and through removal addresses) and found that adopting multiple strategies led to the identification of larger sets of siblings and so increased the possibility of placing a child with one or more siblings.

Qualitative studies also highlight reliance upon siblings as a consistent theme in interviews with fostered children, although a closer look suggests a more nuanced picture: alongside references to siblings as a source of identity and belonging, children also worried about the well-being of siblings (Harrison, 1999). Of course, children are not necessarily happiest when placed together with siblings in a new family. Sibling conflict, competition for adult attention, physical or sexual risk, disproportionate levels of responsibility for a sibling and lack of an established relationship are all complicating factors that need to be considered carefully in making decisions about the importance of co-location (McCormick, 2010).

Another important yet hitherto neglected concern relates to the impact of placements on foster parents' biological children. As noted by Höjer (2007), while foster care is often preferred to institutional care because it offers valuable opportunities for a child to achieve "normality", it should be recognised that these placements also make life less "ordinary" for the sons and daughters of foster carers. In particular, some of the privacy of the home is lost in order to succeed in the public task of foster care. Sons and daughters of foster carers may also take on responsibilities towards foster siblings, or develop close relationships with them, only to have these ruptured when the foster child moves to another family. In a more recent review of the international literature, Höjer, Sebba & Luke (2013) offer a number of key take-home messages. These concerned: (a) the importance of involving children in the decision to foster; (b) keeping children informed about the nature of fostering, perhaps using peer network support groups; (c) foster carers devoting regular "protected" time to their biological children; (d) ensuring that younger children are not overloaded with unwanted information; (e) providing a channel of communication for children to express their own difficulties and ensuring that these are treated as valid concerns; and finally (f) preparing children for the end of a foster placement.

Delayed childbearing and the rise of the only child

In the United States, between 1970 and 2006, the percentage of women having a first child above the age of 35 years increased nearly eightfold (from one in 100 to approimately one in 12; Mathews & Hamilton, 2009). This shift towards delayed parenthood has continued in the past decade: for example, in 2014 the UK Office of National Statistics reported that for the first time, more babies in the United Kingdom were born to mothers over 35 than to mothers under 25 (21% versus 20% respectively; Office for National Statistics, 2014). Together, these trends provide an interesting counterpoint to the view, common in today's media, that children today are growing up too fast and indeed raise a different set of concerns about reproductive fitness.

Specifically, depletion and ageing of egg cells mean that, biologically, the optimal period for a woman to have children is between ages 18 and 30 years (Te Velde & Pearson, 2002) and so from this perspective the rise of delayed parenthood is worrying. Recently, a Dutch team of researchers (Habbema, Eijkemans, Leridon, & Te Velde, 2015) have modelled age-related declines in success rates for couples trying for a baby. Reassuringly, for couples happy with just one child their results indicated a 75% chance of success at age 37 (and a 50% chance of success at age 41). However, to have a 90% chance of having two children their results indicated that couples should start to try to conceive by age 31 (with IVF) or by age 27 (with no IVF) and three to four years sooner for couples hoping for a three-child family. Clearly then, an almost inevitable consequence of the delayed onset of parenthood is an increase over time in the proportion of children growing up without siblings. In the section below, we therefore summarise the evidence on whether this matters for children's development and well-being.

What is the impact of being an only child?

As noted in Chapter 9 in relation to China's one-child policy, only children have historically been viewed in a negative light. In the late 1800s, the American psychologist, G. Stanley Hall famously likened being an only child to "a disease in itself" (Fenton, 1928, p. 547). Similar concerns about the impact of being raised as an only child were subsequently voiced by other psychologists (Brill, 1922; Fenton, 1928), who emphasised the dangers of over-indulgent parenting for children's adjustment, autonomy and capacity for altruism. These beliefs about only children were also in line with public opinion through much of the twentieth century. In a large-scale survey conducted in 1972, 80% of White Americans indicated that they thought only children were disadvantaged (Blake, 1974). Historically, these negative views may have arisen due to external factors that influenced the likelihood of having a one-child family: for example, Falbo (1982) argued that factors such as marital instability, parental death and economic hardship contributed to the likelihood of families having just one child. Although negative views of only children were widespread (and continue to this day to some extent), a meta-analysis of psychological evidence does not support the view that only children are worse off than children with siblings (Falbo & Polit, 1986). Specifically, only children do not appear disadvantaged in terms of achievement, intelligence, adjustment, sociability or personality; indeed, outcomes for only children are typically better than those for children from large families.

More recently several studies have examined whether one-child families differ from multiple-child families in the extent to which they enjoy social support from close personal relationships with other family members. In the United States, Trent and Spitze (2011) analysed data from the National Survey of Families & Households ($N = 13,007$) and reported that, compared with adults who grew up with siblings, those who grew up without siblings engaged in fewer social activities with relatives (a mean difference of seven visits per year), with this difference being particularly clear for those who didn't grow up with both parents. The authors note, however, that this contrast may reflect the fact that individuals who grew up without siblings tend to have fewer relatives than children who grew up with siblings, rather than a group differences in sociability. In support of this view, Trent and Spitze (2011) found no group differences in the frequency of social activities with non-relatives (e.g., neighbours, friends and co-workers).

In contrast, using data from 25 different countries, Gondal (2012) showed that, across countries, individuals raised as single children had smaller and less personal social support networks as adults and relied more heavily on their parents and neighbours for financial support. In short, falling fertility rates appear linked to a changing pattern of social support in which parental roles are more sustained (if only as a source of instrumental rather than emotional support). Linked to this theme of ripple effects on social relationships, other researchers have investigated whether children raised without siblings are at increased risk of peer victimisation. Supporting this view, a survey of 2,552 Spanish adolescents showed that, on average, rates of peer victimisation were higher for children without siblings and for children with four or more siblings (Piñero-Ruiz, López-Espín, Cerezo, & Torres-Cantero, 2012). What is not clear, however, is whether these group differences reflect contrasts in the objective frequency of victimisation, or in children's interpretations of challenging experiences with peers.

Overall, however, the results from a broad range of studies of sibling status appear somewhat equivocal and highlight the difficulties in drawing causal conclusions about the outcomes associated with being a sibling. Falbo, Kim and Chen (2009) examined the effects of sibling status on health in later life and concluded that there were no differences between only children and children with siblings once socio-economic status, adolescent aptitude and educational achievement were taken into account. Moreover, as we hope the previous chapters have made clear, sibling relationships show striking contrasts in quality, such that it is almost certainly a mistake for studies to rely on simple markers such as the presence or absence of a sibling.

Does family size affect sibling relationship quality?

Coupled with the general shift towards delaying parenthood, age-related declines in fertility mean that families are getting smaller. That said, the advent of birth control, does mean that to some extent at least, parents have been able to choose the number of children in their family. This choice raises the question of how well the saying "the more the merrier" applies to sibling relationships. Early theoretical work by

Rosenberg (1982) indicated that children might indeed benefit socially from growing up alongside several siblings, the argument being that this social milieu has the advantages of multiple role models, reduced general anxiety in parents and children and reduced likelihood of either adults or individual children having inappropriate levels of social dominance.

At an empirical level, however, these ideas have proved very difficult to test. In a review of this field, Newman (1996) concluded that there is at least some evidential support for the notion that ties of affection are stronger in larger families, but noted that much of this evidence comes from studies involving college students, raising obvious concerns about the extent to which retrospective reports evoke rose-tinted memories. Underscoring this view, other researchers have suggested that sibling conflict may be more frequent in larger families, because siblings may compete for more limited resources (Goodwin & Roscoe, 1990). Perhaps then a fairer conclusion is that there are both positives and negatives associated with growing up in a large family, and the relative salience of each may depend both on what aspects of relationship quality are in focus and on when the questions are asked.

Overall, the above findings suggest that the answer to any question about the benefits of larger families is likely to include an element of "swings and roundabouts". It may also be that the benefits vary for different family types. In particular, there may be a different set of considerations in play in families raising a child with a disability. For example, in a study of relationships in families raising a child with a hearing impairment, Bat-Chava and Martin (2002) noted that larger families were, on average, characterised by more positive sibling relationships. More significantly, however, both the overall scarcity of direct evidence and the prevalence of confounding factors (e.g., socioeconomic status, ethnicity, religious affiliation) mean that the evidence base is simply not strong enough to warrant any clear conclusions.

Does parental division of household work affect sibling relationships?

Chapter 4 of this book was devoted to family systems theory, which highlights the interconnected nature of family relationships, through processes such as spillover or compensation. However, much of the burden of parenting is linked to more general household chores (cooking, cleaning, shopping, managing finances etc.) and thus the extent to which these chores are shared equitably between parents may also contribute to parents' well-being and hence have an indirect effect upon sibling relationship quality.

Even for couples with relatively progressive values, the transition to parenthood typically sees a strengthening of the traditional division of labour, as women take on more unpaid work and men take on more paid work (e.g., Craig, 2006; Sayer, 2005). As documented by Neilson and Stanfors (2013), in Nordic countries this pattern changed in the 1990s, however, such that parenthood began to affect men and women more similarly. In a subsequent large-scale analysis of between-country contrasts in how parents spend their time (on weekdays and at weekends), Neilson and Stanfors (2014) used data from more than 50,000 respondents in Germany, Italy and Canada to show that, for weekdays at least, parenthood in these three countries continues to reinforce traditional divisions of labour. That said, the same data set also showed that fathers in Germany and Canada (but not Italy) were becoming more involved in domestic work at the weekends.

Several studies have shown that more egalitarian division of household chores is linked to greater satisfaction in marital relationships (e.g., Ozer, Barnett, Brennan, & Sperling, 1998) and that this association is at least in part explained by perceptions of fairness (e.g., Mikula, Riederer, & Bodi, 2012). Moreover, the extent to which fathers are involved in childcare has also been shown to relate to positive child outcomes, such as self-esteem, academic achievement and adjustment (e.g., Deutsch, Servis, & Payne, 2001; Wilson & Prior, 2011). More recently, Dawson, Pike and Bird (2015) adopted a cross-informant design and reported that sibling relationship quality was also associated with more egalitarian division of parental chores. Interestingly, while parents' gender-related attitudes were also assessed in this study, these proved unrelated to sibling relationship quality. Thus, it is parents' actual behaviour rather than their attitudes that appears influential for sibling relationship quality. Further, this association between the division of household tasks and sibling relationship quality was not a result of changes in the marital or parent-child relationship. In discussing this latter finding, Dawson et al. (2015) offer the tentative suggestion that parental cooperation in household tasks provides a direct model for siblings to adopt when interacting together. This intriguing proposal is a promising avenue for future research, ideally within a longitudinal design and a sample of sufficient size and diversity to examine how cultural and socioeconomic differences may influence the strength of this modelling effect. For now, however, the reader may be interested in an excerpt of a conversation (taken from Dunn & Hughes, 2014), which follows a dispute between an older sibling, David, and his 36-month-old sister, Megan, who are trying to draw their mother into a tug-of-war dispute over Megan's toy vacuum cleaner, which David has just managed to repair.

David to Mother:	I wanted to do it. Because I fixed it up. And made it work.
Mother to David:	Well, you'll have to wait your turn.
Megan to Mother:	– switched.
Mother to Megan:	Are you going to let David have a turn?
Megan to Mother:	I have to do it. Ladies do it.
Mother to Megan:	Yes, ladies do it. Yes, and men do it sometimes. Daddy sometimes does the hoovering, doesn't he?
Megan to Mother:	But I do it sometimes
Mother to Megan:	Yes, but Daddy does it sometimes, so you let David do it. (p. 36)

While this excerpt provides a neat example of how competition between siblings may serve to accelerate younger siblings' cognitive development (at 36 months, Megan's appeal to gender roles is quite mature), it is also worth noting that the mother counters Megan's gendered argument with a point about the overlap between mothers' and fathers' responsibilities – indirectly then, the sibling dispute serves as a "pedagogical moment", to coin a phrase used by educationalists. Second, it is the father's involvement in household chores that enables the mother to introduce this more advanced view of gender roles to her children in a way that is accessible and concrete, providing another example of the complex interplay between family influences on children's development. Complexity is also a clear motif in the next two sections of this chapter, in which we provide a brief outline of how the rise of "modern families" may influence the nature of sibling relationships.

Siblings and gamete donation

Falling fertility rates have, alongside the rapid increase in more diverse family forms (e.g., same-sex parent families) resulted in growing demand for gamete donation as a means of starting a family. In addition, legal changes (related to more open adoption procedures) now give individuals the right to know the identity of their donor parent. This in turn has had some unexpected consequences. For example, in a survey of 587 parents with donor conceived children, Hertz and Mattes (2011) showed that the internet is altering how kinship is discovered and formed. Further support for this view comes from the finding that a growing number of adolescents and young adults conceived via egg or sperm donation have begun to seek contact with their "donor siblings" (e.g., Freeman, Jadva, Kramer, & Golombok, 2009).

At this point it is worth noting that there is very little regulation of the maximum number of births from any one sperm donor. The guidance from the American Society for Reproductive Medicine states a limit of 25 live births per population area of 850,000, but monitoring and legal enforcement of this guidance is so far lacking (The Practice Committee of the American Society for Reproductive Medicine and the Practice Committee of the Society for Assisted Reproductive Technology, 2013). As a result, one of the many reasons adolescents might want information about their "donor siblings" is to avoid the possibility of incest, although the primary motivation for contact appears to be simple curiosity (Freeman et al., 2009).

In a pioneering study of this phenomenon, Jadva, Freeman, Kramer and Golombok (2010) documented the experiences of 165 offspring of gamete donation who initiated a search for donor siblings and noted that this search was often triggered by key life events, such as becoming a teenager or an adult, getting married, or having children. A similar trigger effect has previously been noted for adopted children (e.g., Crawshaw, 2002). Interestingly, in Jadva et al.'s (2010) study, three quarters of the offspring seeking contact with donor siblings were female, highlighting the potential importance of gender differences in individuals' desire to make contact with siblings. A similar gender difference has been reported for other groups: in a study of adults who had been adopted, Feast and Howe (1997) noted that women appeared more interested than men in searching for their genetic relations. Similarly, a study of children in out-of-home care showed that two thirds of girls, but only two fifths of boys wanted more contact with their siblings (Lundström & Sallnäs, 2012). A direction for future research would therefore be to examine whether women are, in general, more inclusive than men in their definition of sibling.

Another recent study of the experiences of adolescents conceived by sperm donation in contacting and meeting donor siblings highlights the potential benefits of such contact for identity formation (Persaud et al., 2017). Specifically, in-depth interviews with 23 adolescents conceived by sperm donation (and living in lesbian-mother households) showed that contact with donor siblings was typically perceived as either "normal/neutral" or a unique and positive experience that was integrated into their identity. Indeed, more than half of the adolescents reported that they valued being able to get to know individuals who share half of their DNA. For others, particularly those raised without "social siblings" (i.e., siblings growing up together in the same family), this contact with donor siblings provided the opportunity to find someone who could fill a perceived missing role in their family. Interestingly, only a subset of these adolescents expressed an interest in meeting the sperm donor himself, suggesting that they did not feel the absence of a father figure, but were simply interested in meeting others who were not only genetically related to themselves but also shared the rather unique identity associated with donor conception. In short, this research provides a very contemporary example of the way in which siblings can provide support when family circumstances set children apart from their peers.

Complex families lead to more fluid definitions of siblings

As mentioned in relation to foster care, given the growth of complex families, a natural extension to the question of how sibling relationship quality might vary with family size is the question of who counts as a sibling (see also Chapter 9, for cultural differences in definitions of siblinghood). Interestingly, epidemiological data suggests that a substantial proportion of individuals will give different answers to this question at different points in their lifespan. For example, a study of 9,400 adults aged 19 to 95, surveyed across an interval of approximately five years, showed discrepancies in the reported number of siblings for 31% of participants, with figures going up for 15% and down for 16% (White, 1998).

Interestingly, while fluctuations in reported number of siblings were most common among individuals with complex family histories, they were also evident in non-complex families. In other words, some respondents will, if left to their own devices, use widely different definitions of who is a sibling. This fluidity echoes an idea expressed by a famous nursery rhyme character in *Through the Looking Glass*: "'When I use a word,' Humpty Dumpty said, in rather a scornful tone, 'it means just what I choose it to mean – neither more nor less" (Carroll, 1871, p.80). From a research perspective, this lack of consistent definition is problematic. Legal definitions of family relationships (e.g., for the purposes of resolving disputes about the distribution of estates) are more precise: for example, co-residence for a minimum period of two years is typically required to ascribe a parental relationship between a stepparent and stepchild (Glick, 1990). However, for siblings, co-residence appears to be only part of the story. For example, in the Netherlands Kinship Panel Study,

Pollet (2007) found variation in levels of social investment (i.e., contact with, and concern for siblings) between different types of siblings: specifically, levels of investment were highest for full siblings, then maternal half siblings (who were raised together), while paternal half siblings showed the lowest levels of investment. Viewed alongside the minimal effects of sibling status described earlier, this finding highlights the importance of relationship *quality* rather than quantity. As White (1998) concluded, discrepancies are a useful reminder of the ways in which study participants actively define their own families.

In many ways then it appears that, as a society, we have come full circle, with a return to original ideas of kinship reflecting functional as much as biological ties. Nevertheless, our prediction is that sibling relationships will have an enduring importance. Reflecting this, our hope is that research in this field continues to grow and to address fresh topics of societal relevance. Our prediction is that these topics will span the life course. For example, the very beginnings of the sibling relationships are likely to be affected by changes in both reproductive technologies and in social attitudes to new family forms. Likewise, technological solutions to geographical barriers and increases in longevity may each lead to a growing importance of sibling relationships in late adulthood. Between these two extremes, future generations are likely to encounter more turning points (e.g., changes at work and in the home) than in the past, such that sibling relationships may become increasingly important as a source of stability amid the twists and turns of life. Thus, by leading to fresh perspectives, societal changes should add depth and insight to future research on sibling relationships.

Take-home messages

1. The past few decades have seen dramatic increases in children's exposure to TV, DVDs and digital devices, but very little is known about how these might affect sibling relationships. Preliminary findings indicate that playing video games can strengthen sibling relationships but may also induce conflict in some circumstances.

2. Investigations of whether different family structures lead to contrasts in sibling relationship quality have produced mixed results, which may reflect between-study contrasts in mean sample age. For preschoolers, sibling conflict is higher in single-mother households but does not differ between intact and stepfamilies. For older children, sibling relationship quality is less positive in complex families.

3. Findings from studies of children in foster care indicate that co-locating siblings is generally (but not always) beneficial. There is therefore a need to raise awareness among child welfare workers of the ways in which siblings can support each other in times of stress.

4. Very little is known about the impact of foster care on the carers' biological children: while fostering offers a valuable opportunity for looked-after children to achieve a "normal" life, these placements also make life less ordinary for the carers' own children.

5. Secular trends in delaying parenthood are likely to result in more children growing up without siblings. However, existing evidence indicates that children without siblings should not be considered "at risk". It is the quality of the family relationships (rather than the simple presence of a sibling) that is most likely to matter for children's outcomes.

6. However, adolescents without siblings may be at greater risk of peer victimisation and adults without siblings typically show smaller and less personal social networks

7. Likewise, there is not sufficient evidence to draw clear conclusions regarding whether overall family size is related to average contrasts in sibling relationship quality.

8. Slowly but steadily, the division of household chores is becoming more egalitarian. Extending previous work showing benefits of this shift for marital relationships, recent evidence suggests that sibling relationships are more cooperative when fathers contribute more equally to domestic tasks.

9. Delayed parenthood has led to falling fertility rates and a rapidly rising number of children conceived through gamete donation; follow-up studies reveal that these children are at least as interested in finding their donor siblings as in finding their donor parent.

10. The growing complexity of family forms has led to an increased fluidity in definitions of a sibling: co-residence is clearly important, but other factors that affect the functionality of the sibling relationship also appear important.

References

Bat-Chava, Y., & Martin, D. (2002). Sibling relationships of deaf children: The impact of child and family characteristics. *Rehabilitation Psychology, 47*, 73–91. doi:10.1037/0090-5550.47.1.73.

Blake, J. (1974). Can we believe recent data on birth expectations in the United States? *Demography, 11*, 25–44. doi:10.2307/2060697.

Brill, A. A. (1922). *Psychoanalysis – Its theories and practical applications*. Philadelphia: Saunders.

Buist, K. L., Deković, M., & Prinzie, P. (2013). Sibling relationship quality and psychopathology of children and adolescents: A meta-analysis. *Clinical Psychology Review, 33*, 97–106. doi:10.1016/j.cpr.2012.10.007.

Carroll, L. (1871). *Through the looking glass*. London: Puffin Classics.

Casey Family Programs National Center for Resource Family Support. (2003). *Siblings in out-of-home care: An overview*. Retrieved from http://www.hunter.cuny.edu/socwork/nrcfcpp/downloads/sibling_overview.pdf.

Chapman, M.V., Wall, A., Barth, R. P., Biemer, P., Runyan, D., Webb, M., Dowd, K., Griffith, K., Kinsey, S., Weeks, M. Byron, M. Z., Cano, G., Green, R., Herget, D., Langer, M., Liu, J., Lytle, T., McCracken, R., Mierzwa, F., Suresh, R. & Wallace, I. (2004). Children's voices: The perceptions of children in foster care. *American Journal of Orthopsychiatry, 74*, 293–304. doi: 10.1037/0002-9432.74.3.293.

Coyne, S. M., Jensen, A. C., Smith, N. J., & Erickson, D. H. (2016). Super Mario brothers and sisters: Associations between coplaying video games and sibling conflict and affection. *Journal of Adolescence, 47*, 48–59. doi:10.1016/j.adolescence.2015.12.001.

Craig, L. (2006). The money or the care: A comparison of couple and sole parent households' time allocation to work and children. *Australian Journal of Social Issues, 40*, 521–539.

Crawshaw, M. (2002). Lessons from a recent adoption study to identify some of the service needs of, and issues for, donor offspring wanting to know about their donors. *Human Fertility, 5*, 6–12. doi:10.1080/1464727992000199691.

Dawson, A., Pike, A., & Bird, L. (2015). Parental division of household labour and sibling relationship quality: Family relationship mediators. *Infant and Child Development, 24*, 379–393. doi:10.1002/icd.1890.

Deater-Deckard, K., Dunn, J., & Lussier, G. (2002). Sibling relationships and social-emotional adjustment in different family contexts. *Social Development, 11*, 571–590. doi:10.1111/1467-9507.00216.

Deutsch, F. M., Servis, L. J., & Payne, J. D. (2001). Paternal participation in child care and its effects on children's self-esteem and attitudes toward gendered roles. *Journal of Family Issues, 22*, 1000–1024. doi: 10.1177/019251301022008003.

Dunn, J., Deater-Deckard, K., Pickering, K., & Golding, J. (1999). Siblings, parents and partners: Family relationships within a longitudinal community study. *Journal of Child Psychology and Psychiatry, 40*, 1025–1037. doi:10.1111/1469-7610.00521.

Dunn, J., & Hughes, C. (2014). Family talk about moral issues: The toddler and preschool years. In C. Wainryb and H. E. Recchia (Eds.), *Talking about right and wrong: Parent-child conversations as contexts for moral development* (pp. 21–43). New York: Cambridge University Press.

Dunn, J., & Kendrick, C. (1982). *Siblings: Love, envy, and understanding.* London: Grant McIntyre Ltd.

Ewoldsen, D. R., Eno, C. A., Okdie, B. M., Velez, J. A., Guadagno, R. E., & Decoster, J. (2012). Effect of playing violent video games cooperatively or competitively on subsequent cooperative behavior. *Cyberpsychology, Behavior, and Social Networking, 15*, 277–280. doi:10.1089/cyber.2011.0308.

Falbo, T. (1982). Only children in America. In M. Lamb, & B. Sutton-Smith (Eds.), *Sibling relationships: Their nature and significance across the lifespan* (pp. 285–304). Hillsdale, NJ: Lawrence Erlbaum Associates.

Falbo, T., Kim, S., & Chen, K.Y. (2009). Alternate models of sibling status effects on health in later life. *Developmental Psychology, 45*, 677–687. doi:10.1037/a0013941.

Falbo, T., & Polit, D. (1986). A quantitative review of the only child literature: Research evidence and theory development. *Psychological Bulletin, 100*, 176–189. doi:10.1037/0033-2909.100.2.176.

Feast, J., & Howe, D. (1997). Adopted adults who search for background information and contact with birth relatives. *Adoption and Fostering, 21*, 8–15. doi:10.1177/030857599702100204.

Fenton, N. (1928). The only child. *Journal of Genetic Psychology, 35*, 546–556. doi:10.1080/08856559.1928.10532171.

Freeman, T., Jadva, V., Kramer, W., & Golombok, S. (2009). Gamete donation: Parents' experiences of searching for their child's donor siblings and donor. *Human Reproduction, 24*, 505–516. doi: 10.1093/humrep/den469.

Glick, C. (1990). The spousal share in intestate succession: Stepparents are getting shortchanged. *Minnesota Law Review, 74*, 631–659.

Golombok, S. (2015). *Modern families: Parents and children in new family forms.* Cambridge: Cambridge University Press.

Golombok, S., Zadeh, S., Imrie, S., Smith, V., & Freeman, T. (2016). Single mothers by choice: Mother-child relationships and children's psychological adjustment. *Journal of Family Psychology, 30*, 409–418. doi: 10.1037/fam0000188.

Gondal, N. (2012). Who "fills in" for siblings and how? A multilevel analysis of personal network composition and its relationship to sibling size. *Sociological Forum, 27,* 732–755. doi:10.1111/j.1573-7861.2012.01343.x.

Goodwin, M., & Roscoe, B. (1990). Sibling violence and agonistic interactions among middle adolescents. *Adolescence, 25,* 451–467.

Habbema, J. D. F., Eijkemans, M. J. C., Leridon, H., & Te Velde, E. R. (2015). Realizing a desired family size: When should couples start? *Human Reproduction, 30,* 2215–2221. doi:10.1093/humrep/dev148.

Harrison, C. (1999). Children being looked after and their sibling relationships: The experiences of children in the working in partnerships with 'lost' parents research project. In A. Mullender (Ed.), *We are family: Sibling relationships in placement and beyond* (pp. 65–90). London: British Agencies for Adoption and Fostering.

Hegar, R. L. (2005). Sibling placement in foster care and adoption: An overview of international research. *Children and Youth Services Review, 27,* 717–739. doi:10.1016/j.childyouth.2004.12.018.

Hegar, R. L., & Rosenthal, J. A. (2009). Kinship care and sibling placement: Child behavior, family relationships, and school outcomes. *Children and Youth Services Review, 31,* 670–679. doi:10.1016/j.childyouth.2009.01.002.

Hegar, R. L., & Rosenthal, J. A. (2011). Foster children placed with or separated from siblings: Outcomes based on a national sample. *Children and Youth Services Review, 33,* 1245–1253. doi:10.1016/j.childyouth.2011.02.020.

Herrick, M. A., & Piccus, W. (2005). Sibling connections: The importance of nurturing sibling bonds in the foster care system. *Children and Youth Services Review, 27,* 845–861. doi:10.1016/j.childyouth.2004.12.013.

Hertz, R., & Mattes, J. (2011). Donor-shared siblings or genetic strangers: New families, clans, and the internet. *Journal of Family Issues, 32,* pp. 1129–1155. doi:10.1177/0192513X11404345.

Hetherington, E. M., & Clingempeel, W. G. (1992). Coping with marital transitions: A family systems approach. *Monographs of the Society for Research in Child Development, 57,* 1–242. doi: 10.1111/j.1540-5834.1992.tb00298.x.

Höjer, I. (2007). Sons and daughters of foster carers and the impact of fostering on their everyday life. *Child and Family Social Work, 12,* 73–83. doi:10.1111/j.1365-2206.2006.00447.x.

Höjer, I., Sebba, J., & Luke, N. (2013). The impact of fostering on foster carers' children. Oxford, UK: Rees Centre for Research in Fostering and Education. Retrieved from http://reescentre.education.ox.ac.uk/about-us/impact-of-fostering-on-foster-carers-children/.

Jacobs, K., & Sillars, A. (2012). Sibling support during post-divorce adjustment: An idiographic analysis of support forms, functions, and relationship types. *Journal of Family Communication, 12,* 167–187. doi:10.1080/15267431.2011.584056.

Jadva, V., Freeman, T., Kramer, W., & Golombok, S. (2010). Experiences of offspring searching for and contacting their donor siblings and donor. *Reproductive BioMedicine Online, 20,* 523–532. doi:10.1016/j.rbmo.2010.01.001.

Jones, C. (2015). Sibling relationships in adoptive and fostering families: A review of the international research literature. *Children and Society, 30,* 324–334. doi:10.1111/chso.12146.

Keller, H., Borke, J., Yovsi, R., Lohaus, A., & Jensen, H. (2005). Cultural orientations and historical changes as predictors of parenting behavior. *International Journal of Behavioral Development, 29,* 229–237. doi:10.1177/01650250544000017.

Lery, B., Shaw, T. V., & Magruder, J. (2005). Using administrative child welfare data to identify sibling groups. *Children and Youth Services Review, 27,* 783–791. doi:10.1177/0165025054400017.

Lundström, T., & Sallnäs, M. (2012). Sibling contact among Swedish children in foster and residential care—Out of home care in a family service system. *Children and Youth Services Review*, *34*, 396–402. doi:10.1016/j.childyouth.2011.11.008.

Mathews, T. J., & Hamilton, B. E. (2009). *Delayed childbearing: More women are having their first child later in life.* Hyattsville, MD: National Centre for Health Statistics. Retrieved from https://www.cdc.gov/nchs/data/databriefs/db21.pdf.

Mikula, G., Riederer, B., & Bodi, O. (2012). Perceived justice in the division of domestic labor: Actor and partner effects. *Personal Relationships*, *19*, 680–695. doi:10.1111/j.1475-6811.2011.01385.x.

Neilson, J., & Stanfors, M. (2013). Re-traditionalisation of gender relations in the 1990s? The impact of parenthood on gendered time use in three Scandinavian countries. *Journal of Contemporary European Studies*, *21*, 269–289. doi:10.1080/14782804.2013.815467.

Neilson, J., & Stanfors, M. (2014). It's about time! Gender, parenthood, and household divisions of labor under different welfare regimes. *Journal of Family Issues*, *35*, 1066–1088. doi: 10.1177/0192513X14522240.

Newman, J. (1996). The more the merrier? Effects of family size and sibling spacing on sibling relationships. *Child: Care, Health and Development*, *22*, 285302. doi:10.1111/j.1365-2214.1996.tb00431.x.

Noller, P., Feeney, J. A., Sheehan, G., Darlington, Y., & Rogers, C. (2009). Conflict in divorcing and continuously married families: A study of marital, parent-child and sibling relationships. *Journal of Divorce and Remarriage*, *49*, 1–24. doi:10.1080/10502550801971223.

O'Connor, T. G., Dunn, J., Jenkins, J. M., Pickering, K., & Rasbash, J. (2001). Family settings and children's adjustment: Differential adjustment within and across families. *British Journal of Psychiatry*, *179*, 110–115. doi: 10.1192/bjp.179.2.110.

Office for National Statistics. (2014). *Births by parents' characteristics in England and Wales.* London: Office for National Statistics. Retrieved from http://www.ons.gov.uk/people populationandcommunity/birthsdeathsandmarriages/livebirths/bulletins/birthsby parentscharacteristicsinenglandandwales/2014tab-Main-points.

Ozer, E. M., Barnett, R. C., Brennan, R. T., & Sperling, J. (1998). Does child care involvement increase or decrease distress among dual-earner couples? *Women's health (Hillsdale, N.J.)*, *4*, 285–311.

Persaud, S., Freeman, T., Jadva, V., Slutsky, J., Kramer, W., Steele, M., Steele, H., & Golombok, S. (2017). Adolescents conceived through donor insemination in mother-headed families: A qualitative study of motivations and experiences of contacting and meeting same-donor offspring. *Children and Society*, *31*, 13–22. doi:10.1111/chso.12158.

Piñero-Ruiz, E., López-Espín, J. J., Cerezo, F., & Torres-Cantero, A. M. (2012). Number of siblings and school victimization. *Tamaño de la fratría y victimización escolar*, *28*, 842–847. doi:10.6018/analesps.28.3.156091.

Pollet, T.V. (2007). Genetic relatedness and sibling relationship characteristics in a modern society. *Evolution and Human Behavior*, *28*, 176–185. doi:10.1016/j.evolhumbehav.2006.10.001.

The Practice Committee of the American Society for Reproductive Medicine and the Practice Committee of the Society for Assisted Reproductive Technology. (2013). Recommendations for gamete and embryo donation: A committee opinion. *Fertility and Sterility*, *99*, 47–62. doi:10.1016/j.fertnstert.2012.09.037.

Rosenberg, B. (1982). Life span personality stability in sibling status. In M. Lamb & B. Sutton-Smith (Eds.), *Sibling relationships: Their nature and significance across the lifespan* (pp. 167–224). Hillsdale, NJ: Lawrence Erlbaum Associates.

Sayer, L. C. (2005). Gender, time and inequality: Trends in women's and men's paid work, unpaid work and free time. *Social Forces*, *84*, 285–303. doi: 10.1353/sof.2005.0126.

Tarren-Sweeney, M., & Hazell, P. (2005). The mental health and socialization of siblings in care. *Children and Youth Services Review, 27*, 821–843. doi:10.1016/j.childyouth.2004.12.014.

Te Velde, E. R., & Pearson, P. L. (2002). The variability of female reproductive ageing. *Human Reproduction Update, 8*, 141–154. doi:10.1093/humupd/8.2.141.

Trent, K., & Spitze, G. (2011). Growing up without siblings and adult sociability behaviors. *Journal of Family Issues, 32*, 1178–1204. doi:10.1177/0192513X11398945.

White, L. (1998). Who's counting? Quasi-facts and stepfamilies in reports of number of siblings. *Journal of Marriage and Family, 60*, 725–733. doi: 10.2307/353541.

Wilson, K. R., & Prior, M. R. (2011). Father involvement and child well-being. *Journal of Paediatrics and Child Health, 47*, 405–407. doi:10.1111/j.1440-1754.2010.01770.x.

GLOSSARY

between-family variation	Variation in a given construct between families, or between children from different families. Most sibling studies assess between-family variation in sibling relationship quality because they compare sibling relationships across different families.
effect size	A quantitative measure of the size of a difference between groups or the strength of association between two variables. Effect sizes have many advantages over statistical significance testing, as they are not influenced by sample size. As a general rule of thumb, an effect size of 1 standard deviation is equivalent to an IQ difference of approximately 15 points.
heterotypic continuity	A phenomenon where an underlying developmental process stays the same over time but the specific manifestations of that process change at different points in development. For example, siblings who get on well early in life generally continue to share a good relationship as they grow up, but how this relationship quality is manifest will vary with age.
measurement invariance	A statistical property indicating that a construct has the same factor structure, factor loadings and item intercepts across two or more groups. Measurement invariance indicates that the same construct is being measured within each group. Establishing measurement invariance is an important first step when making comparisons across cultures, as the meaning of a particular behaviour or response may be culture specific.

within-family variation   Variation in a construct between children in the same family. For example, in families with three or more children it is possible to compare the quality of a child's relationship with each of his or her siblings.

INDEX